OUR ENEMIES WILL VANISH

Yaroslav Trofimov is the chief foreign-affairs correspondent of *The Wall Street Journal* and was a finalist for the Pulitzer Prize in international reporting for two consecutive years, in 2022 and 2023. Before covering the Russian war on Ukraine, he reported on most major conflicts of the past two decades, serving as the Journal's bureau chief in Afghanistan and Pakistan and as a correspondent in Iraq. He holds an MA from New York University and is the author of two critically acclaimed books, *Faith at War* and *The Siege of Mecca*.

ALSO BY YAROSLAV TROFIMOV

Faith at War

The Siege of Mecca

OUR ENEMIES WILL VANISH

The Russian Invasion and Ukraine's War of Independence

Yaroslav Trofimov

MICHAEL JOSEPH

PENGUIN MICHAEL JOSEPH

UK | USA | Canada | Ireland | Australia
India | New Zealand | South Africa

Penguin Michael Joseph is part of the Penguin Random House group of companies
whose addresses can be found at global.penguinrandomhouse.com

First published in the United States of America by Penguin Press,
an imprint of Penguin Random House LLC 2024
First published in Great Britain by Penguin Michael Joseph 2024
001

Copyright © Yaroslav Trofimov, 2024

The moral right of the author has been asserted

Brief portions of this work originally appeared in news articles written by the author
and published in *The Wall Street Journal* during 2022 and 2023

Photographs in insert by Manu Brabo
Book design and map illustrations by Daniel Lagin
Printed and bound in Great Britain by Clays Ltd, Elcograf S.p.A.

The authorized representative in the EEA is Penguin Random House Ireland,
Morrison Chambers, 32 Nassau Street, Dublin D02 YH68

A CIP catalogue record for this book is available from the British Library

HARDBACK ISBN: 978–0–241–65544–3
TRADE PAPERBACK ISBN: 978–0–241–65545–0

www.greenpenguin.co.uk

The best among us have died for us.

PAUL ÉLUARD, 1942

CONTENTS

PART 3 ▪ RESISTANCE

PART 4 ▪ DESTRUCTION

PART 5 ▪ VICTORY IN THE NORTH

PART 6 ▪ DONBAS

PART 7 ▪ ATTRITION

PART 8 ▪ LIBERATION

CAST OF PRINCIPAL
CHARACTERS

UKRAINE

Volodymyr Zelensky, president

Valeriy Zaluzhny, commander in chief of Ukrainian Armed Forces

Oleksandr Syrsky, commander of Ukrainian Ground Forces

Dmytro Kuleba, foreign minister

Oleksiy Danilov, secretary of National Security and Defense Council

Kyrylo Budanov, commander of GUR military intelligence service

Mykhailo Podolyak, presidential adviser

Petro Poroshenko, former president

Vsevolod Kozhemiako, commander of Khartiya battalion

Maria "Vozhata," medic in Carpathian Sich battalion

Mykola Volokhov, commander of Terra unit

Kyrylo Berkal, Azov Regiment officer

Valentyn Koval, Himars battery commander

Anna Zaitseva, wife of Azovstal defender

Yulia Paevska, medic and former prisoner

Ihor Skybiuk, commander of 80th Brigade

Ihor Terekhov, mayor of Kharkiv

Kirill Stremousov, collaborator in Kherson

RUSSIA

Vladimir Putin, president

Sergei Shoigu, minister of defense

Valeriy Gerasimov, chief of General Staff

Sergei Lavrov, foreign minister

Yevgeny Prigozhin, head of Wagner paramilitary organization

Ramzan Kadyrov, leader of Chechen Republic

Sergei Surovikin, commander of Russian forces in Ukraine

Igor Girkin, former FSB colonel and former minister of defense of Donetsk "people's republic"

OTHER COUNTRIES

Joe Biden, president, United States

Boris Johnson, prime minister, United Kingdom

Emmanuel Macron, president, France

Olaf Scholz, federal chancellor, Germany

Stevo Stephen, *Wall Street Journal* head of risk

Manu Brabo, photographer

PROLOGUE

On the sunny afternoon of February 23, 2022, Kyiv was still a city at peace. As I walked up the steep hill into the Pechersk government quarter, municipal workers put up billboards advertising upcoming concerts. Cherry-liquor bars, a favorite of young Kyivites, were already full, with folk-rock music blasting. Parents took photos of their children enjoying pony rides around the park. In the domed parliament building, Ukrainian lawmakers gathered to debate emergency wartime legislation.

A few blocks away, I was meeting with President Volodymyr Zelensky's predecessor and one of the main leaders of the Ukrainian opposition, Petro Poroshenko. A chocolate-industry tycoon who had badly lost the 2019 election, Poroshenko was battling corruption charges that he decried as politically motivated. He had just been barred by the courts from traveling outside the Kyiv region. Our meeting had originally been scheduled for later in the week, but I had received a call: "Come right away."

Dressed in a tailored suit, Poroshenko offered me an espresso in his office and reminisced about how Ukrainian society had united after the 2014 revolution against the authoritarian rule of President Viktor Yanukovych. Back then, Russia had captured Ukraine's Crimean Peninsula and tried to bite off the nation's entire southeastern half, an Italy-sized belt of land running from Odesa to Kharkiv, by fomenting pro-Russian insurrections.

Moscow's attempts had failed everywhere except Donbas, Yanukovych's home, where a direct Russian intervention carved out two proxy statelets, the Donetsk and Luhansk "people's republics." Russian president Vladimir Putin pretended for eight years that Moscow wasn't directly involved in the conflict. But two days earlier, on February 21, he had recognized these two "republics," with borders that included large territories controlled by Kyiv, and had signed mutual-defense agreements with them. After that, shelling had intensified all over the cease-fire line that ran through Donbas.

The animosity between Poroshenko and Zelensky was visceral. A former comedian, Zelensky used to relentlessly ridicule Poroshenko in his satirical shows. Yet the two politicians had met the previous night to discuss the looming threat from Moscow. Internal strife has repeatedly caused national catastrophes throughout Ukrainian history, as political rivals engaged in petty intrigues and sought foreign help, forfeiting the country's independence. A thirty-year stretch of the late seventeenth century is known to Ukrainians as "The Ruin," for the devastation wrought by the *hetmans* of two competing Ukrainian states who courted Russian, Polish, and Ottoman alliances in their power struggles. In 1918, a descendant of one of these *hetmans*, Pavlo Skoropadsky, carried out a German-sponsored conservative coup against a socialist-leaning Ukrainian republic. The peasant uprisings that broke out as a result provided an opening for the seemingly definitive Russian reconquest of the nation three years later. In 2010, squabbles between pro-Western Ukrainian politicians had allowed a pro-Russian candidate, Yanukovych, to take the country's presidency. This time around Moscow would not be able to exploit Ukraine's internal fissures, Poroshenko assured me.

"There will be unity. Ukraine above all. Unity not around a person or a position, but unity around the nation. As long as the threat of an invasion persists, we must take a moratorium on anything that undermines unity," Poroshenko said. His party's lawmakers, he added, were about to vote for a government bill in parliament to significantly expand Zelensky's powers, something they had previously opposed.

I switched off the recorder and shook Poroshenko's hand. He leaned toward me, lowering his voice.

"It's going to be tomorrow after four a.m.," he said. "I thought I should warn you. You still have time to rush to the airport and hop on a flight out of here."

"Tomorrow?" I asked, unsure. "The war?"

"Yes," Poroshenko nodded. "Now we have the intelligence. That's why parliament is meeting now, and why we are voting for all the things that we used to be so firmly against."

Many prominent Ukrainians, including some senior officials and billionaire oligarchs, were flying out of Kyiv that afternoon, convinced that their country would quickly collapse once confronted by the full might of Russia—a nuclear power with a much bigger and better-armed military, and a war chest of hundreds of billions of dollars in oil and gas revenues. Some hoped to return as part of a new, pro-Russian regime.

Outside Ukraine, hardly anyone believed that the nation had a chance in the face of a Russian onslaught, no matter how valiantly it resisted. For centuries, Russian military power had terrified Europe. As for this place called Ukraine, was it, deep down, a real country after all? A Russian triumph within days was a foregone conclusion, Western intelligence services predicted.

President Joe Biden's administration had already pulled out American diplomats and military advisers, shutting down the sprawling US embassy compound in Kyiv. But the dates that Washington floated for the invasion had come and gone, with nothing more than mockery of American warmongering on Russian TV. To Washington's angst, Zelensky himself and his aides publicly played down the likelihood of a full-scale Russian invasion, unwilling to spook the country's population—and incredulous that Putin would do something so foolhardy. Unlike Putin and some of Ukraine's Western partners, Zelensky knew that Ukrainian soldiers would not surrender—and estimated that the assembled Russian force would be insufficient to capture Kyiv, let alone the entire nation.

I too had clung to hope that it could all be a big bluff, an attempt for Putin to extract last-minute concessions from the West. Stevo Stephen, a former British commando and a friend advising me and my colleagues on security, disagreed. Russian troops had been camping out for weeks in the cold, dark forests around Ukraine, suffering diarrhea, respiratory infections, and vehicle breakdowns in harsh winter conditions. "I did this sort of staging several times myself, and there was not one time when we didn't invade at the end," he mused. "You just don't do it if you don't mean it."

I walked back from the meeting with Poroshenko to Kyiv's Hyatt hotel, through the crowds of the capital's central Khreshchatyk Avenue and past the ancient golden-domed cathedrals of St. Sophia and St. Michael. The usual afternoon traffic clogged the intersections. There was neither panic buying nor lines at the ATMs. Were all these young people in bars unaware of the gathering storm? Or were they just savoring their last, precious moments of peace?

In Washington, foreboding was palpable as Ukraine's foreign minister, Dmytro Kuleba, visited Biden. Welcomed into the White House with a mixture of warmth and sadness, Kuleba felt like he was being diagnosed with stage-four cancer. It seemed like final farewells—for him, and for his country.

Stevo and I stocked up on essentials and withdrew as much cash as possible. I also called my friends on the eastern bank of the Dnipro River that bisects Ukraine, telling them to jump on a train west, to avoid being trapped on the wrong side once the Russians advanced or destroyed the bridges. Manu Brabo, a Spanish photographer on assignment for the *Wall Street Journal*, had just reached the front line in Donetsk. He didn't want to leave and took some convincing that once Russian forces approached Kyiv, nobody would care much about skirmishes in the east. Manu drove as fast as he could, spending the night in the town of Uman, which happened to be where my grandmother was born in 1914, two months into World War I.

Assuming that all the normal communications would be offline by the morning, Stevo and I tested our satellite phones and stowed body armor and helmets by the beds in our rooms.

That day, the presidents of Poland and Lithuania came to Kyiv for a few hours, on one of the last flights before Ukrainian airports shut down. "Be strong," the broad-shouldered Lithuanian president, Gitanas Nausėda, said in English as he shook hands with the diminutive Ukrainian leader outside the pale blue, Baroque Mariinsky Palace. "I am strong," Zelensky replied quietly.

By nightfall, the news of imminent war had spread, and a pall of anxiety descended upon the city. The phones of the soldiers I knew went offline. Hardly anyone was on Kyiv's main Independence Square, or Maidan. A giant neon sign declaring "I Love Ukraine" shone through the falling snow.

My hotel, which barely a week earlier had been packed with French sales executives, was empty, except for my *Journal* colleagues and Sean Penn, who had just spent the afternoon with Zelensky.

We sat with Penn, who was worried but also impressed by the Ukrainian president's demeanor, drinking Negronis in the hotel's bar. On TV, Zelensky made his late-night address. Standing in front of a map of Ukraine, he wore a smart charcoal suit with a white shirt and a black tie. It was the last time he would appear in formal attire that year. Ukraine was ready to negotiate and address Moscow's concerns, he said, but Putin wouldn't take his calls.

"The Ukrainian people want peace. We are different from you, but it is not a reason to be enemies," Zelensky added. Switching to Russian, he spoke directly to the citizens of Russia: "If soldiers try to advance, if someone tries to take away our country and our freedom, our lives and the lives of our children, we will defend ourselves. If you advance, you will see our faces, not our backs."

◆◆◆

I slept with the hotel's window open, the chilly breeze ruffling the curtains, to hear the moment the war began. The thuds were distant but unmistakable in the darkness. One, then another. One more. The wide square outside was empty, projectors still illuminating the golden cupolas of St. Sophia, streetlights reflecting on the wet cobblestones. I looked at my phone. Thursday, February 24. Not yet 5 a.m.

The invasion had started. All over Ukraine, Russian missiles and bombs were falling on Ukrainian military bases, airfields, air-defense batteries, logistics hubs, and government installations. Long columns of tanks, fighting vehicles, artillery, and trucks carrying soldiers poured in from the north, south, and east, sweeping away the useless border fences. They met little initial resistance.

The air-raid siren started to wail as the second wave of Russian missiles approached Kyiv. I ran downstairs to the hotel's basement, which had turned into a bomb shelter. Would I see a city ablaze when I resurfaced? For months, military experts, American and Russian alike, had been predicting a shock-

and-awe bombing run that would decapitate the Ukrainian government, disrupt communications, and overwhelm any organized resistance.

But at sunrise the center of Kyiv was still standing, intact. The phone networks and the internet were still up. The electricity was on. An acrid smell rose from the nearby headquarters of the Ukrainian domestic intelligence agency, or SBU—a granite fortresslike compound where spies were burning files so they wouldn't fall into Russian hands. The wind whisked up fragments of documents. One that floated my way was an officer's wiretap training record. At the back door of the Kyiv municipality building, bleary-eyed secretaries and administrative staff lined up to remove personal belongings from their offices. They didn't want to speak. Kyiv's main avenue, Khreshchatyk, was deserted, except for a new tent across the street from the Zara store that had popped up to recruit volunteers to fight the Russians. Like everything else, the shop was closed. Only a dozen people gathered by the tent.

Jets rumbled above the low, heavy clouds. Nobody knew if they were Russian, but everyone assumed so. There were more distant bangs, and then some more. Frazzled and disoriented, the Hyatt hotel's muscular security men tried to exercise at least some degree of control by suddenly demanding draconian compliance with COVID mask rules. That lasted a couple of hours before they gave up, took off their masks, and went home.

The war did not come out of the blue, but it was hard to believe that Putin had actually launched it. The hotel's staff brought in coffee and a tray of croissants, the last they would bake for a long time, as Putin appeared on Russian TV. Cocky and confident, he announced what he called a "special military operation." He declared his goal to "denazify and demilitarize" Ukraine—denazification being a ludicrous euphemism for replacing the country's elected Jewish president with a puppet of the Kremlin's choosing. Ukraine and Russia, Putin added, should be a "common whole," and Ukrainian soldiers should lay down their arms instead of following orders of the criminal "junta" in Kyiv. As for the West, any attempt to interfere and create obstacles for Russia, he threatened, would provoke an immediate response with "consequences that you have never encountered in your history."

Listening to Putin, I thought of fallen capital cities I had seen over the past two decades: the innards of government buildings spilling onto sidewalks for everyone to see, portraits of rulers and cherished flags trampled in the dirt, as new masters pulled down hallowed statues and rode triumphantly through the streets. Would Kyiv, the city where I was born and had grown up, meet the same fate as Baghdad in 2003, as Tripoli in 2011? As Kabul in the summer of 2021, where I watched the American-trained Afghan National Army dissolve without much of a fight and go home?

Putin's entire invasion plan was premised on expectations that most Ukrainian soldiers would do just that.

FEBRUARY 24, 2022

BELARUS

POLAND

Zhytomyr

• Lviv

UKRAINE

SLOVAKIA

HUNGARY

MOLDOVA

ROMANIA

Nuclear Power Stations

Decommissioned
Nuclear Power Stations

Annexed by Russia in 2014

"People's Republics" controlled
by Russia since 2014–2015

RUSSIA

Chernihiv

Sumy

Kyiv

Dnipro River

Kharkiv

Uman

Dnipro

Luhansk

Donbas

Kryvyi Rih

Donetsk

Mariupol

Kherson

Odesa

Azov Sea

Snake
Island

Crimean
Peninsula

KERCH BRIDGE

Sevastopol

Black Sea

KILOMETERS

0   50   100   150

N

0   50   100   150

MILES

PART 1

DIGNITY

CHAPTER 1

THE "PEOPLE'S REPUBLICS"

Russia's war against Ukraine had begun eight years earlier, with what Ukrainians called their "Revolution of Dignity" and what Moscow described as an American-sponsored putsch.

The initial divorce between Russia and Ukraine, agreed in December 1991, was surprisingly bloodless. At a meeting in a Belarusian forest lodge, Russian president Boris Yeltsin and his counterparts from Ukraine and Belarus decided to dissolve the Soviet Union, respecting each other's territorial integrity. Russia recognized Ukraine's sovereignty over lands that many, if not most, Russians had always considered rightfully theirs, from Kharkiv to Crimea to Odesa.

The Russian-American poet Joseph Brodsky reacted by writing a vitriolic poem wishing that the mighty Dnipro River would flow backward to punish ungrateful and uppity *khokhols*, a Russian slur for Ukrainians. Another Russian Nobel Prize winner, Aleksandr Solzhenitsyn, cried betrayal. But nobody in Moscow seriously tried to stop the breakup. Russia was so magnanimous because it expected Ukraine's independence to be nominal at best, just like that of nearby Belarus. The bonds between the two countries and the two peoples were so tight, after all, that a truly separate and viable Ukrainian state was impossible to imagine—at least in Moscow.

In Belarus, the 1994 election of former collective farm chief Aleksandr

Lukashenko—the only member of the Belarusian parliament who voted against independence—snuffed out any attempt to steer the country westward. Lukashenko brought Belarus into a confederation with Russia, and brutally suppressed the democratic opposition by jailing or outright assassinating opponents.

The authoritarian Yanukovych, a Russian-speaking coal-industry boss and onetime juvenile criminal from Donbas, was supposed to perform a similar role for Ukraine—and he might well have, except that the Ukrainian people revolted twice.

THE FIRST REVOLUTION WAS IN 2004, WHEN YANUKOVYCH, WHO WAS PRIME minister at the time, tried to steal a presidential election by using local bureaucracies to stuff ballot boxes. President Leonid Kuchma, at the end of his second and final term, ordered security forces to remain neutral. Under pressure from protesters, Ukraine's supreme court acknowledged the fraud and ordered another round of elections. This time, Yanukovych lost.

In 2010, a chastened, seemingly changed Yanukovych won the presidency fair and square. In part, he gained power because of unchecked graft and infighting in Ukraine's pro-Western camp. As all Ukrainian presidents had done since independence, Yanukovych promised to seek closer ties with the European Union. He even negotiated a free-trade and political-association agreement with the EU. But, in November 2013, he unexpectedly pulled out of the deal and moved to join a customs union with Russia.

As stunned Ukrainians digested the news, Mustafa Nayyem, a Kyiv journalist of Afghan descent, made the first call for protests. "People, let's get serious," he wrote on Facebook. "Who is ready to come to Maidan before midnight tonight? Likes don't count."

Hundreds of thousands showed up in the following days and weeks. The initially peaceful rallies turned violent when Yanukovych ordered riot police to open fire, and descended into an outright bloodbath on February 20, 2014, with dozens gunned down in central Kyiv. The Ukrainian parliament—including many lawmakers from the president's party—intervened to outlaw the use of force against protesters just as a delegation of European foreign ministers reached a compromise. On February 21, Yanukovych agreed to form a government of national unity with the opposition and to hold presidential elections under international supervision by December.

But the president lost his nerve that night. The Ukrainian security services crumbled and protesters demanded that Yanukovych leave Kyiv by the morning. From his palatial residence, he absconded first to the eastern city of Kharkiv, then to Donetsk, and eventually on to Crimea, where he was picked up by Russian troops and escorted to safety in Russia. The next day, February 22, the Ukrainian parliament declared that Yanukovych had abandoned his constitutional duties. Lawmakers appointed the new opposition-backed speaker as interim president and scheduled a presidential election for May. Moscow called it a coup.

UP UNTIL THAT MOMENT, MOST UKRAINIANS HAD OFTEN BEEN WARY OF Russia's intentions but had not considered Russia a foe. Millions of Ukrainians worked in Russia, which, because of its oil and gas wealth, and because of Ukraine's corrosive corruption, was perceived as a prosperous land of opportunity. Zelensky also spent much of his time in Moscow working as a comedian and was a rising star of Russian state TV.

In the middle of the Ukrainian revolution, Zelensky cohosted Russian TV's 2014 New Year's Day show, watched by tens of millions of people in both nations. He sang and danced onstage, wearing a black tuxedo, a bow tie, and a black top hat.

"New Year, the first day, what awaits us," Ukraine's future president crooned. "Na-na na-na-na." Then he delivered a schmaltzy stand-up routine, comparing the previous night's celebrations to a military campaign. "You can even write military memoirs about it. The New Year's offensive started precisely at midnight with a volley of champagne," he joked. The stars of Russian showbiz howled with laughter in the audience, raising their glasses.

❖

The real military offensive began fifty-seven days later, on February 27, 2014. Russian special forces—operating without insignia and dubbed "little green men"—fanned out from the headquarters of the Russian Black

Sea Fleet in Sevastopol. The base had been leased from Ukraine by Moscow since the Soviet Union's collapse in an agreement that was extended by Yanukovych in 2010. The soldiers seized Crimea's government and legislature buildings, raising Russian flags. Crimean lawmakers, gathered at gunpoint, voted to secede from Ukraine. Ukrainian forces in Crimea didn't offer much resistance, except for singing patriotic songs.

Many military leaders, including the newly appointed commander of the Ukrainian Navy, simply joined the Russians. Hollowed out and thoroughly infiltrated by Russian agents, the Ukrainian military was hardly a fighting force. Only some 6,000 Ukrainian troops were combat-ready, the interim government estimated. When they tried to deploy, they discovered that their armored vehicles lacked batteries. Private businessmen had to pitch in with a few million dollars to fix that.

Russia didn't have military bases in other parts of Ukraine, but it had cultivated a network of sleeper agents, especially inside Ukrainian law enforcement, as well as a legion of pro-Russian politicians. As one of its first moves, the interim government in Kyiv, which held power until Poroshenko's victory in May's presidential elections, passed legislation to limit the use of the Russian language in public, a blunder that made it easier for Putin to posture as the defender of Ukraine's Russian-speakers.

Overnight, Russian flags appeared across cities in eastern and southern Ukraine. Pro-Russian protesters, organized and often armed, tried to seize government buildings, clashing with rival, pro-Ukrainian activists. The police mostly stood by, or even tacitly helped the pro-Russians.

In Kharkiv, an overwhelmingly Russian-speaking metropolis of 1.5 million people, a deadly gun battle erupted in March as Russian and pro-Russian militants stormed the headquarters of a pro-Ukrainian organization. Terror spread to the streets, and pro-Russian thugs assaulted one of Ukraine's most famous novelists, Serhiy Zhadan, beating him with bats in the center of the city.

Even as blood was spilled in Kharkiv, many people in eastern and southern Ukraine remained indifferent, in denial about the consequences of the political confrontation unfolding on their streets.

The Russian takeover of Crimea had been nearly bloodless, and Russian rule, in the minds of many—particularly the retirees, and parts of law enforcement—meant not war but higher salaries, generous pensions, and political stability after years of turmoil. In April 2014, Putin proclaimed that all of eastern and southern Ukraine wasn't historically Ukrainian and should henceforth be known as Novorossiya, or New Russia.

That month, pro-Russian militants seized the regional government headquarters and other administrative buildings in Kharkiv, Donetsk, and Luhansk, hoisting Russian flags and proclaiming three supposedly independent "people's republics." Similar plans in other Ukrainian cities were thwarted by organized pro-Ukrainian groups. In Odesa, this confrontation ended in tragedy after pro-Russian protesters, some of them armed, barricaded themselves in the regional labor union headquarters. On May 2, 2014, after the two sides exchanged firebombs, the building caught fire. A total of forty-eight people died, most of them burned inside the union headquarters.

In Kharkiv, the Russian takeover of the regional government lasted just one night. A special police unit flown from central Ukraine stormed the building at dawn, and the sixty-three founding fathers of the Kharkiv "people's republic" were detained. Things turned out differently in Donetsk and Luhansk. With local police and intelligence services refusing to act or switching sides, the occupied government compounds quickly turned into fortresses, as weapons, explosives, and men in fatigues poured in. Donbas was plunged into war.

⟨∘⟩

The morning of April 12, 2014, five days after the proclamation of the Donetsk "people's republic," Igor Girkin, a retired Russian intelligence colonel with a fondness for reenacting historical battles, led a small group of Russian military veterans to capture the police station in the town of Slovyansk, on the northern edge of the Donetsk region. They quickly distributed the captured weapons to local supporters and took control of the city.

When the Ukrainian military sent creaky fighting vehicles to reclaim Slovyansk, Girkin's men and local pro-Russian supporters blocked the roads. To many Ukrainian soldiers, shooting at fellow Ukrainians was unthinkable. They surrendered six vehicles and even handed over the firing pins of their rifles before being allowed to leave.

The weakness of Ukraine's regular army had been revealed. In response, many Ukrainian civilians organized to protect their broke, dysfunctional state. Unruly militias sprang up, often financed by political parties or oligarchs, some of them with a far-right political history, others affiliated with soccer fan clubs. A powerful network of volunteer groups rose alongside these battalions, drawing on activists who had banded together in revolutionary encampments on Kyiv's Maidan.

The war that spread through Donbas in the following months was bloodier than anyone had predicted. After nearly three months of fighting, Ukrainian forces managed to retake Slovyansk. By then, thousands of heavily armed volunteers, including Russian intelligence and military personnel, had thronged into Donetsk and Luhansk from Russia. Suddenly, these self-proclaimed "people's republics" possessed large tank and artillery formations. When the Ukrainian Air Force tried to ferry troops and supplies to a garrison in the Luhansk airport in June, Russian proxies shot down a Ukrainian Il-76 transport plane, killing all forty-six people aboard. A month later, a Russian Buk missile launcher shot down a Malaysian Boeing 777 airliner, mistaking it for another Ukrainian resupply run and killing 298 people, most of them Dutch citizens. Girkin by then was the Donetsk "people's republic" minister of defense, and has since been sentenced to life imprisonment in absentia by a Dutch court.

Instead of higher salaries and economic prosperity, the Russian intervention brought devastation to Donbas. Russian men with guns took over. Properties were seized by gangs. Soon, even the oligarchs who had once supported Yanukovych and flirted with Russia were no longer able to stay. Moscow didn't need them anymore. As jobs and services disappeared, and fighting continued, more than half of the roughly four million people in the Russian-controlled parts of Donbas fled the region—to other parts of Ukraine, to Russia, or to the West. Those who remained were mostly too poor, too old, or too sick to move.

❖

Throughout 2014, the more success the Ukrainian Army achieved, the more directly Russia became involved, although Putin insisted the fighters were all local oppressed coal miners and tractor drivers. In February 2015, elite Russian units tipped the scales in the last major operation of that campaign, the Battle of Debaltseve. Thousands of Ukrainian forces desperately fought to break out, sustaining heavy casualties as Russian troops captured the town.

Russia's show of strength meant that Ukraine had to accept a cease-fire on Moscow's terms. With Ukrainian forces facing a catastrophe in Debaltseve, Poroshenko, Putin, and the leaders of Germany and France flew to the Belarusian capital, Minsk, for peace talks. The so-called Minsk-2 agreement that they signed in February 2015 ended large-scale hostilities in Donbas, with both sides pulling back heavy artillery and stopping offensive operations. The rest of the deal, which foresaw a comprehensive political settlement, was never implemented.

For a while, this limbo suited everyone. Viewed in Moscow with contempt, President Barack Obama had pursued a "restart" with Putin shortly after the Russian invasion of Georgia in 2008 and saw no reason to get involved beyond mild sanctions. He refused to provide any weapons to Kyiv, and the Minsk-2 agreement relieved any pressure on him to help Ukraine defend itself. Ukraine, Obama explained in an interview with *The Atlantic* the following year, "is going to be vulnerable to military domination by Russia no matter what we do."

Instead, Obama focused on working with Moscow to achieve his foreign policy priority, the Iran nuclear deal. Germany was free to build the lucrative Nord Stream 2 pipeline that would provide cheap Russian gas, and the ability to distribute it to the rest of Europe.

Putin ended up with authority over one-third of Donbas, including two of its three main cities, Donetsk and Luhansk. For Ukraine, the frozen conflict in Donbas was an open wound preventing integration with the West and stunting economic development. Yet Kyiv also gained precious time to rebuild its institutions and thwart—for the time being, at least—Putin's "New Russia" ambition to swallow the entirety of Ukraine's south and east. By occupying Crimea and parts of Donbas in 2014, Russia acquired 7 percent of Ukrainian territory—but forfeited the sympathy of most Ukrainians, likely for generations. According to the United Nations, 4,400 Ukrainian troops, 6,500 Russian proxies and Russians, and 3,400 civilians on both sides died in Donbas in 2014 and 2015.

———

IN THE AFTERMATH, POROSHENKO FOCUSED ON BEEFING UP THE UKRAI-
nian military, with the United States, Britain, and Canada teaching thousands of Ukrainian soldiers and officers the NATO doctrine. Volunteer units
were incorporated into national security forces. In a major psychological shift,
Ukrainians gained the right to travel to the EU without a visa, with $29.99
budget flights to Paris or Vienna making European weekends routine even
for students on limited incomes—and reorienting the society further away
from Russia. Russian TV was no longer able to broadcast in Ukraine, Russian
pop music was taken off the air, and flights to Russia were discontinued.

Having further entrenched Ukrainian as the national language and
achieved the recognition of the Ukrainian Orthodox Church's independence from Moscow by Bartholomew, the Ecumenical Patriarch of Con-
stantinople, Poroshenko campaigned in the 2019 presidential election under
the patriotic slogan "Army, Language, Faith."

By then the conflict in Donbas was simmering far away, with only occasional bouts of violence, and most Ukrainian voters cared more about rising prices and the rampant graft that continued under his rule. Zelensky,
famous for playing an accidental president in the TV series *Servant of the
People*, ran as an uncompromised outsider who would bring peace with
Russia.

"I will tell you about the Ukraine of my dreams: it's the Ukraine where
the only shooting will be the fireworks at weddings and birthdays," his elec-
toral manifesto began. "Where there are no announcements 'Work in Poland.' But in Poland, there are announcements, 'Work in Ukraine.'" Lower
down, in the fine print, he also promised to pursue membership in NATO,
and not to relinquish an inch of Russian-occupied land.

Zelensky, then forty-one, won by a landslide with 73 percent of the vote,
carrying twenty-four of Ukraine's twenty-five regions, with only Lviv in the
west voting for Poroshenko. Zelensky's party, Servant of the People, also secured an absolute majority in parliament. The opposition parties that advocated for closer ties with Russia gained only 49 of the 450 seats, thanks
mostly to districts in Ukrainian-controlled parts of Donbas.

One of Zelensky's first moves in office was to cancel the Independence Day military parade, featuring tanks and missile launchers rumbling down Khreshchatyk, and instead hold a lighthearted concert with a hip-hop performance. He secured a popular prisoner exchange with Putin, and violence along the cease-fire line in Donbas all but disappeared. According to the UN, in the first two full years of his presidency, only fifteen civilians died because of direct hostilities in Donbas.

Despite Russian pressure, Zelensky continued to aspire for Ukraine to join NATO. He refused the constitutional reforms, which Moscow insisted were required by the Minsk-2 accords, that would have given Russian proxies in Donbas a veto over Kyiv's foreign policy. In July 2021, Zelensky replaced the head of the armed forces, appointing General Valeriy Zaluzhny, forty-eight, a veteran of the war in Donbas. A broad-shouldered man with an easygoing smile, Zaluzhny was Ukraine's first top military commander without a past in the Soviet military, and without any former classmates and comrades serving under Russian colors. In a TV interview shortly after assuming command, Zaluzhny joked that he would love to ride on Moscow's Red Square and Arbat pedestrian boulevard—in a Ukrainian tank.

The same month, Putin published a lengthy treatise called "On the Historical Unity of the Russians and Ukrainians," in which he argued that Ukraine is an artificial country that could only be sovereign in partnership with Russia. He had the article read out to every member of the Russian Armed Forces. Weeks later, Putin started complaining about the imaginary "genocide" of Russian-speakers in Donbas and ordered troops to start deploying along Ukraine's borders.

Central Intelligence Agency Director William Burns, who flew to Moscow to meet Putin in November 2021, came home convinced that an invasion was inevitable. "Don't you know that Ukraine is not even a real country?" Putin had told Burns all the way back in 2008, when the future CIA chief served as the American ambassador to Moscow. This conviction, at the core of Putin's worldview, had now crystallized into a determination that Russia faced a unique window of opportunity, tactically and strategically, to eliminate Ukrainian statehood. At their meeting, Putin told Burns that Ukraine was too weak and divided to resist, and the Europeans were too risk-averse to interfere. As for Biden's America, Putin had decided that it was impotent after the Taliban takeover of Afghanistan. As the year drew to a close, the Russian president was certain that his modernized and upgraded Russian army would score a quick and decisive victory, at a minimal cost.

CHAPTER 2

"LOVE IT OR NOT, ENDURE IT, MY BEAUTY"

When I arrived in Kharkiv in late January 2022, the tail end of a Russian Smerch rocket stuck diagonally out of the ground in the central Freedom Square, one of Europe's largest plazas. Brought to Kharkiv as a reminder of the bloodshed that had occurred more than a hundred miles to the southeast, in Donbas, it was a warning about the fragility of the city's new peace. "Is Kharkiv Next?" wondered a sign placed nearby, featuring World War II quotes from Winston Churchill and Charles De Gaulle. Just across the street stood the regional government building where pro-Russian militants had attempted unsuccessfully to challenge the writ of the Ukrainian state in 2014.

These traumatic events seemed like a forgotten nightmare. A hipster cocktail bar and a Nordic fusion restaurant had opened nearby, and the city exuded a sense of busy, confident prosperity. The brand-new Nikolsky shopping mall on Kharkiv's main street, with its oyster bars, virtual-reality playgrounds, multiplex cinemas, and a plethora of high-end branded stores, could have been found in Dubai, London, or Singapore. At night, central Kharkiv was illuminated with blue, yellow, and pink lights beneath the domed spire of the Assumption Cathedral and the Constructivist jumble of Derzhprom, the 1920s skyscraper that once housed the Soviet Ukrainian government.

———

UNLIKE IN 2014, THIS TIME THERE WAS LITTLE THREAT FROM WITHIN. THE hardcore pro-Russian militants had either all escaped to Donbas, where many died in the ranks of Russian-run military formations, or had emigrated to Russia. The city had become a home to some 100,000 refugees from Russian rule. Putin's promise of a "Russian Spring" was now a byword for banditry and economic collapse, not higher pensions and salaries. Even politicians from parties sympathetic to Russia acknowledged that fact. "There are no fools anymore," said Sergey Gladkoskok, leader of the Russia-friendly opposition in the Kharkiv legislature. "People see that things are bad in Donetsk and Luhansk, and that things are good here. They have war over there and we have peace over here."

Kharkiv mayor Ihor Terekhov was outraged by Zelensky's suggestion, made in a *Washington Post* interview, that the city, Ukraine's second largest, could be quickly captured by Russia in the event of an invasion. "Kharkiv is and will be a Ukrainian city," Terekhov responded indignantly on January 21. "Anyone who attempts to seize Kharkiv must realize this: not just the Kharkivites will be defending their beloved city, but all Ukrainians."

In the administration building, a framed Ukrainian flag and a memorial plaque at the entrance reminded visitors of the events of 2014. The new governor, Oleh Syniehubov, initially welcomed me to his office on January 26, before being politely reminded by security that with war clouds gathering, he could no longer host guests in areas that contained classified information. We walked over to a nearby conference room, where he delivered an optimistic assessment: "It's not 2014, when the army, let's admit it, didn't really exist, and the loyalties of the police were often unclear." In 2022, Syniehubov added, Ukraine was more ready than ever. "What we really don't need now is panic," he said, echoing Zelensky. The city was normal and the only hint of trouble was that luxury vehicle brands had stopped shipping new cars to Kharkiv showrooms. Those were the first places to be looted in Donetsk and Luhansk in 2014.

———

A NEW LAW CAME INTO EFFECT AT THE START OF JANUARY, ESTABLISHING the Territorial Defense, a volunteer force to protect local communities. These civilian volunteers were supposed to be trained and commanded by professional officers, providing backup to the 205,000 uniformed troops in the Ukrainian military. The effort was slow, however. Some volunteers showed up for a few hours of training using wooden guns, or listened to a brief first-aid course, but the force was small and seemed unprepared for combat. Mykhailo Sokolov, the chief noncommissioned officer of the Territorial Defense brigade formed for Kharkiv, was a grizzled, war-battered veteran. He spoke of great enthusiasm among the locals: "Of course we will all defend our homes, our spouses, our children, our mistresses—with weapons in our hands. Nobody knows our terrain, our byways, or hidden paths better than us, and this will allow us to spring up surprises on the enemy." But the brigade's temporary headquarters, in a hastily restored former vocational school, was nearly empty. A functioning military unit it was not.

The only people spending their days getting ready for war were the veterans of the volunteer battalions in Donbas, many of whom had joined far-right political movements. In a sweaty Kharkiv sports hall where tough young men lifted weights, boxed, and wrestled, a muscular man who wore a mustacheless goatee introduced himself. Kostyantyn Nemichev was the head of the Kharkiv defense committee, a body uniting several volunteer units that he said could deploy over 1,000 fighters on three hours' notice.

As a nineteen-year-old fan of Kharkiv's FC Metalist soccer club, Nemichev had fought in the city's street clashes in the spring of 2014. Later that summer, he joined the war for Donbas as a soldier for the volunteer Azov Battalion, which ousted Russian proxies from the southern city of Mariupol. Everything was different now, he told me.

"Our army is prepared, and it no longer needs volunteer units. It's ready for war," he said. "But our government is not ready, it's trying to keep silent about the conflict. People on the streets don't know what to do, where to run, what to take, if there is shelling, if there is bombing, if there is a Russian offensive tomorrow."

In 2014, the mood in Kharkiv had been 70 percent sympathetic to Russia, with only a third of the population identifying with the Ukrainian cause, Nemichev estimated. But this proportion had since flipped, with most of Moscow's remaining supporters driven by a sense of nostalgia for their Soviet youth, rather than Putin's "Russian world" irredentism. "There are no pro-Russian forces on the streets anymore."

What would his fighters do, should Russian tanks roll across the border? "If the Russian Army enters, it will have a hard time penetrating Kharkiv. They will try to surround it, to shell it, and will bet on pro-Russian forces waking up and destabilizing Kharkiv from within," he replied. "Our task is to quell these separatist movements while the army does its job. And once we have secured the city, we will obviously join the army on the front line."

Unlike almost everyone else in Kharkiv, Nemichev and his men believed that war was unavoidable. "If Putin is bargaining and doesn't get what he wants, he must invade," he told me. "If he retreats without invading, his political career will be over. His entire career is built on conflict."

⊰⊱

Ever since coming to power in the final hours of 1999, Putin had focused on building up Russia's armed forces. He turned what had been an army of conscripts that struggled against separatist rebels in Chechnya, a Caucasus republic smaller than New Jersey, into a professional force supposedly comparable to the American military, with its expeditionary capabilities. He also transformed the celebrations of the 1945 Soviet victory over Nazi Germany into Russia's national religion, a unifying social glue in a country with many ethnic minorities and a fast-growing Muslim population. Every year on May 9, the high-pomp parade through central Moscow included the ever-more-sophisticated weapons in Russia's arsenal: the Armata tank, declared to be impervious to Western weapons; the Yars intercontinental ballistic missile; the Zemledeliye long-distance mine-laying launcher. Europe's thirst for Russian gas and oil had filled Moscow's coffers with cash: by January 2022, the Russian central bank sat on $643 billion in international reserves. With his macho aura and fervent defense of "traditional values,"

Putin was a hero to the seemingly ascendant European nationalist right, and to parts of the Republican Party in the United States.

He had reason to be smug. His 2008 invasion of Georgia had been cost-free. Western sanctions had been lifted quickly, and four years later a Putin-friendly government took power in Tbilisi, the Georgian capital. Russia's 2015 military intervention in Syria, which the Obama administration had predicted would result in a messy quagmire akin to the Soviet debacle in Afghanistan, had also been a resounding success. Using airpower and incurring minimal casualties, the Russians ensured the survival of President Bashar al-Assad in the face of an Islamist insurgency.

The same couldn't be said of the American client state in Afghanistan. In August 2021, even as US forces remained in Kabul, the Afghan army on which American taxpayers had spent more than $80 billion collapsed in days. President Ashraf Ghani, a former American citizen whose children never moved to Kabul, fled to the United Arab Emirates, and the Taliban seized power triumphantly. I had walked through the center of the Afghan capital on the final day of the Afghan republic, watching as government employees emptied ministry buildings, taking home their personal items, and as soldiers hurriedly discarded their uniforms, donning civilian clothes.

One country that agreed to help rescue Afghans who had worked with the West was Ukraine. In mid-August 2021, Zelensky's administration sent Ukrainian military planes to the Kabul airport, which was still controlled by American Marines, and dispatched special forces troops into hostile city territory to pick up the evacuees. Weeks later, when I returned to Kabul, the Taliban were already driving around the country in American Humvees and MRAPs and flying a Black Hawk over the city.

The combination of Russia's proven military prowess and the bitter aftertaste of America's debacle in Afghanistan meant that in the months before the Russian invasion, few in Washington, and even fewer in Paris and Berlin, held faith in Ukraine's ability to resist. If Kyiv was doomed, the reasoning went, there was no point in supplying Ukraine with heavy weapons that would quickly fall into enemy hands.

Washington rushed several planeloads of arms to Ukraine just as it began shutting down the American embassy in Kyiv in January 2022. These weapons, however, were more suitable for behind-the-lines insurgency operations than for a conventional war between two modern mechanized armies. The United States supplied ninety Javelin shoulder-fired antitank missiles—a potent weapon, but not nearly enough to match the thousands of Russian tanks arrayed on the border. With American permission, the Baltic states sent a few Stinger man-portable air-defense missiles, a weapon that America had provided to Afghanistan's mujahedeen in the 1980s. Britain, in perhaps the most consequential commitment, shipped about 2,000 short-range antitank missiles known as NLAWs.

But Ukraine's pleas for heavier weapons were falling on deaf ears. When Estonia tried to send Ukraine a handful of Soviet-designed D-30 howitzers that it had purchased from East German stocks, Berlin vetoed the move. "Our restrictive position is well known and is rooted in history," German foreign minister Annalena Baerbock said when she visited Kyiv in late January. She was referring to Germany's shameful history in World War II, of course. Yet Berlin had concluded it should not be helping Ukraine, which had lost more than seven million lives, or nearly one-fifth of its population, because of the war that Germany had unleashed in 1939. Those victims included my great-grandfather, murdered by the Nazis in Kyiv in 1941.

Instead of sending arms, German chancellor Olaf Scholz and French president Emmanuel Macron kept calling Putin, hoping that concessions by Ukraine, such as Zelensky returning to the Minsk-2 agreement on Russian terms, could somehow avert the war.

But Putin was already openly savoring Ukraine's impending death. "Love it or not, endure it, my beauty," he said about Ukraine at a February 7 press conference with Macron in Moscow. It was a play on a well-known song by the Russian punk rock band Red Mildew, popular during his younger years in the 1980s and 1990s. "The beauty's lying in a coffin, and I've crept up to fuck her," the song's full lyrics went. "Love it or not, keep sleeping, my beauty."

CHAPTER 3

THE LAST DAYS OF PEACE

I n mid-February, with the war just ten days away, most Ukrainians remained strangely nonchalant. No panic buying or hoarding, no mass exodus from the country. The currency was stable. The idea of full-scale
hostilities ravaging Kyiv was so outlandish, so hard to imagine, that people
simply refused to entertain it.

With myriad contingencies on his mind, Stevo had already purchased
a carload of camping gear in Kharkiv's new mall, in case we ended up sleeping rough. At his urging, I went shopping for hiking boots in the sprawling
sporting goods store on Kyiv's Antonovych Street.

"What kind of hiking do you expect to be doing?" the smiling sales-
woman asked me.

"I need them for the war," I said.

She looked at me like I was insane. Stevo advised me to buy leather. "It
doesn't burn as easily when you're hit," he explained.

THE CIA DIRECTOR, WILLIAM BURNS, SECRETLY FLEW TO KYIV, MEETING
Zelensky to warn him that Russia had planned a strike on the Ukrainian
capital via Belarus—and the Ukrainian president's assassination. The United
States possessed granular intelligence about Russian preparations, and Biden
had asked Burns to lay it all out in Kyiv. "They spoke about the physical

liquidation of our leadership, about the creation of filtration and concentration camps," Zelensky's national security adviser, Oleksiy Danilov, later recalled. "But what could we do? Since October, we kept asking: give us weapons. But they didn't really give weapons to us."

Though Zelensky took Burns's private warnings seriously, the Ukrainian government continued downplaying the risk of war in public. The Ukrainian president was worried that an outbreak of panic could precipitate an economic collapse and imperil military preparations. But there was also genuine disbelief that Russia could try to take over Ukraine with only the 200,000 troops on the border. Slightly bigger than metropolitan France, Ukraine spans more than 800 miles from one end to another. The working theory in Kyiv was that the coming war would likely center on the East, a much larger but still limited version of the 2014–2015 conflict over Donbas.

"They would need as many troops just for Kyiv, with all its hills, the river, the terrain. No way would they invade with so few men," one senior Zelensky adviser said in early February. Indeed, by historical standards, the forces gathered by Putin were tiny. In 1939, the Soviet Union sent more than twice as many soldiers to invade Finland—which had a population of 3.7 million at the time, or one-twelfth of Ukraine's. The Soviets still failed to capture Helsinki.

The disconnect between American and Ukrainian perceptions, explained Major General Kyrylo Budanov, the head of Ukraine's GUR military intelligence, was because the Americans had access to high-level human and signals intelligence sources and knew what Putin was being told by his generals. The Ukrainians had plentiful sources lower down in the Russian Armed Forces and bureaucracy, and knew that the generals were lying to Putin about their army's preparedness.

Still, in secret, the Ukrainian military was getting ready. The military's commander in chief, Valeriy Zaluzhny, ordered units to disperse around the country, ostensibly for training exercises, and moved air-defense batteries and military aircraft from their bases to new, hidden locations. Publicly, however, things proceeded as normal. "I was afraid that we would lose the element of surprise," Zaluzhny recalled later. "We needed the adversary to think that we are all deployed in our usual bases, smoking grass, watching TV, and posting on Facebook."

The secrecy was so tight that neither Washington nor many senior officials in the Zelensky administration knew what the Ukrainian military was doing. "We were pessimistic about Ukraine holding out in part because the Ukrainians didn't share any of their preparations or planning with us," a senior Pentagon official told me later. "And the preparations and plans that they did share with us were military deception. The military leadership was preparing to defend the country, but in revealing those plans to us, they worried that it would get back to their political leadership, which was in denial that the invasion would happen."

While the Ukrainian military managed to keep the Americans in the dark, how well could it protect its secrets from the Russian spies who had thoroughly infiltrated the country? "The Russian intelligence network operating here has been installed a long time ago. We haven't eliminated all of it, there is more work to do," Danilov, the national security adviser, told me in mid-February. "Their mission from Moscow Center is simple: destroy, destroy, destroy. They have no other mission except destroying us as a nation."

The Russians openly counted on that fifth column—particularly within the armed forces. Ukraine would put up only a fleeting resistance in case of war, Sergei Markov, the director of the pro-Kremlin Institute for Political Studies in Moscow and a former Putin adviser, predicted shortly before the invasion. "Most of the Ukrainian Army will quickly switch to the side of the Russian Federation, raising our flags," he said. "The population will also overwhelmingly support Russia."

❖

In the second week of February, I drove to the Russian border in the northern region of Chernihiv, studying the thick forests around the road on the way, imagining where the best locations would be for small Ukrainian units with their Javelins and NLAWs.

Local Donbas war veterans, Territorial Defense commanders, and active-duty military officials had just met behind closed doors in Chernihiv's conference hall to discuss organizing the resistance. They had few illusions.

"There will be artillery and missile strikes that will destroy critical infrastructure and military facilities. That is exactly what we are preparing for," said one of the participants, Maksym Konashevych. Regardless of what happened in Kyiv, the fight would go on, he said. "Our goal is clear: even if the leadership of the country tells us to surrender, we will not surrender. Everyone counts only on themselves, on their friends, on their family, on their comrades in arms."

Recently retired major general Serhiy Kryvonos, who had served as the chief of staff of Ukraine's special forces during the war for Donbas and later as Zelensky's deputy national security adviser, addressed the gathering on how to best prepare Chernihiv's defenses. How could Ukraine, with its rudimentary air defenses and outdated warplanes, resist the full strength of Russia's professional military? I asked.

"Russia's professional military?" Kryvonos scoffed. "You're trying to scare a doggie with a sausage. We beat them before, and we will beat them now. Look at Afghanistan: the Taliban had nothing to fight with, but they ended up forcing the United States to withdraw. What is most important is not the military hardware, but the motivated, trained people. No army in the world could ever overcome a motivated people."

When I pointed out that America's war in Afghanistan lasted two decades and caused an untold number of Afghan deaths, the major general's answer was quick: "Ukraine is ready to fight a long time," he said. "Yes, we are preparing to fight one of the biggest armies of the world, and there will be losses. We can lose a battle, even a campaign. But the Russian army will never triumph over the Ukrainian people."

PART 2

INVASION

CHAPTER 4

"WE WILL FIGHT. WE WILL NOT SURRENDER."

Before dawn on February 24, 2022, Volodymyr Radchenko, a noted orthopedic surgeon in Kharkiv, and his wife, Gelya, were shaken out of bed by loud explosions. They looked out of their second-floor window to see the horizon lit up with fires and trails of missiles. The couple had built a spacious house in the village of Velyki Prokhody north of the city because they sought clean air for their son, Sashko, who had suffered from respiratory problems in his childhood. Russia was so close that from their balcony they could see the forested strip marking the international border.

Radchenko's wife, a computer engineer, initially thought the Russians had drunkenly set off fireworks. Then their phones buzzed with messages from friends elsewhere in Ukraine. "Rush, rush, we have to leave," Radchenko told her. "The war has begun."

Their passports were handy: the documents were near expiration and the couple had planned to travel to Kharkiv to renew them. They grabbed what they could and, still in their pajamas and nightgowns, jumped into the car with sixteen-year-old Sashko. Gelya's mother, Tetyana, refused to leave. "You'll come back for the weekend, right?" she asked her daughter as the car sped off. The highway was empty, but some trees were already felled by shelling, as if a tornado had ripped through.

The Russian tanks appeared on the streets of Velyki Prokhody fifteen minutes later. Behind them, more and more Russian troops poured into the country from all directions, some of them setting up in the Radchenkos' backyard. Tetyana and her daughter were now living in two different worlds, separated by a front line. Millions of Ukrainian families were about to meet the same fate, some staying under occupation, others fleeing farther and farther away from their homes.

Vasyl Romanika, the mayor of the town of Boromlya, not far from the Russian border in the northern Sumy region, spent three entire days sitting in his office, watching the Russian armor drive by. He tried to count at first, but there were just too many tanks, howitzers, armored personnel carriers, and trucks. Bypassing the regional capital, Sumy, and other secondary cities, these troops, displaying "Z" tactical markers, streamed toward their main prize: Kyiv. So did a Russian force with "V" markings that invaded from Belarus, making its way along the right bank of the Dnipro from the northwest. A third group, its tanks and artillery daubed with "O" markings, advanced along the left bank of the Dnipro, bypassing Chernihiv and heading toward Kyiv's eastern suburbs. Hundreds of missile and bomb strikes hit cities all over Ukraine—including Uman, where Manu was sleeping. He was jolted out of bed by the blasts at a nearby Ukrainian military base.

Russian Black Sea Fleet warships sailed toward the Ukrainian coastline that morning, with the fleet's flagship, the cruiser *Moskva*, approaching the rocky Snake Island that sat off the Danube delta marking the Romanian border.

⟺

Putin had been presented several options for the campaign. The most logical one would have concentrated Russian forces in the east, surrounding and annihilating the cream of the Ukrainian Army stuck in Donbas. A war limited to Donbas would have likely elicited only limited Western reaction. It could have also been won relatively quickly, causing a political crisis in Kyiv and a possible collapse of the Zelensky administration. Ukraine's foreign minister, Dmytro Kuleba, told me, "If Russia had done so, I'm afraid the position of our partners would have been different and the logic of the Minsk process—based on the idea of concessions to avoid a big war—would have still been enforced."

But Putin wanted much more: all of Ukraine.

"Out of the several options that Putin had before the war, and we knew very well what these options were, he ended up choosing the toughest—and the worst for him," said Major General Budanov, the GUR military intelligence chief. "Russian experts had repeatedly warned him that this option is the least preferable one and must be carefully weighed. But he picked the cruelest one."

Putin's war plan to capture Kyiv in a speedy blitzkrieg was premised on an obsessive idea, fueled by reading the wrong history books during months of self-isolation during the COVID pandemic. He believed that Ukraine was an artificial state, and that its people—and soldiers—wouldn't fight when faced with the overwhelming strength of the Russian military. Documents later found on dead and captured Russian officers showed that Moscow expected the whole war to wrap up in ten days, with a new collaborationist regime installed in Kyiv and most of the country pacified under Russian control. The group with "V" markings that invaded via the exclusion zone of the 1986 Chornobyl nuclear disaster on the right bank of the Dnipro was the primary force tasked with seizing Kyiv. In the second, "O"-marked, group streaming to Kyiv from the northeast, a large part consisted of the Russian National Guard—an internal security force that, according to captured plans, would be mopping up protests and detaining Ukrainian elites in the occupied capital.

Putin's war plan was being kept secret even from Russian battalion tactical group commanders on the ground in Belarus, who received their marching orders only hours before crossing the border. Ukrainian intelligence officers observing these units didn't see the invasion until it was too late to redeploy their own forces from Donbas. The deception put Kyiv in mortal peril. No major Ukrainian units confronted the huge Russian column from Belarus on the right bank of the Dnipro as it made its way through the marshlands and forests of the nuclear exclusion zone around Chornobyl.

"The volume of that invasion from Belarus was unexpected. On the eve of it, none of our partners forecasted such a sizable invasion force, as surprising as it seems now," acknowledged Zelensky's senior adviser, Mykhailo Podolyak.

Though overall the Russian invasion contingent was roughly the same size as the Ukrainian military, in the first days of the war Russian troops outnumbered Ukrainian soldiers twelve to one on the Kyiv front. Ten Ukrainian brigades—about half of Ukraine's available maneuver forces at the time—were in Donbas.

Ukraine's defenses were even weaker in the south, where the open terrain allowed Russia to use its air superiority to annihilate resisting Ukrainian units. The Russian military took full advantage of this imbalance in the first hours of the war, fanning out from Crimea and seizing vast areas.

◆◆◆

On February 24, Zelensky had only just gone to bed after a long night in the office when the warning came that Russian artillery units along the border were preparing for shelling. He woke up his wife, Olena, an architect who had spent years working as a scriptwriter for his comedy shows. "You must explain everything to the children, because it is war," he told her before rushing back to the presidential headquarters on Bankova Street atop the Pechersk hill. It was the last time he would see his daughter and son for months.

There was hardly anyone on Bankova when Zelensky returned to his desk. Once fully briefed by the military, he got British prime minister Boris Johnson on the line. It was still the middle of the night in London. Like other Western leaders, Johnson had been told by advisers that Ukraine's fight was futile. "Some of the defense intelligence people were saying: look, this is going to be very one-sided. The Russians are just going to roll through," Johnson recalled. The universal Western assumption, he added, was that the years ahead would be spent supporting a guerrilla campaign in occupied Ukraine, making it hard for Putin to hold what he had conquered.

Still, Johnson offered support—and a haven. "For God's sake, find a way of looking after yourself," the British prime minister said he told Zelensky. "If there is anything we can do to help you find somewhere to be safe, then we want to do it." One possibility, Johnson explained to me, was to set up a Zelensky government-in-exile in London, the way a Polish government-in-exile had been established there after the Nazi and Soviet invasions of 1939: "I thought his survival was pretty indispensable to Ukrainian resistance."

Zelensky wasn't interested. He wanted the West to help ensure the survival of Ukraine, a commitment of a different order of magnitude.

"We will fight," Zelensky told Johnson. "We will not surrender."

As Ukraine's national security council gathered in the Bankova compound at 7 a.m., Zelensky's own security detail and a few aides also urged him to move to another, safer location in the city—or to leave Kyiv altogether. The president refused to consider the proposal. "Try to tell me this one more time, and that will be the end of you here," he told one senior aide, who was privately convinced that the Russians could be in central Kyiv within hours.

At around 8 a.m., Ukrainian lawmakers gathered in the domed parliament building, a ten-minute walk from Bankova. They were disheveled, some of them in tracksuits and with suitcases, nervously scrolling their phones for updates. Unlike the previous day, when faction leaders had made long speeches before voting in emergency laws, there was no time for debate. The parliament's speaker, Ruslan Stefanchuk, brought in two decrees from Zelensky, one declaring martial law and another ordering a general mobilization. The lawmakers approved the legislation, which among other things banned foreign travel for men under sixty. Fifteen minutes later, they dispersed. The police started issuing Kalashnikov assault rifles to every member of parliament who wanted one.

Some of these lawmakers and other officials walked over to the presidential headquarters, where Zelensky briefed them on the morning's events and stressed the need to maintain the government's legitimacy. Suddenly, his security detail burst in, warning that Russian special forces hit squads had already infiltrated Pechersk, aiming to assassinate the president and other senior officials. In addition, they warned, there was a high risk of a Russian missile strike on the building. The meeting ended abruptly. Zelensky was rushed to his underground bunker.

Gathering the cabinet via a secure video link, Prime Minister Denys Shmyhal ordered ministers not directly involved in the country's defense to leave Kyiv for western Ukraine, to ensure the government's continuity should Russia capture the capital. Those ministers who remained in Kyiv sent their deputies away as backup.

The foreign minister, Kuleba, was in the air, flying on a Turkish Airlines plane from New York to Kyiv when the invasion began. The plane had Wi-Fi, so he texted his assistant to rebook the connecting flight to Warsaw instead. After he landed in Poland, he briefed Zelensky on his conversations with Biden and other US officials. "If everyone gives us a week or ten days," Kuleba told Zelensky, "it means that we have to survive by all means, whatever it takes." Zelensky asked him to go to western Ukraine, rather than Kyiv, as part of the backup cabinet plan.

Danilov, the national security adviser, worried that morning about whether the machinery of the Ukrainian state would hold together. "The first day of war is the hardest one. The problem of the first day of the war is that you don't know how people will behave," he recalled. "How many will run away scared, and how many will stay put to carry out their duties? This is something you can't be sure of ahead of time. Humans, they are weak creatures by nature."

❖

At around 10 a.m., Zelensky made his first address to the nation since Russia invaded. Unlike the previous night's speech, which had been recorded by a professional TV crew, it was filmed vertically on his phone. Zelensky stood in a rumpled blazer in front of a gilded frame in his office, the collar of his white shirt unbuttoned.

"Today, Putin started a war with Ukraine, with the entire democratic world. He wants to destroy my country, our country, everything that we have built, everything that we are living for," Zelensky said. "We need, together, to save Ukraine and the entire democratic world."

Once Zelensky was done with the recording, he resumed calling foreign leaders, trying to rally international support. The call with France's Macron, which the French government released later, showed just how chaotic the morning was.

"We hear that they sent [Russian] special forces everywhere in Kyiv," Macron said in English.

"Everywhere. In Kyiv, in Odesa, and from Belarus. So we fight everywhere on our territory. It is not the same like it was in 2014," Zelensky replied.

"It's clear. It's total war," Macron said, bringing his hands together and frowning as he processed the information. "Okay. Okay."

"Emmanuel, it's really important that you speak with Putin, and it's important to make an antiwar coalition," Zelensky implored him.

France, unlike the United States and the United Kingdom, still operated an embassy in Kyiv. Macron offered Zelensky refuge in the diplomatic compound should Russian special forces overrun the city. The Ukrainian leader politely declined the offer.

As Zelensky and Macron spoke, dozens of Russian combat helicopters carrying some of Moscow's best-trained troops took off from Belarus. They were headed toward the Ukrainian capital.

CHAPTER 5

UKRAINE BARES ITS TEETH

With the Russian Army possessing an overwhelming advantage in artillery, long-range rockets, and aircraft, as well as cruise missiles that could hit anywhere in Ukraine, the priority of the Ukrainian military leadership was to preserve the country's ability to resist after Moscow's first strike. It was imperative to stall the Russians long enough for the mobilization, the deployment of reserves, and the expected foreign aid to make a difference.

As Russia attacked along ten different axes, General Zaluzhny made a strategic decision to trade land for time. Defending Kyiv was the absolute priority: if the capital fell, nothing else would matter. Instead of fighting for every village and getting wiped out by Russia's superior firepower, Ukrainian troops pulled back to more defensible positions, aiming to bleed the Russians as much as possible along the way. Zaluzhny's orders to the troops were to "show teeth"—and there was little hesitation to open fire, unlike in 2014. "For eight years, we were morally preparing to start killing the enemy, instead of waiting for it to calm down and leave us be," he recalled. In the forests north and east of Kyiv, Ukrainian units started to ambush the Russian columns and take the first prisoners. Videos of frightened captured Russian soldiers, with their red armbands, quickly appeared on social media and Ukrainian TV, raising the nation's morale.

Following the centralized Soviet doctrine, Russia's army is strictly hierarchical. Key decisions are made at the very top, even local operations require layers of approvals, and initiative is often punished rather than rewarded. A former KGB intelligence service lieutenant colonel who skipped mandatory military service in his youth, Putin was at the pinnacle of this pyramid, directly running the war and making tactical military decisions. The culture of hiding errors meant that the information reported up the Russian chain of command was biased toward exaggerating successes and minimizing problems, a flaw that prevented the Russian military from quickly adjusting once it encountered unexpected setbacks.

Zelensky had never served in the military either, but once the war began, he delegated command of operations to Zaluzhny and other generals while maintaining broad oversight. "He doesn't need to understand military affairs any more than he needs to know about medicine or bridge building," Zaluzhny explained in a *Time* magazine interview. In the previous eight years, Western advisers had helped shift the Ukrainian military's once-Soviet doctrine toward NATO standards. The new organizing principle was known as "mission command"—the idea that once the top commander's overall intent was clear, units were free to execute their missions as they saw fit, without asking for additional permission.

Running an army this way requires a high degree of trust, something that comes more naturally in a democracy. It was the secret to Ukraine's resilience.

"This is what saved Ukraine at the outset of the war. When the offensives began on many operational directions, one of the goals of the Russians was to overwhelm Ukraine by the quantity of engagements. If the approach had remained centralized, Ukraine wouldn't have been able to manage it. The command systems would have been overloaded, and commanders would have had to make a multitude of decisions without knowing what is happening on the ground, without being able to visit the troops," said Andriy Zagorodnyuk, who headed the reforms project at the ministry of defense under Poroshenko and served as Zelensky's defense minister in 2019 and 2020. "It would have been catastrophic."

Russian leaders suffered from a fatal blind spot when it came to Ukraine:

believing that Russians and Ukrainians are one people, they assumed that the Ukrainians thought just as they did. In a war between a big Soviet army and a small Soviet army, the outcome would have been preordained. But the Ukrainians, it turned out, had a different mindset—and a different plan.

⁂

In the first hours of the war, information was scarce. Wild rumors proliferated. Russia's ministry of defense announced that first morning that it had succeeded in destroying the Ukrainian air-defense system and the Ukrainian Air Force, and that Russian troops were facing little to no resistance. "Units and soldiers of the Armed Forces of Ukraine are fleeing their positions en masse, leaving their weapons behind," it said.

Ever since 2014, the Kremlin had cultivated a class of militaristic propagandists, some of them affiliated with Moscow newspapers and TV channels, some operating solely on social media. Many of these *voenkors*, the Russian shorthand for military correspondents, had followings in the hundreds of thousands or even millions on Telegram, the social media platform owned by Russian-born entrepreneur Pavel Durov, who had emigrated to Dubai after run-ins with the Kremlin.

The morning of February 24, the *voenkors*—many of whom added a "Z," which had been adopted as a symbol of the Russian invasion, to their handles—were euphoric. Kharkiv had already fallen, they wrote, and Odesa was mere hours away. By the day's end, the Ukrainian state would be no more. A meme circulated describing the mock timetable of the Russian-Ukrainian war; it foresaw an invasion after breakfast, a Russian military parade on Kyiv's Khreshchatyk after lunch, and celebratory fireworks after dinner.

Girkin, the former defense minister of Donetsk, was living in Moscow by then. He had garnered a large social media audience as a fiercely nationalist military affairs commentator who sometimes criticized the Kremlin. He took a more cautious tone than most *voenkors*. "So, the war that was inevitable since 2014 has begun," he wrote the morning of February 24. "I sincerely wish the Russian Army a quick and decisive victory. If only because the only thing that is worse than a victorious war is a lost war. And because the Putins come and go, while Russia remains."

———

STEVO AND I DROVE AROUND CENTRAL KYIV SHORTLY AFTER 10 A.M. THERE was no sign of Russian special forces anywhere, and not much Ukrainian military presence either. Every business except for grocery stores and pharmacies was shuttered. In a sprawling MegaMarket store, bleary-eyed Kyivites packed the trunks of their cars with necessities—canned food, candles, big bottles of drinking water. While cheaper items had begun to run out, the store was brimming with luxuries. There was a fish tank with live sturgeon and lobsters, fresh pineapples and strawberries from South Africa, the finest Italian prosciutto, and French cheeses. We filled our bags with PowerBars, cans of tuna, dried mangoes, and beef jerky.

With the country's survival uncertain, I had expected that everyone would want dollars instead of hryvnia, the Ukrainian currency. But there was no longer an official exchange rate—and nobody wanted to speculate. I could still pay with Apple Pay, the cashier told me helpfully. People all around lined up at the checkout, quietly and stoically, making it a point of pride to maintain civility and order.

Oleksandr Trembach, a surgeon, told me he was determined to stay put in Kyiv, along with his wife, mother-in-law, daughter, son-in-law, and three grandchildren, even as many neighbors fled that morning. "We will overcome this evil. Ukrainians are strong," he said as he bought salt, chicken, and yogurt. "If need be, we will be shooting at the Russians from every window. We know how."

We had another mission that morning. While all the *Journal*'s Afghan reporters who found shelter in Ukraine the previous August had already resettled in Canada, Sahar, a young Afghan actress who had arrived with them, was still in Kyiv. With an unrestrained desire to help everyone he could, Stevo had secured an invitation for her to attend a film festival in Spain, but her passport was stuck in the Spanish embassy.

It was a beehive of activity as diplomats and security staff tried to organize the evacuation of Spanish citizens living in Ukraine and their families. Buses were lined up in front of the compound, and grim-faced Spanish officials paced with printouts of names and addresses. Children wailed. "We only deal with the Spanish nationals now," one of the embassy staffers

barked when I asked for Sahar's passport. I lost my cool and unloaded on
another muscular Spanish official who looked like he was military or security personnel. "She just fled the Taliban, and if the Russians come here,
they will hand her over and kill her," I said in broken Spanish. "Señor, do
you have any honor?"

The man looked at me, asked for the full name, and came back with Sahar's passport ten minutes later. "What on earth did you tell him?" she
asked me, incredulous.

By lunchtime, most of the Hyatt hotel's staff had deserted. Food was
limited, too. We ate what we could, while Sean Penn planned his departure
from Kyiv at the next table, as Telegram channels started pumping out
frightening videos of Russian helicopters. The choppers were firing flares on
all sides, crossing the wide reservoir on the Dnipro north of Kyiv, and flying into the city's Hostomel Airport.

CHAPTER 6

"RUSSIAN WARSHIP, GO FUCK YOURSELF"

Russia's air assault troops, known as VDV, are the pride of its military. They have a long history of daring strikes and train extensively in securing enemy airfields. If Russia were to gain full control of a Kyiv airport on day one of the war, landing transport planes with troops and equipment there, the Ukrainian capital would be at Moscow's mercy.

That Russia would try to seize Hostomel was known in advance to the CIA, whose director had briefed Zelensky and Ukrainian commanders in the run-up to the war. British special forces had placed sensors and cameras in the area. The Ukrainians already had their own separate intelligence confirming the plan, but the scale of the Russian attack still caught them by surprise.

Located on the northwest edge of Kyiv, just ten miles from the capital's ring road, Hostomel, with its 2.4-mile-long runway, is suitable for planes of all sizes. It was used mostly by Antonov, the Ukrainian aircraft manufacturer. The heaviest aircraft ever built, the Antonov-225 Mriya, or Dream, was under repair and remained parked in a Hostomel hangar after the company flew most of its other planes to Europe in the hours before the invasion began.

Kyiv has two other airports, used for commercial aviation. The main one, Boryspil, is located outside the city on the left bank of the wide Dnipro River and would be unsuitable for mounting an attack because all the government institutions sit on the higher right bank. The Ukrainian military worried more about the Russians landing airborne troops in Zhuliany, a smaller airport located wholly within the city—less than three miles from the ministry of defense.

Ukraine's National Guard, which reports to the ministry of interior rather than the ministry of defense, was responsible for Hostomel. Some 200 guardsmen, three-quarters of them young conscripts doing mandatory service, were deployed at the Guard's base on the edge of the airport compound. The previous night, airport staff had put trucks across the runway, to prevent any planes from landing. Before dawn, the brigade's senior non-commissioned officer—a Donbas war veteran who went by the call sign Stolytsia, or Capital, because he's a native of Kyiv—jumped into a car to inspect and reinforce positions around the airstrip. Minutes after he was gone, a Russian missile struck the Guard's base. It missed the barracks, hitting the parade grounds instead. By then, most of his men were already deployed in small groups around the airport.

At 10 a.m., a fleet of nearly forty Russian helicopters flew low over the Dnipro reservoir, which is known as the Kyiv Sea because it is more than seven miles wide. This stealthy approach allowed them to evade Ukrainian air defenses until they approached Kyiv's northern outskirts. Two helicopters were shot down there, but the remaining choppers, shooting flares to divert missiles, banked right. They appeared above Hostomel before 11 a.m., with Ka-52 and Mi-24 gunships laying fire to protect the heavy Mi-8 troop transporter helicopters packed with the VDV's best. Two Russian fighter-bomber jets swerved in and out, lobbing missiles into the National Guard's outposts.

The National Guard troops in Hostomel didn't have the American Stinger missiles—only a small number had been supplied to Ukraine before the war began, and these had been dispatched to other units. Still, the Ukrainians could defend the airfield with antiaircraft guns and 1960s-vintage Soviet-designed shoulder-fired Igla missiles. They fired all they had at the enemy, including Kalashnikov rifles and machine guns. Three Russian helicopters, including two armored Ka-52 flying fortresses, went down in flames. Lieutenant Serhiy Falatiuk was surprised when he managed to shoot down the first chopper with his Igla. "They burn!" he shouted. "You can hit them!" Three other choppers were damaged over Hostomel and pulled away. But the swarm of Russian aircraft was too numerous, and the Ukrainian defenders ran out of antiaircraft missiles. Most of the Russian helicopters managed to land, disgorging nearly 300 VDV troops who quickly seized strategic terrain and took over the airport's headquarters, with its Soviet-built underground bunkers that provided cover against artillery.

The implications of the Russian takeover in Hostomel were potentially catastrophic. That morning, Russian Il-76 transport planes were already taking off with VDV troops and their armored vehicles in the northern city of Pskov. An entire brigade or two of Russia's best forces could be airlifted to the doorstep of Kyiv within hours, with Hostomel providing a gateway for a devastating attack on the city. Russia's main invasion force, meanwhile, was already moving overland from Chornobyl.

The Ukrainian National Guard unit in Hostomel possessed some light artillery at its base on the other side of the airfield. The troops lobbed salvoes of mortars at the landing strip, hoping to damage it enough to prevent the Il-76 transporters from landing. As Russian helicopter gunships continued the attack, the guardsmen and a small special forces detachment, which had rushed to help them, pulled back toward Kyiv. Several Ukrainian troops were taken prisoner inside Hostomel. This three-hour battle, and the decision to shell the landing strip, bought valuable time for Kyiv's defense.

Once the National Guard withdrew, the VDV troops—who wore no identifying markers except for orange-and-black stripes of the St. George's ribbon, a symbol of Russian military valor—deployed at the checkpoint on the entrance to the Hostomel compound. A CNN reporter, Matthew Chance, drove up shortly thereafter, assuming that the soldiers at the gate were Ukrainian. He asked them, "Where are the Russians?"

"We are the Russians," the men replied. Stunned, he noticed the St. George's colors. The Russians shooed him away as gunfire erupted.

The Ukrainians were desperate to dislodge the VDV from Hostomel and sent fresh forces to counterattack. At dusk, Ukraine's 95th Air Assault Brigade, based in nearby Zhytomyr, ferried its own troops by helicopter to the airport's periphery. Other units hauled artillery by road. The Ukrainian Air Force, which had hidden and dispersed its planes during the Russian missile strikes that morning, sent jets to bomb Hostomel's runway. The planes carrying Russian VDV reinforcements couldn't land. Though inferior to Russia's modern aircraft, Ukrainian MiG-29s continued to fly because Russia's ministry of defense, believing its own victorious reports about having destroyed the Ukrainian Air Force, had told Russian troops to assume that any planes in the air were Russian.

By nightfall, Zelensky appeared on TV once again. This time, he was dressed in an olive drab shirt. The Russians were pinned down in Hostomel, he said, and he had given orders to destroy them. He put the day's events in perspective. "What we are hearing today is not the explosions of missiles, the sound of combat, and the roar of aviation, but the sound of a new iron curtain coming down and isolating Russia from the civilized world," Zelensky said. "Our national mission is to make sure that this curtain doesn't come down on our, Ukrainian, territory."

President Biden made a call to Kyiv that afternoon—in the American morning of February 24. His advisers wavered about whether they should be disturbing Zelensky but decided that they had to offer support. He could always decline the call, after all. Zelensky was patched in quickly, and the tone of his voice left some of the Americans distraught. The Ukrainian president implied to Biden that this could be their last conversation, as the Russians were trying to kill him. He didn't exude steely confidence in Ukrainian victory. Some Biden administration officials were convinced after the call that Zelensky would flee Kyiv within hours.

Beyond Hostomel, the Russians advanced everywhere except the established front line in Donbas—north from Crimea, south from Belgorod and Bryansk, and west from Rostov. They were already on Kharkiv's ring road, having reached the southern port city of Kherson, and seized the Kakhovka Dam on the Dnipro. Roads leading out of Kyiv to Poland were jammed with fleeing civilians. Train tickets sold out, and Ukrainian Railways put up special, free evacuation trains west.

In Austria, Kharkiv businessman Vsevolod Kozhemiako, ranked by *Forbes* as the country's eighty-eighth-wealthiest man, with a prewar fortune of $100 million, cut short his family vacation at the Lech ski resort. A close friend of Volodymyr Radchenko, the surgeon from Velyki Prokhody, Kozhemiako dropped off his wife and children in Vienna and headed to the

Ukrainian border, one of the few people to cross eastward as hundreds of thousands escaped to the west. Most of the others returning to Ukraine were men like him, who decided that they couldn't live with themselves if they sat out the fight. How can I not go? he kept thinking. Within days, tens of thousands of Ukrainian men living and working in Europe or the United States had made the same journey, abandoning their jobs and families to fight for their homeland.

❖

I n the Black Sea, Russian warships approached the tiny Snake Island where a garrison of some eighty Ukrainian troops, most of them border guards and Marines, was posted. The rocky outcrop, where legend says Achilles is buried, sits in a strategic position just over twenty miles from the coasts of Ukraine and Romania, overlooking the shipping lanes from Odesa and traffic up the Danube. Its defenders had only light weapons and antiaircraft guns—nothing to protect them from the firepower of the cruiser *Moskva*, the patrol ship *Vasily Bykov*, and Russian naval aviation. With its array of antiship and antiaircraft missiles, and more than 500 sailors on board, *Moskva* was the most powerful vessel in the entire Black Sea.

The Russian warships used VHF channel 16, the international distress frequency, to broadcast their demands to Snake Island's garrison. "It is clear that the United States of America will fight until the last Ukrainian," the Russians began. "If you refuse to take part in a fratricidal war and choose the right side, you will have an opportunity to arrange your life as a civilian or to continue serving in the Armed Forces of the Russian Federation, with the prospects of career advancement, stable wages, the solution of personal problems, and a high military pension at retirement, living in a single big country."

Hours later, the Russian tone became more menacing: "Your chances of survival are zero. Think of your families and loved ones who expect you at home alive." With no surrender agreement forthcoming, Russian warplanes carried out a strike on the island, and then another.

As Ukrainian border guard staff on the mainland listened to this radio traffic, the Russians tried again. "I am the Russian warship, I propose to lay down your weapons and surrender to avoid bloodshed," the voice on the radio said. This time, a Ukrainian trooper on Snake Island had had enough. "Russian warship," he responded, "go fuck yourself!"

Shortly thereafter, transmissions from Snake Island ceased as Russia landed its forces. Ukrainian officials assumed the worst. In his address late that night, Zelensky said that all the border guards on the island had been killed after refusing to give in. The radio transmission's recording spread like wildfire. "Russian warship, go fuck yourself" turned into the instant rallying cry of Ukrainian resistance.

In truth, Snake Island's entire garrison ended up being taken prisoner by the Russians, with some released later in POW exchanges and many others spending more than a year in captivity. But it took weeks for the legend of their heroic deaths to be disproven. In the meantime, the response of the Snake Island border guard inspired thousands of Ukrainian soldiers all along the front lines.

⊹⊹⊹

That afternoon, February 24, Manu arrived in Kyiv after his long trip from Donbas via Uman, disheveled and exhausted. He had expected to spend just a few days there and had left his suitcase in Kyiv's Holiday Inn hotel. But the hotel was now locked, all its staff gone. I had to lend him a spare pair of jeans.

We took a drive through Kyiv's streets after nightfall. Khreshchatyk remained brightly illuminated, the windows of fashion stores sparkling with lights and neon signs reflecting in the asphalt. There were no other cars, no other people to be seen anywhere. It was before 8 p.m., but it seemed like the dead of night.

Hostomel, Ukrainian officials reported at the time, had been retaken from the Russians. Zaluzhny projected optimism. "We are fighting. It will be hard, but we will hold out. The Russian blitzkrieg has failed. They will wash in their own blood," Ukraine's top general said.

At first light, Manu and I headed over to Hostomel to see for ourselves.

CHAPTER 7

"WE ARE ALL HERE"

Sirens sounded in the middle of the night as another wave of Russian airstrikes hit Kyiv before dawn on February 25. A high-rise on the left bank of the Dnipro was struck and caught fire. The Hyatt's basement shelter was full, with cots for families with children. They had hoped an international hotel would be the safest place in town. Staff prepared a rudimentary breakfast on plastic trays. There were no more elaborate buffets with five varieties of smoked fish, fresh pineapples and strawberries, and a selection of cheeses. Sahar, the actress, stayed with us in the hotel, with the few belongings she had brought from Kabul, as Stevo organized a convoy of cars toward the Polish border.

Devoid of traffic, cities shrink. That morning, Manu and I sped through the empty avenues of Kyiv to the capital's northwestern edge, seeing almost no military presence and encountering no checkpoints. It was only on the ring road that we ran into several BMP-1 tracked fighting vehicles, which roared out of the forest and onto the highway, mixing with civilian cars right next to a giant statue of a soccer ball wrapped in Ukrainian and Polish colors—a relic from the 2012 European Championship cohosted by the two neighboring nations.

After turning left into the Hostomel municipal boundaries, we spotted other cars U-turning and careening at high speed. A lone BMP blocked the road, just before a bridge over the Irpin River. "We're trying to get to

Hostomel airfield," I told a soldier who stood in front of us. The man was agitated, waving his rifle. "Go, go, go now!" he shouted. "The Russians are coming, they'll be here anytime. We're about to blow up the bridge." A volley of machine-gun fire burst through the air. We dove for cover and ran back to our car. Ukrainian announcements of retaking Hostomel were clearly premature. Overnight, Russian columns making their way from Chornobyl had advanced through the nuclear exclusion zone, their forward elements linking up with Russian VDV troops holed up in Hostomel's bunkers. The previous day's clashes, and the Ukrainian artillery's fire, however, had sufficiently damaged the runways to prevent Russian reinforcements from landing. The Russians still didn't have enough of a force for a decisive assault on the Ukrainian capital, or the ability to fly one in.

We drove for a few minutes back to the ring road that marked Kyiv's city limits. The weather was warm, and the snow had melted. Close to a hundred Ukrainian volunteer fighters were gathering along the road in a strip of forest, its deciduous trees all leafless. Commanded by a handful of uniformed officers, they were digging shallow trenches, preparing to confront Russian tanks. Most didn't have helmets, let alone body armor; they wore blue jeans and baseball caps. Clustered close to each other, in defiance of basic military tactics, they didn't seem to have any weapons heavier than Kalashnikov rifles. They would have had no chance against a Russian helicopter run, or a tank. Spotting me snapping a photo, the commander shooed us away. He didn't want pictures or interviews. This was not the time.

Elsewhere in the city, Mykola Volokhov, a Donbas war veteran and amateur bike racer who had just graduated from law school, gathered his friends, many of them also former fighters. In previous months, they had spent their weekends participating in medieval tournament reenactments, usually as fifteenth-century Flemish knights. "It was small groups against small groups—good training," he recalled. Immediately, they started planning for urban combat against a more formidable foe, creating small mobile teams that would roam Kyiv's streets in civilian vehicles, armed with machine guns, antitank missiles, and rocket-propelled grenades. They received their weapons that day, after signing up for the Territorial Defense.

❖

Several SUVs stood in the Hyatt's driveway, engines running, getting ready to depart toward Lviv. My *Journal* colleagues had been ordered by the paper's management to move to the relative safety of western Ukraine. Sahar was departing, too. Sean Penn was already gone. Stevo gave Sahar his body armor for the trip. He had two extra plates, but no Kevlar carrier vest for himself. Every morning thereafter, until we found a spare carrier a few days later, would begin with Manu and me securing these plates around Stevo's torso with half a roll of duct tape.

Only Stevo, Manu, and I stayed in the empty, darkened hotel lobby once the convoy got going. It was a slow ride because hundreds of thousands of Kyivites hit the same highway that day. Usually, it takes under six hours to drive to Lviv. My colleagues and Sahar got there more than two days later, after one of their cars broke down.

We sat in the lobby, lights switched off to save energy, and scrolled Telegram and Twitter for news. The situation wasn't encouraging. In the northeast, Russian columns that bypassed Chernihiv had already reached the edge of the Kyiv suburb of Brovary. In the early afternoon, a presumed Russian military vehicle was spotted in Kyiv's northern neighborhood of Obolon, losing control and running over a civilian sedan. Viktor Medvedchuk, the head of Ukraine's main pro-Russian party, who had been under house arrest pending a treason investigation, used the disarray to escape, likely smuggled out by his bodyguards.

Medvedchuk wasn't just a friend of Putin, he was family: in 2004, the Russian president had become the godfather of his daughter Daryna. The disappearance was ominous. Should Russia take Kyiv, I thought, Medvedchuk would be the lead candidate to head Ukraine's new puppet regime. There were other candidates, of course. Yanukovych, the fugitive former president, had already made his way to Minsk, hoping for restoration.

It would be stupid to be stuck in Kyiv in case it became surrounded by the Russians, I argued. The communications would go down, and we would be unable to file stories about the war as Ukrainians made a stand somewhere west of the city. So in the late afternoon, we packed our SUV and decided to drive south—close enough to come back in the morning, but far enough to be outside the potential encirclement zone. We made our way through suburban roads hugging the Dnipro and hit the empty highway to Odesa. At the highway junction, a column of Ukrainian reinforcements passed us heading in the other direction toward the capital, with dour soldiers sitting atop the armor of several BMPs. Every car on the road honked, people stopping to come out and raise their fists and wave at the troops. "It's good to see soldiers going to Kyiv, not leaving it," I told Stevo. "These boys are gonna fight," he replied.

We drove past the town of Vasylkiv, where an air-force academy on the main road, just across from a military airfield, had been bombed the previous day. Rudimentary barricades made of sandbags, tractors, and trucks started appearing on the highway, manned by local villagers with hunting rifles. These, too, would stand no chance against a Russian tank, Stevo noted.

Once we hit a thirty-five-mile distance from Kyiv, I started looking for a place to stay. Google Maps churned out a fishing lodge, with the owner's cell-phone number. I called him and he met us at the pond, by a mock road sign indicating the presence of witches. A former military pilot, he was suspicious at first, making sure we weren't Russians, before he gave us a two-bedroom timber cottage overlooking the water. "Don't drive out at night," he warned. "The guys around here are setting up ambushes everywhere in case the Russians come down, and they may shoot you by mistake." A village woman would bring us *varenyky* dumplings and some fried fish for dinner.

Once he was gone and we had settled on the porch, we heard a deafening sound above us. A MiG-29 fighter jet. Russian? But when the plane tipped its wings, we could see the Ukrainian *tryzub*, the country's trident-like coat of arms, glistening in the sun. Despite Russia's claims of destroying Ukraine's air force and air defenses in the first hours of the war, Ukraine still retained the ability to operate its military aircraft. Another jet flew above us minutes later, and then another.

In Kyiv, Zelensky's aides sandbagged the windows of the presidential building on Bankova, with the security detail also placing machine guns in the openings and stocking ammunition on the ornate parquet floor. They prepared to defend the compound against Russian infiltrators. "This may be the last time you see me," the Ukrainian president said as he spoke by video-conference with leaders of the European Union. Some proposed to spirit Zelensky out of Kyiv, to set up a government in western Ukraine or even abroad, but he refused flat out. "I need ammo, not a ride," is how his reply was reported that day. Zelensky didn't utter these words at the time, his spokesman told me, but it was the mindset in Kyiv.

Zaluzhny also received a call from General Mark Milley, the chairman of the US Joint Chiefs of Staff, asking whether he wanted American help to leave Kyiv. Zaluzhny refused. "I don't understand you," the Ukrainian general replied. "For me the war started in 2014 . . . I didn't run away then, and I'm not going to run away now."

Millions, however, were running. Fourteen-hour lines had formed on Ukraine's border with Poland—even before the wave of refugees escaping Kyiv managed to reach the frontier. Western governments were stunned by the speed of the Russian advance, and mindful of Putin's warnings not to interfere in the conflict. Only Poland moved quickly, sending several truck-loads of ammunition and weapons overland to Ukraine. Kuleba, the Ukrainian foreign minister, was invited by Polish president Andrzej Duda to attend Poland's national security council meeting on February 24 before he headed back into Ukraine the next day. The Polish government, like other NATO allies, had been told by the alliance's intelligence that a swift collapse of the Ukrainian state was near certain. Still, Warsaw refused to give up. "The Poles believed in us more intuitively than fact-based, because all the facts spoke against us at the time," Kuleba said.

The mood was very different in other European capitals. "Nobody was giving the Ukrainians any chances," Boris Johnson recalled. "If this is going to happen, the best thing is that maybe it should happen quickly," a senior aide to German chancellor Olaf Scholz told him at the time. "Maybe they won't resist, and maybe our problem will be solved." Ukrainian ambassador Andrij Melnyk received a puzzled reply when he pushed a senior German minister to start shipping weapons and to impose sanctions on Russia. What was the point? the minister wondered, according to Melnyk's recollection. The Ukrainian state had only a few more hours left, and Berlin would have to find an accommodation with Kyiv's new masters.

"It all looked very strange at the time; there was an absolute bewilderment on the part of our partners," Zelensky's adviser, Mykhailo Podolyak, told me. "They didn't comprehend what was going on. The first impression seemed that everyone was shocked but also trying to distance themselves from the war, disbelieving Ukraine's ability to effectively defend itself."

⋯

Assuming that Zelensky's capitulation was within sight, Putin offered negotiations in Belarus on February 25—hoping for a Minsk-3 agreement to seal Ukraine's future as a Russian satrapy. He also addressed Ukrainian military commanders, most of whom were receiving a flood of private messages from Russia, and openly solicited a coup against Ukraine's elected government. "Take power into your own hands, it looks like it will be easier for us to find an agreement with you than with that gang of drug addicts and neo-Nazis that has lodged itself in Kyiv, taking hostage the entire Ukrainian people," Putin urged in a televised appearance. Russian TV, meanwhile, was already reporting that Zelensky had fled. Scrolling the news, the Ukrainian president decided that he needed to make a stand.

As darkness fell on the Ukrainian capital, Zelensky and his closest aides—Prime Minister Shmyhal, Chief of Staff Andriy Yermak, adviser Podolyak, and parliament majority leader David Arakhamia—walked out to the square in front of the presidential headquarters. Zelensky's security guards had just fired their weapons at suspected Russian infiltrators, and casings still littered the ground. Holding his phone in a selfie mode, Zelensky made a thirty-two-second speech, with the three simple words that meant everything.

"*Vsi my tut*," he said. "We are all here."

"Our soldiers are here, the citizens of our society are here, we are all here, defending our independence, our state. And that is how it will be."

⋯

Our choice of accommodation wasn't the most fortunate. As we slept in the fishing lodge, Russian planes dropped airborne troops into the nearby forest. We heard distant explosions. Unbeknownst to us, the Russians had converged on the Vasylkiv military airport at dawn, trying to seize the facility so that Russian planes could use its runway—essentially cutting off Kyiv from the south and completing the city's encirclement. Vasylkiv's panicked mayor said in a call to Ukrainian TV that heavy fighting was under way on the town's central street, with many casualties.

At breakfast, the lodge's owner offered to call his friends in Vasylkiv to find out who controlled the town. Nobody picked up, he came back to tell us half an hour later, but the highway to Kyiv that skirted Vasylkiv seemed clear. We drove out cautiously, stopping on the roadside after seeing several Ukrainian troops jump over the railing and head down a forest path. They raised their guns at us and didn't want to talk. At the gas station down the road, where a huge line of cars had gathered, a battered Lada sedan pulled up, with five Ukrainian soldiers in body armor, Kalashnikov rifles wedged between their knees. "Who's in Vasylkiv?" I asked them. "We are, we've just smashed them," one of the soldiers told me, flashing a thumbs-up.

Slowly, we drove into town. The sun shone on the empty streets. Ukrainian troops milled by the airfield's entrance on the main street, and there was evidence of overnight fighting everywhere—broken glass, pockmarked buildings, destroyed billboards. The Russians, however, were nowhere to be seen. Vasylkiv was back under firm Ukrainian control.

The main highway between Kyiv and Poland had been severed by advancing Russian forces that night, just hours after my colleagues and Sahar finally made it to western Ukraine. In the confusion, some of Ukraine's own forces inside Kyiv were mistaken for Russians, and hit by nervous, untrained Territorial Defense fighters. Carcasses of burned-out vehicles, reported to be Russian but in truth Ukrainian, were left under overpasses for weeks. With all the bridges west of the city blown up, the main Russian force was halted—for now. Kyiv, however, had been cut off from the west, north, and east. Only the Odesa highway to the south provided a lifeline for resupply—and a potential route for escape.

Chapter 8

THE WAR WON'T BE
A WALK IN THE PARK

The morning of February 26, day three of the war, I noticed a large crowd as I passed the entry checkpoint back to Kyiv on the Odesa highway. Hundreds, maybe thousands, of men and women had gathered by the horse-racing track to the left of the road. People were patiently waiting in a long line that snaked around the compound. They were volunteers for the Territorial Defense. As I tried to cross the road toward them, two unsmiling middle-aged men barred my way. They asked me to say *"palianytsia,"* a type of Ukrainian bread and a word that Russians are allegedly unable to pronounce correctly. Satisfied that they weren't dealing with a Muscovite, they let me proceed.

"There is nowhere for us to run. We must defend our homeland, our family," said one of the men in the line, a human resources administrator at a big corporation.

"Everyone who wanted to escape has already run away," echoed his neighbor, Misha, a thirty-five-year-old information technology worker. A Russian missile had hit near his condo that morning, he said. "This was the last drop for me," he explained. "There is no point trying to hide; we need to strike back and push them out, back to where they came from."

I squeezed inside the racetrack, elbowing my way through the crowd behind two uniformed officers. Ammunition boxes, Kalashnikov rifles, and rocket-propelled grenades were piled up on the stands, with cars and vans driving up. Volunteers filled the trunks with the weapons, packed the vehicles, and sped off to the front. It seemed as if the entire city had risen to fight against the invaders. The mood was determined, calm, and businesslike. The emotion that hung in the air was wounded pride: "How dare they," rather than fear.

"There is no way the Russians can take Kyiv now," I told Manu as we walked out.

"*No pasarán!*" he agreed, invoking a phrase from the Spanish Civil War.

The same scenes were repeating all over Kyiv. Oleksandr Melnychuk, an opera soloist in the Kyiv Opera and Ballet Theater, picked up a gun to join a Territorial Defense unit on the northern outskirts of the city. There weren't enough Kalashnikovs for everyone, and so he faced some of Russia's most elite units with his own hunting rifle.

◆◆◆

In the afternoon, we gave up on the Hyatt, which was running out of food, and moved into a duplex Airbnb apartment on Antonovych Street. Apart from the doorman and one elderly lady who stubbornly stayed behind, we were the only residents of the elegant nineteenth-century building. It used to be impossible to find parking on that street, but there were only a handful of cars left now. We stocked up on groceries and booze in the small basement shop that remained open across the street. The two middle-aged women who ran it normally lived in Bucha, a town abutting Hostomel. Afraid to travel home, they slept in their shop. A basement strip club around the block had also turned into a bomb shelter. So had a dive bar a couple of doors down from the apartment. In the bar, a big yellow flag hung above the counter, with the combination of the Ukrainian *tryzub*, the Jewish Star of David, and the inscription "Together until the end" in Ukrainian and Hebrew. As the barman made us free espressos—the only item currently on offer—I read the news on my phone. Kyiv's military administration was declaring a curfew from that Saturday afternoon until Monday morning, aiming to root out Russian infiltrator cells. We wouldn't be able to step outside for thirty-six hours or so, at the risk of being shot on sight.

As the night fell and Manu started cooking dinner, the rattle of gun battles erupted all over Kyiv. Some sounded close, less than a mile away. Then electricity in the building went out, and with it the internet. I wondered aloud whether we had made the wrong decision and should have stayed in the fishing lodge after all. Would we wake up to Russian tanks rolling down Antonovych Street?

"We will probably be surrounded by Monday. Though who knows," I texted Stevo, who was in his upstairs bedroom. "Huh. Then we will go to plan B. Be under siege and or face capture," he replied. I sent back a shrug emoji: "*Che sarà, sarà*"—what will be will be.

"Cocktail?" Stevo wrote four minutes later. "Sure," I replied. We met with Manu in the kitchen and concocted vodka tonics—the only beverage with available ingredients.

The electricity came back on half an hour later.

None of us particularly liked the idea of Russian captivity. With my Ukrainian roots, I couldn't expect mercy. Neither would Stevo, with his military past. Manu had already spent forty-five days as a prisoner of the Qadhafi regime in Libya. For that whole time, he hadn't been allowed to brush his teeth. He now performed a thorough brush every time before we left the apartment.

DURING THE NIGHT, ONE SMALL RUSSIAN SPECIAL FORCES UNIT IN CIVILIAN clothes got close enough to the parliament building to open fire. Another had taken over an unfinished high-rise on a major central intersection, firing into the compound of Zaluzhny's General Staff.

Volokhov and fellow former Flemish knight impersonators were sent that evening to the fortresslike Kyiv city government headquarters on Khreshchatyk. The ten-story building had served as one of the main protesters' strongholds during the 2014 revolution. A protester at the time, Volokhov was intimately familiar with its layout. "The information we had that night was that the Russians had broken through, that a tank column was about to enter Khreshchatyk, and that we had to get ready for urban combat," he said. "We were expecting Russian helicopters to launch an airborne assault on the street at any time."

A helicopter did indeed fly over the building, shooting flares. Nobody knew whose. Volokhov raced to the roof, fearing that the Russians might drop off paratroopers there. He wished he had land mines, but there weren't any in the compound. He made do with blocking off access from the rooftop. He and his men scouted the building and decided that the best firing positions would be on the third and sixth floors.

In the middle of the night, Volokhov received a call from the municipality's officer in charge: "The Russians are here. Do your thing."

Volokhov and his men broke down the doors of sixth-floor offices and took positions with a clear line of fire to their target: a police van that had rolled up into a side street. Someone somewhere reported that the vehicle had been taken over by Russian special forces infiltrating the area. A fighter with an NLAW missile crouched by one window. Another set up a machine gun. "Fire only on command," Volokhov ordered them as he measured the distance to the van.

Behind them, one of the municipality secretaries walked into the room, her phone in her hands. "Can I film you?" she asked as she stood behind the fighter with the NLAW, unaware of the potentially deadly back blast.

"Yes, lady, you can, but if you stand within twenty meters behind the missile, you may have a bit of a problem," he said.

"Okay, then I will film from the corner," she replied meekly.

Volokhov didn't order the missile to be fired. Russians using a single police van to attack Khreshchatyk didn't make any sense, he reckoned. He made a few calls, and it turned out that this was genuine Ukrainian police. The officers in the van never knew how close they had been to death.

When we woke up on the morning of February 27, Kyiv was still solidly in Ukrainian hands, with no more gunfire. The Russian tank column and helicopter assaults never materialized. The only sounds of war we could hear were the distant thumps of artillery on the northern and western outskirts. Putin's blitzkrieg plan had failed.

The airborne landing in Hostomel three days earlier had proved futile. Zelensky remained ensconced on Bankova. The Ukrainian state didn't collapse. Reinforcements were beefing up Kyiv's defenses. Russia was about to get its nose bloodied.

While Russian propagandists continued to exult at what they believed to be an imminent Russian victory, Girkin, the former FSB intelligence service colonel, sounded notes of concern. "It looks like the leadership has now realized that war with the so-called Ukraine won't be a walk in the park," he wrote.

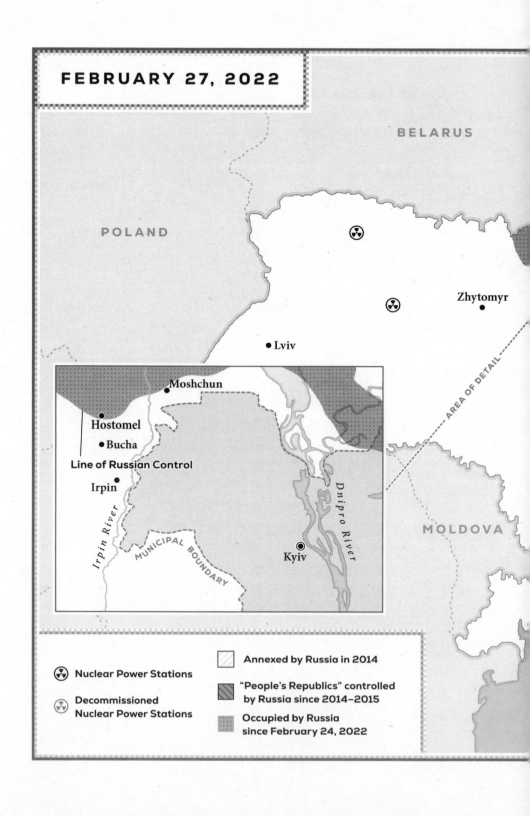

FEBRUARY 27, 2022

BELARUS

POLAND

Zhytomyr

Lviv

Moshchun

Hostomel

Bucha

Line of Russian Control

Irpin

Irpin River

MUNICIPAL BOUNDARY

Dnipro River

Kyiv

AREA OF DETAIL

MOLDOVA

Nuclear Power Stations

Decommissioned
Nuclear Power Stations

Annexed by Russia in 2014

"People's Republics" controlled
by Russia since 2014–2015

Occupied by Russia
since February 24, 2022

KILOMETERS
0   50   100   150

0   50   100   150
MILES

N

RUSSIA

● Chernihiv

Sumy ●

Okhtyrka ●

Kharkiv ●

UKRAINE

Kupyansk ●

Luhansk ●

Donbas

● Uman

● Dnipro

Kryvyi Rih ●

Donetsk ●

Voznesensk ●

Enerhodar ●

Mariupol ●

Kherson ●

Odesa ●

Azov Sea

Dnipro River

Kyiv ◎

Crimean
Peninsula

KERCH BRIDGE

Snake
Island

Sevastopol ●

Black Sea

PART 3

⊶▣⊷

RESISTANCE

CHAPTER 9

BLACK HAWK DOWN
WITHOUT BLACK HAWKS

On the morning of February 27, day four of the war, the main news came from Kharkiv. A Ukrainian TV correspondent there, broadcasting live on all Ukrainian networks, was suddenly anonymous. Her face wasn't shown onscreen. The Russians had entered the city, she said, perhaps for good. She could not risk being identified, detained, and possibly shot.

Once the Russian blitzkrieg on Kyiv hit a snag, Kharkiv, on the northern edge of eastern Ukraine, and Mariupol, on its southern shore, gained vital importance. Apart from being major transportation and industrial hubs, the two cities were indispensable gateways for Russian attempts to encircle and wipe out Ukraine's most capable units in Donbas. By seizing both cities, Russia would be able to launch a giant pincer movement, capturing the bulk of eastern Ukraine in one swoop.

As Russian columns rumbled through Ukraine, the attitude of local mayors and officials was crucial. Ukraine's recent administrative reform had devolved many powers to local communities, so these mayors often possessed formidable authority and could mobilize their constituents as well as the resources of local businesses. Some used all their influence, digging improvised fortifications, raising volunteer units, and coordinating defenses. Others did nothing, waiting to see which way the wind would blow. A few, often recruited by Russian intelligence beforehand, actively collaborated with the invaders.

Because the Russians had expected little initial resistance, even relatively minor obstacles forced them to pause, giving Ukrainian reinforcements time to arrive. In the battle for Kharkiv, two towns on the city's flanks highlighted the choice.

After Russian columns reached the crossroads town of Kupyansk southeast of Kharkiv, a Russian battalion commander gave the mayor, Hennadiy Matsegora, an ultimatum: surrender or see your city demolished. Elected from a party favorable to Russia, Matsegora immediately capitulated.

In a video address to Kupyansk's citizens on February 27, Matsegora said he wanted to avoid the destruction of infrastructure that the municipality would never be able to rebuild. The Russians, he added, would ensure law and order. They wouldn't interfere with Kupyansk's daily activities, he promised, as long as nobody engaged in "provocations."

"Our lives will depend on us, on our actions, on the reputation that we will earn now. Courage, leave the basements and the bomb shelters," Matsegora urged. The Russians drove into Kupyansk unopposed, taking over the huge railway node and using it to supply their forces from Russia. Scores of enraged local citizens, waving Ukrainian flags, tried to attack the mayor's car on Kupyansk's main road, but the town's fate was sealed. In the following months, Kupyansk would become the seat of the Russian occupation for that part of Ukraine.

In Okhtyrka, another road and rail hub, to the northwest of Kharkiv, the Russians tried a similar approach. That town's mayor, Pavlo Kuzmenko, refused invitations to collaborate. Still, as one Russian column headed toward Kyiv and another aiming for Poltava rumbled into Okhtyrka on the first day of the war, Russian soldiers didn't expect a fight. "They seemed certain that nobody would attack them," Kuzmenko told me.

As the Russians reached Okhtyrka's central roundabout, they were ambushed by local Territorial Defense volunteers and a handful of engineering troops based in the city. These volunteers had little training and had only read the instructions of their RPG-18 Mukha rocket-propelled grenades for the first time earlier that morning. But they managed to destroy several Russian fighting vehicles and trucks. The Russians retreated beyond a river on Okhtyrka's edge to regroup and prepare another push.

This courage won time for a train carrying hardened troops of the Ukrainian Army's 93rd Brigade to arrive in Okhtyrka. They jumped into battle straight from the train station, securing most of the town and blowing up the bridge. In the following days, the Russians took revenge on the city using aviation, artillery, and missiles. The first strike, on February 25, targeted a kindergarten. Five people who had just left a shelter for some fresh air died as Russian Grad rockets slammed into the courtyard. The next day, a Russian airstrike using thermobaric bombs flattened the building of the engineering unit, where Territorial Defense recruits and other soldiers had gathered. Some seventy troops were killed and the nearby power station was disabled. Days later, Mr. Kuzmenko's municipality building was also turned into rubble, as was the town's main museum. But although nearly surrounded, Okhtyrka refused to fold.

⋯

Kharkiv's mayor, Ihor Terekhov, also received Moscow's offers of collaboration in exchange for generous financial benefits under a future Russian regime. The Russians had reasons to be hopeful he would accept. Terekhov was far from a Ukrainian radical. He spoke only Russian, including when performing official functions that in theory should only be carried out in Ukrainian. Appealing to older residents still in thrall of Soviet nostalgia, he had spent the previous year opposing attempts to remove a monument to Marshal Georgiy Zhukov, the Soviet commander in World War II, and to rename Zhukov Avenue in the city. Three times a court ordered the renaming, and three times Terekhov got the city council to vote to restore the Soviet name, restarting the court process anew. The monument to the "Great Marshal of Victory" would stand in the city for eternity, he had promised. But all of that had been peacetime politics. Like Okhtyrka's mayor, Terekhov rejected the Russian proposals. In Kharkiv, the Russians were going to face a ferocious fight.

The Donbas veterans and other militias I had seen training in January had already organized themselves into armed units, with the help of the SBU intelligence service and GUR military intelligence. Azov veteran Kostyantyn Nemichev, the former head of the volunteers' Kharkiv defense committee, had become a leader in one of the most notorious and secretive units, Kraken, which operated under the authority of GUR. Regular troops from Ukraine's 92nd Mechanized Brigade, based in nearby Chuhuyiv, had also entered the city. Kharkiv's Territorial Defense was no longer armed with just wooden rifles.

NOT ONLY DID THE RUSSIANS NOT HAVE A PROPER PLAN FOR CAPTURING Kharkiv, but they were so sure the population was overwhelmingly on their side that many of them had brought along parade uniforms, expecting to be greeted as liberators.

The morning of February 27, the Russian assault force was meant to consist of *spetsnaz*, or special forces, troops from the 2nd Special Purpose Brigade, the Russian National Guard, and the 25th Motor Rifle Brigade. Lacking reliable communications, however, the Russian *spetsnaz* and the Guard moved on their own in light vehicles, while the 25th Brigade, with their heavy armor and tanks, stalled behind. Before dawn, just over a dozen Tigr armored vehicles and armored Kamaz trucks containing a few hundred Russian special forces sped on snow-covered streets into the residential areas of northern Kharkiv, moving toward the center. The streets were blocked with barricades made of tires, some of which had been set ablaze. Social media lit up with videos from local civilians of this relatively small invasion force meandering through the courtyards of Kharkiv high-rises.

The response of local defenders was swift. Rocket-propelled grenades and gunfire rained down on the Russians from every corner. One group began to retreat, hiding behind their vehicles as they reversed slowly. Another column of armored Tigrs was ambushed on Kharkiv's Shevchenko Street. Russian soldiers abandoned their vehicles and fled on foot up the road, seeking refuge in a school, a sturdy neoclassical-style three-story building painted dirty yellow. They reacted with disdain to Ukrainian offers of surrender. "Soon, our main force will be in Kharkiv, and you will be the ones surrendering," one of the Russians shouted, according to the recollections of Ukrainian defenders.

"Glory to Ukraine!" one Ukrainian soldier exclaimed, salvaging war booty from one of the Tigrs—RPGs, ammunition, and backpacks with medical kits. Importantly, the Russians had also left behind some of their radios, a mistake that allowed the Ukrainians to listen to Russian traffic, and to impersonate Russian officers.

Firing from the school's windows, the Russians killed the crew of a BTR-4 armored personnel carrier of Ukraine's 92nd Brigade. After that, the Ukrainians showed no mercy. A tank, firing from a park across the road from the school, smashed shells into the building's windows. As the Russians tried to break out, their company commander was fatally injured. Many others were killed that afternoon. Some managed to escape under the cover of darkness; several others were captured. A helmet-camera video recorded by a Ukrainian soldier inside the school showed Russian troopers' bodies sprawled in the burning building. "Dogs who came to our land, fuck you," he cursed.

A Russian survivor's account of the day compared it to the American debacle in Mogadishu in 1993. Except that the Russians, unlike the Americans at the time, couldn't rescue their troops with helicopters and air support. "It was Black Hawk Down without the Black Hawks," said the Russian, who, like other survivors, was traded months later for Ukrainian POWs.

"I don't know what they were expecting," Ukrainian major Oleh Koshevyi, one of Kharkiv's defenders, told me a few days after the failed Russian assault. "In 2014, lots of people here were running with a Russian flag and would have greeted Russian soldiers with flowers. They must have thought the same would happen now, that once they enter the city the population would split in half, with one half supporting them. Instead, everyone has united against them."

Kharkiv held.

CHAPTER 10

SOUTHERN BETRAYAL

Russia's complacency in Kharkiv stemmed in part from rapid success in Kherson, another regional capital of 300,000 people at the mouth of the Dnipro River in southern Ukraine.

There, instead of organizing resistance, the leadership of the SBU intelligence service flung open the gates and welcomed the enemy. Some senior officials secretly worked for Moscow, providing information about Ukrainian defenses and minefields on the way from Crimea. The SBU head of Crimean affairs, Oleh Kulinich, who spent much of his time in Kherson, and the head of the Kherson SBU counterterrorism unit were later detained by Ukraine and charged with treason. Zelensky also later stripped the SBU's Kherson regional head, General Serhiy Krivoruchko, of rank and branded him a traitor.

Kherson turned out to be Ukraine's vulnerable underbelly. Twelve days before the Russian invasion, Zelensky himself visited an exercise involving 1,300 troops in the town of Kalanchak, along the highway to the regional capital from Crimea. "We're not afraid of anyone, there is no panic, everything is under control," he told journalists after watching security forces perform a helicopter assault. "It's important that we are prepared, and we are."

But on the first day of the invasion, the Kherson governor, the regional head of police, and top security commanders all fled the region. There was no resistance in Kalanchak, and a Ukrainian artillery unit that was supposed to prevent Russian advances along a narrow isthmus from Crimea withdrew. There were no trenches, no fortifications made ahead of time. The Ukrainian Army's 59th Motor Rifle Brigade, responsible for this part of the front, was busy with exercises on the eve of the invasion and hadn't been ordered to deploy. In the first hours of the offensive, it was practically helpless against Russian airstrikes, and found itself outflanked by Russian VDV paratroopers from the rear.

Soldiers from the 59th Brigade, the 80th Air Assault Brigade, and other decimated Ukrainian units pulled back from the southern steppe, fighting their way out of encirclement and leaving behind burning tanks and BMPs. Unable to reach superior headquarters in Kyiv, their commanders decided that trying to defend Kherson was pointless. Instead, they headed thirty miles north to the next regional capital, Mykolaiv, hoping to halt the Russian onslaught there. The nearly mile-long Antonovsky Bridge over the Dnipro, the only direct route into the city of Kherson from the south and the gateway to the rest of the Ukrainian coast, was left intact by retreating forces. This was one of Ukraine's biggest blunders in the entire war.

"The Russian tanks and vehicles showed up here like they were traveling on a red carpet, and were near Kherson in just a few hours," said Volodymyr Mykolaenko, who served as mayor of Kherson from 2014 to 2020. "Kherson has been sold out." When Mykolaenko went to Kherson's military headquarters on the first morning of the war, the commandant wouldn't receive him. By lunchtime, almost all the officials were already gone.

Mykolaenko's predecessor as mayor, businessman Volodymyr Saldo, didn't leave Kherson that day. Recruited by the Russians before the war, he was preparing for an important role under the new regime.

UKRAINE'S TURKISH-MADE BAYRAKTAR TB2 DRONES MANAGED TO DESTROY the initial Russian column headed toward the Antonovsky Bridge into Kherson, halting the advance for a day. But when the Russians regrouped and managed to cross, only about a hundred untrained volunteers, plus a handful of stragglers from the regular military, were left to defend the city. Armed only with Kalashnikov rifles, some twenty hand grenades, Molotov cocktails, and two ancient Mukha RPGs, they were no match for the invaders.

The volunteers prepared an ambush for the Russians, lying in wait under lilac bushes and acacia trees in Kherson's Buzki Park, along the Mykolaiv Highway. Plastic bags with Molotov cocktails—bottles of incendiary liquid named after the Soviet foreign minister during World War II—were prepositioned under the trees throughout the park. These men had no uniforms and wore jeans and tracksuits, with blue-and-yellow ribbons to identify each other. A local journalist and activist, Kostyantyn Ryzhenko, urged them to go home. Any attempt to attack the Russian military without proper weapons was doomed, he warned. The volunteers didn't listen.

The next day, a column of Russian BMP and BTR fighting vehicles rolled into Kherson, flying huge Russian flags, and headed toward Buzki Park. The Russians never got close enough for the Molotov cocktails to be useful. Their heavy machine guns started firing into the park from hundreds of yards away, tearing through trees and bodies. After one Ukrainian Mukha managed to hit and damage a Russian fighting vehicle, a Russian tank joined the fray. It was carnage. "For the Russians, this battle was like shooting in a shooting gallery," said one of the few survivors, Stanislav Vazanov. Like many other volunteer fighters in Buzki Park, he had never fired a weapon before.

The surviving Ukrainians fled under fire, some hiding for months and others, like Vazanov, making their way to Mykolaiv. Dozens of bullet-riddled bodies, several missing limbs or heads, lay on the snow for days, eaten by dogs. Russian commanders decided to make some money and demanded cash from families that wanted to retrieve their relatives' corpses. Having easily secured Kherson, the Russians pushed farther north, toward Mykolaiv and, beyond it, Odesa and Kryvyi Rih.

✜

Home to 630,000 people, Zelensky's hometown of Kryvyi Rih stretches some eighty miles from one end to the other. Snaking between ore mines, steel plants, parks, and gritty residential neighborhoods, it straddles the main routes toward central Ukraine. Losing it would have been catastrophic.

The Russians had reasons to count on cooperation by Mayor Oleksandr

Vilkul. A deputy prime minister under Yanukovych, and the son of the city's previous Russia-friendly mayor, Vilkul was long associated with deeper ties with Moscow. In 2019, he ran on behalf of the pro-Russian opposition in the presidential elections, against Zelensky and Poroshenko, garnering 4 percent in the first round.

The Russians and their proxies reached out to him as soon as the war began. The first, private, call was from Vitaliy Zakharchenko, Yanukovych's minister of interior, who had fled to Russia alongside the deposed president in 2014. The second message came publicly from Oleg Tsaryov, a former parliament member from the region, who also escaped to Moscow in 2014. "Our troops are already near Kryvyi Rih," Tsaryov wrote on his social media, praising what he described as Vilkul's traditionally pro-Russian position. "Collaboration with the Army of the Russian Federation means saving the city and the lives of its inhabitants."

But Vilkul had other plans. Like many other elected community leaders with pro-Russian sympathies before the war, he didn't waver about his loyalty when the invasion threatened his hometown. "Fuck yourself, traitor, along with your owners," he replied publicly to Tsaryov. Growing a beard and donning a uniform with a black skullcap that made him look like an Afghan mujahedeen commander, Vilkul used the municipality's extensive resources to defend Kryvyi Rih as Russian columns sped toward the city from the south.

"There was no army here at all when the war began," he recalled a few weeks later. "We had one battalion of territorial defense, in the process of formation, six hundred troops of the National Guard, and two mortars. That's all."

On the second day of the war, a Russian Il-76 transport plane and two fighter jets flew low over the Kryvyi Rih airport, attempting to land airborne troops. But Vilkul's municipality had already blocked the landing strip with dump trucks.

On February 26, the Russian column of some 300 tanks, armored BTRs and BMPs, Ural troop transporters, and artillery approached Kryvyi Rih from the southwest. Vilkul ordered a fleet of heavy Belaz mining trucks, their tires shot out, to block the highway. Warm weather had melted the snow and turned the ground muddy. "We were lucky that the Russians couldn't travel on dirt roads then, only on asphalt," Vilkul told me.

Spotters in the town of Bashtanka along the way allowed Ukrainian assault helicopters to strike the Russian column, inflicting considerable damage. Hours later, when the lead vehicles of the column got stuck in front of the Belaz barricades, just a few hundred yards from the entrance to Kryvyi Rih, Ukrainian helicopter gunships hit it again. Unprepared for such resistance, the Russians, running low on fuel and ammunition, turned back. They abandoned valuable equipment, including Grad multiple-launch rocket systems. Vilkul quickly found some retired officers trained in how to use Grads, and the launchers were turned around to attack their former owners. Municipal digging crews erected ever stronger fortifications around the city. After that initial failure, the Russians were never able to approach Kryvyi Rih again.

"The Russians and their imperial mania of greatness . . . They thought that everyone who speaks Russian is awaiting Russia here. But it turned out that the Russian-speaking Ukrainian patriotism is no weaker than the Ukrainian-speaking Ukrainian patriotism," Vilkul mused as he showed me graphic videos of these clashes. "Look at who is fighting at the front lines? . . . We are on our own land and have nowhere to retreat. We must fight and we must win."

CHAPTER 11

ASSAULT ON THE
CITY OF MARY

Mariupol, or the City of Mary, was founded by the Russian Imperial Court in the late eighteenth century as a home for the Orthodox Greeks from newly conquered Crimea and the Ottoman Empire. An industrial port on the Azov Sea with a massive steel plant, it was a multiethnic hodgepodge of nearly half a million people as the war began. Not as prosperous or sophisticated as Kharkiv, it was still one of Ukraine's biggest cities. Since 2014, it had learned to live in tense proximity with the Russian-controlled "people's republic" of Donetsk, absorbing tens of thousands of refugees from the occupied region.

In January 2015, Russian proxies had blanketed Mariupol's eastern neighborhoods with rockets, killing some thirty civilians, including children. Like the rest of the Ukrainian-administered Donbas in following years, Mariupol had received an infusion of investment, with new restaurants, stores, and hotels opening on its waterfront. Stevo managed to get food poisoning from eating oysters in a swanky Mariupol restaurant in January, perhaps the last person to do so for many years to come. Refugees from Russian-held Donetsk brought with them money, new skills, and new businesses. But the sense of looming violence was never far away. The entire side wall of a fifteen-story Mariupol high-rise had been painted over with a giant fresco of a six-year-old girl, Milana Abdurashytova, clutching a teddy bear. She had lost her mother, and her leg, in the Russian shelling of 2015.

The controversial Azov Regiment was born in the battles for Mariupol in 2014 and 2015. Some of its early leaders had neo-Nazi connections, and the unit had adopted a modified version of the Wolfsangel runic symbol that was popular with the European far-right. Hundreds of other Ukrainians, however, joined Azov simply because they wanted to defend their country. Unlike the regular army at the time, the unit seemed well-run and efficient. Jewish billionaire Ihor Kolomoisky, then the governor of the nearby Dnipropetrovsk region who would later emerge as a key Zelensky supporter, was among Azov's early backers. The links between some Azov members and white supremacist groups in the United States and elsewhere, however, were a godsend for Russian propaganda. In 2018, the US Congress banned American military assistance to the group.

The Azov of 2022, however, was very different from its earlier version. Having been integrated into Ukraine's National Guard, it had grown from a single battalion to a full regiment. Command had passed from its founder, far-right politician and former parliament member Andriy Biletsky, to a full-time National Guard officer, Lieutenant Colonel Denys Prokopenko, better known under his call sign Friend Redys, or Radish. (Azov's soldiers and officers address each other with the egalitarian "friend," a tradition that harks back to the Ukrainian Riflemen of a century earlier.)

"The Kremlin's propaganda calls us Nazis and fascists, and themselves liberators who have come to 'de-Nazify' Ukraine," Azov, the main military unit deployed in Mariupol, said in a statement as the invasion began. "We despise Nazism and Stalinism because our country has suffered the most from these totalitarian regimes and their deceitful ideologies." Azov's soldiers included Jews and Muslims, and speakers of both Ukrainian and Russian, it added.

❖

Ten days before the invasion, Prokopenko called on fellow Azov officers to craft a plan for the city's defense. One of these veterans was Kyrylo Berkal, better known under his call sign Friend Kirt. A Chinese-speaking travel agency entrepreneur who once enjoyed beachfront life in Phuket, Thailand, Berkal returned to Ukraine to fight in 2014. A major in the Ukrainian

National Guard, he headed Azov's training academy. Prokopenko had given him a mission impossible: to cobble together a battalion-sized force among the Azov trainees, border guards, policemen, and other leftover troops. The new battalion's job would be to control one of Mariupol's four areas of defense, Sector C, in the northern part of the city.

"There were fifty-two of our men in the academy, and we had to absorb some four hundred additional people who didn't have any clue about what to do when at war," Berkal recalled. Worse, Mariupol's authorities and the management of local industries didn't allow Azov to prepare any fortifications, to dig trenches, or even to scout industrial plants for possible defensive positions. "Until the first missiles started to rain, all we could do was just play with the maps," Berkal said. There were no stockpiles of additional ammunition, fuel, or food.

On February 24, Berkal noticed reports of massive shelling east of the city early in the morning. He decided this was his last chance to take a quick nap. As soon as he shut his eyes, however, the first Russian missiles slammed into Mariupol. He didn't get to sleep again for several days. The initial strikes focused on air defenses and communications towers, sparing Azov's barracks. Within an hour, Berkal and other Azov commanders rushed to fortify Mariupol's neighborhoods and industrial zones with trenches, firing nests, and defensive walls. The military was now in charge, and civilian laws no longer applied.

That morning, Mariupol mayor Vadym Boychenko projected confidence. "The most important thing now is to keep calm and not to succumb to panic," he said in a briefing broadcast on local TV. "I have looked into the eyes of our soldiers, and I am fully confident." Shortly thereafter, he escaped the city with most of his team. There was no organized evacuation for Mariupol's other civilians.

YULIA PAEVSKA, A FIFTY-THREE-YEAR-OLD PARAMEDIC AND VOLUNTEER known under her call sign Tayra, had arrived in Mariupol the day before. So had three Ukrainian journalists from the Associated Press who would be the only international reporters to chronicle Mariupol's tragedy.

Russian warplanes, operating with near impunity, dropped bombs on

Mariupol's residential neighborhoods, and Russian multiple-launch rocket systems and artillery started pounding the city. Having served long tours as a military medic in Donbas, Paevska immediately offered her help at Mariupol's 555th Military Hospital, setting up a triage tent for the bloodied soldiers and civilians brought to the facility.

"The Russians began flattening neighborhood after neighborhood, as if working under a plan. We had fifty to seventy wounded coming to the hospital in the first day, and soon it turned to some two hundred heavily injured people a day, and we stopped counting the lightly injured ones," Paevska said. Most of these injuries were caused by shrapnel from air bombardments and shelling.

Power, water, and heating networks went out quickly across the city. Few in Mariupol were prepared for war. Soon, law and order began to break down, with looters storming groceries and shopping malls. The malls didn't last long anyway, targeted by the next wave of Russian strikes.

"People were dazed. Nobody believed it would happen. The TV was telling them until the last day that everything is fine. Why they were told this, I don't know. But it's a human trait—you refuse to believe in something bad, no matter how terrible your situation is, you still hope for the best. It's a coping mechanism," Paevska mused later.

She understood early on that Mariupol was likely to be surrounded but decided to stay anyway: "They needed my help."

In the first days of the war, the Ukrainian Marines' 36th Brigade stood its ground on the front line nearly twenty miles east of Mariupol, despite relentless pounding by the Russian Air Force. A massive Russian push, however, broke through Ukrainian lines farther to the north, near the town of Volnovakha.

Azov's men hadn't tried to blow up the highway bridge from the north because they expected Ukrainian units in Volnovakha to fall back to Mariupol. But only small, scattered groups of Ukrainian soldiers showed up, with Russian reconnaissance units in hot pursuit.

On that highway, Azov fighters in pickup trucks found themselves face-to-face with a column of four Russian BMP-3s, formidable armored vehicles with deadly 100mm cannons. The battle was decided in seconds, as in a shootout. Azov's men whipped out their antitank missiles, hit the Russian BMPs before they had a chance to swing their turrets, and swerved away at full speed. In the morning, drone reconnaissance showed that the four BMPs had been abandoned. Berkal drove to the spot, stripping weapons from the damaged vehicles and recording Azov's first victorious video of the war, with a message to the advancing Russians: "Welcome to hell!"

The main thrust of the Russian force, the 150th Motorized Rifle Division, wasn't far behind. Berkal's men attempted to blow up the bridge but failed without the required explosives. They had only ten antitank mines, not nearly enough to create an obstacle. Instead, they mixed the real mines with some sixty similar-looking but harmless training mines. The resulting minefield looked convincing, at least from afar. "We fooled them," Berkal recalled. He also ordered two tanks to open random fire from a big industrial complex on the edge of the highway, imitating a much larger force. For a while, the Russians were deterred.

Azov's commander, Prokopenko, released the first of many video addresses on the second day of the war, his helmet covered by blue masking tape. "I order every fighter of the Azov regiment to fight until the end," he said. "We will destroy the Russians in the air, on land, and in the sea."

AZOV CHOSE THE HUGE AZOVSTAL STEEL PLANT COMPOUND AS ITS BASE, a city within the city that had its own warren of underground bunkers and piers. Seeking protection, many Mariupol civilians headed there too. Anna Zaitseva and her three-month-old son, Svyatoslav, moved with her parents and other civilians into one such bunker. She would only see her husband, Kirill, who had just joined Azov, twice after that. With Ukrainian air defenses eviscerated, Russian planes dropped as many as one hundred bombs a day on Mariupol. "Our life seemed like a horror movie—or a computer game, where you needed to reach a higher level every day," she recalled. Once the baby formula, heated by a candle, ran out, soldiers started bringing her cow's milk and sugar to keep Svyatoslav alive. Her father braved shelling to step outside to boil water. "Every day, it was a true act of heroism for his grandson's sake."

Azov had been training to repel a seaborne assault, or an attack from the familiar directions—the east and the north. The soldiers hadn't expected the Russians to arrive from their rear, from the west. With every hour, Russian forces that had fanned out from Crimea were getting closer and closer, sweeping through the coastal steppes of Kherson and Zaporizhzhia with little resistance.

On the morning of February 27, they linked up with the Russian armies coming from the north and the east. The city was surrounded. The Russians expected that Mariupol would fall within days. After all, its defenders could no longer be resupplied with ammunition or food. They were outgunned. Resistance seemed futile. But Azov had different ideas.

❖

On February 27, Russian soldiers also failed in their initial attempt to enter Bucha, a leafy Kyiv suburb adjoining Hostomel. A long column of armored fighting vehicles, trucks, and artillery had arrived from Belarus and started driving along the town's Vokzalna Street toward the neighboring town of Irpin and, beyond it, Kyiv. Once the Russians crossed the railway tracks and were wedged between rows of family homes, Ukraine's Bayraktar drones hovering over the town fired their missiles at the first and last vehicles, trapping the column. Soldiers and Territorial Defense fighters waiting in ambush obliterated the rest with antitank weapons. The Russian survivors fled Bucha, leaving behind dozens of burning vehicles, ammunition, and the bodies of their comrades.

An irate middle-aged resident of the neighborhood recorded the immediate aftermath on his phone, walking from one smoldering Russian armored vehicle to another, stepping over collapsed electric utility poles, pulverized trees, and unexploded shells. "Burn in hell," he cursed. "They've come here. And now look at what is left of them. Just spare parts."

That video, shared on social media and broadcast all day on Ukrainian TV, helped puncture the myth of Russia's invincibility. Soon, a catchy pop song became the national sensation. "We have one comment to all of their arguments: Bayraktar," the lyrics went, along with a video clip of footage of exploding Russian columns.

Ukraine's slow-flying Bayraktars wouldn't be effective against a modern army with sophisticated air defenses, the Russians had said over and over before the war began. But the Russian Army was in disarray.

Still, Ukraine needed all the help it could get. Citing the Russian attacks on Ukrainian cities, Zelensky issued an appeal to the entire world. Citizens of any country, he said, were welcome to come to Ukraine and join its armed forces, serving in the new International Legion.

"It's not just an invasion of Russia in Ukraine, it's the beginning of a war against Europe. Against the unity of Europe. Against elementary human rights in Europe. Against all rules of coexistence on the continent."

CHAPTER 12

"I WAS BORN IN KYIV, AND I WILL DIE IN KYIV"

The curfew in Kyiv was lifted on Monday, February 28, day five of the war. I looked out the window. The streets were just as empty as the previous day, snow falling slowly from the lead-colored clouds. In the courtyard behind our apartment, several men were loading a car with ammunition and rifles.

It felt wrong to wear on the streets of my own hometown the vest and the helmet that I had donned hundreds of times in Iraq, Afghanistan, and other war zones. By the Botanical Garden where I used to go on dates in high school and planted my awkward first kiss. By the museum where I used to spend afternoons gazing at French Impressionist paintings. By the cinema where as a teenager I had watched Fellini's movies, their more sensual scenes removed by Soviet censors. The city that invaders had come to take had been my home. The Russians thought it was theirs, in a country that they believed didn't exist, part of a nation they told themselves had been invented. Kyiv seemed on its deathbed, listless, bled of its people. How dare they, I thought.

We drove westward. New billboards with the country's new motto, "Russian warship, go fuck yourself," had been erected. Others, also in Russian, targeted Russian troops should they enter the city. "Russian soldier, how are you going to be able to look in your children's eyes? Stop!" they implored. Flipping Putin's World War II rhetoric, some billboards quoted a fa-

mous Soviet song about the Nazi invasion of 1941: "On June 22, precisely at
4 a.m., Kyiv was bombed, and we have been told that the war has begun,"
they read.

We saw no other cars as we barreled along the highway fringed by pine
forests. "Fuck my life," Stevo cursed. We all knew from experience that when
roads are completely empty in war zones, there is usually a reason. With relief, we spotted several soldiers and a tank, flying Ukrainian colors, on the
roadside. They waved us down. "The bridge has been blown up, and there
are Russians on the other side," one of them said.

We stopped to chat with the tank crew, which was loading up with
shells that had been strewn on the curb. The tank crew members were old,
probably in their late fifties, and they went about their business with calm
detachment. "Don't linger here too long," one of them said, pointing to a
crater nearby. "A Russian shell landed there not long ago." Two civilian volunteers arrived in a car full of hot food. Like most other Ukrainian units,
these tank crews now had civilian sponsors who would take care of their
needs. Earlier in the day, one of the volunteers told me, they had brought a
welder from Kyiv to fix a broken part in the tank. The previous day, sleeping bags and mats. "We help the boys with what we can."

Artillery exchanges resumed in the area, with plumes of smoke rising
into the sky. The tanks revved their engines and moved into the forest. We
pulled back and kept going along the ring road, toward the Hostomel junction. Instead of Territorial Defense volunteers, we spotted pickups with
well-equipped Ukrainian special forces troops, some of them carrying
sniper rifles. They were in a good mood, bragging of how they had destroyed
three Russian armored vehicles. Chechen troops loyal to strongman Ramzan Kadyrov were on the other side of the front line, they said. His bearded
private militia, the well-equipped *kadyrovtsi*, were technically part of the
Russian National Guard—and notorious for their cruelty.

As we drove back into the city, away from the front line, we relaxed. In
neighborhood after neighborhood, Territorial Defense fighters piled up old
refrigerators, furniture, and even broken bikes to create barricades and
checkpoints. At night, during curfew, these barriers were manned by armed
guards looking for Russian infiltrators. During the day, some had just unarmed guards, or no guards at all. At one of them, we didn't stop fast enough.

One of the men jumped up, his face contorting, and thrust his Kalashnikov through the front-side window into Manu's face. "Chechen, Chechen!" he screamed. Manu had a long beard, almost *kadyrovtsi*-long, and I couldn't fault the soldier's logic. It took a minute for explanations and for apologies.

"Manu, you are shaving this thing down as soon as we get home," I said as we drove off.

"Brother, I sure am," he replied. "I don't want to die." He kept his word.

Coming down the highway ramp, we were stuck behind a battery of Pion 203mm howitzers, the biggest artillery pieces possessed by Ukraine or Russia. We nervously looked at the sky, expecting a Russian plane or missile to strike such a prize target. But nothing happened. The howitzers slowly made their way through Kyiv in broad daylight, followed by bright orange municipal trucks carrying ammunition. The battery must have arrived from another city, and its ability to move around brought home for the first time Russia's failure to establish air superiority, let alone air supremacy, over Ukraine. Ukraine was turning out to be much stronger—and Russia much weaker—than even the most optimistic analysts had predicted.

With a range of more than twenty miles, these Pions zeroed in on the Hostomel runway, making it impossible for Russia to land reinforcements there. The Mriya, Ukraine's Dream aircraft, was also damaged beyond repair. Russia's costly success in establishing the Hostomel bridgehead on day one of the war had proved strategically irrelevant after all. In the following days, helped by Ukrainian spotters, the Pions and other artillery methodically targeted Russian positions around Kyiv.

⋄⊪⋄

The two-night curfew spooked many of those who had stayed behind, and the Kyiv train station was packed. "We are preparing for the worst. We see how things are escalating, and it's becoming scary," said Nikita Darnostup, a twenty-eight-year-old computer graphics designer. "I really want to believe that we will be able to see Kyiv again, one day."

"This is complete surrealism," said his partner, Ulyana Panteleyeva, twenty-seven, with a sigh. Both had already fled once, escaping their hometown of Donetsk after the Russian occupation of 2014. "I never imagined we would have to go through this for a second time," Ulyana said, tears coming to her eyes. They left for Lviv that afternoon. Refugees from Donetsk and Luhansk, I noticed, were usually among the first to flee. They knew what happened once the Russians took over.

Elsewhere in Kyiv's otherwise empty neighborhoods, long, patient lines formed outside the remaining grocery stores. Inside the stores, alcohol sections had been cordoned off with tape: overnight, the Kyiv municipality had banned booze and warned that looters would be shot on sight. I didn't witness that happening, but in some smaller towns suspected looters were tied to electric utility poles for public shaming.

I spoke to three young women who had just joined the line, expecting to wait at least an hour for their turn. A twenty-three-year-old post office worker, Valeria Voytenko, said that her fiancé was battling the Russians in Kharkiv. "He has already lost one of his fighters. A child, only twenty years old, and already gone. I don't even know how to express my support to him," she said. "What do you say in this situation? So sorry for the boys. They are so young, some just eighteen or twenty years old. They are all afraid, but they all keep fighting."

Unlike the couple at the train station, none of these three women planned to leave the city. "I was born in Kyiv and I will die in Kyiv. If they give us weapons, we will go shoot too," Valeria said. But weapons were hard to get now. One of their friends had spent the previous two days in line at a Territorial Defense office, she said. The man and his buddy were taking shifts in the line, with one sleeping while the other waited.

None of the three women had doubts about the eventual outcome of the war. "We will fight to the last one," said Yana Kamun, a twenty-year-old manicurist. "And we have faith that Ukraine will win."

IN WESTERN CAPITALS, THERE WAS FAR LESS OPTIMISM. US SENATORS received an intelligence briefing that day, a warning that Kyiv was on the verge of being surrounded, making further deliveries of Western aid impossible. Macron called Putin, asking him to stop attacks on civilians and civilian infrastructure, and to allow the remaining routes in and out of Kyiv to stay open. Putin agreed, the French president announced with relief. But of course, just weeks earlier Putin had also assured Macron that he wouldn't invade in the first place.

A Ukrainian delegation arrived in the southern Belarusian city of Gomel on February 28 for the first round of peace talks with Russia since the invasion began. The day before, Zelensky had extracted a promise from President Aleksandr Lukashenko that there would be no bombing of Ukraine from Belarusian soil during the meetings. It's not clear whether Lukashenko had any power to deliver. Belarus was now effectively a Russian protectorate, and Russian troops there didn't have to ask for any permission.

The Russians expected a full Ukrainian surrender in Gomel. The chief Russian representative, former culture minister Vladimir Medinsky, recited a long list of demands. It included Ukrainian troops handing over all their tanks and artillery to Russian forces and cutting down the Ukrainian Army to some 50,000 men armed only with rifles and pistols. Moscow wanted a different, Russian-friendly government installed in Kyiv, the arrest and trial of "Nazis," the restoration of Russian as Ukraine's official language, and Russian control over Ukraine's foreign policy. Medinsky even demanded that city streets named after Ukrainian national heroes hostile to Russia be returned to their old, Soviet names.

A less polished member of the Russian delegation, deputy defense minister Colonel General Alexander Fomin, told the Ukrainians in blunt terms what would happen if they refused. "We will keep killing and slaughtering you," he said, according to one of the Ukrainian negotiators, Zelensky's adviser, Mykhailo Podolyak.

"We listened to them, and we realized that these are not people sent for talks, but for our capitulation," Podolyak recalled. "They had no understanding of the country that they had invaded, and of our resources. They had no idea how to negotiate." The Ukrainians, he added, agreed to the meeting so they could try to understand Russia's true intentions—and push for humanitarian cease-fires and brief truces that would gain Kyiv time.

There was little progress in Gomel, but the two delegations agreed to reconvene after consultations in their capitals. The war went on.

CHAPTER 13

"EVERY THIRD PERSON IN MY SHELTER IS JEWISH"

On the morning of Tuesday, March 1, the live video feed from Kharkiv's Freedom Square recorded moderate traffic outside the regional government headquarters. A handful of cars were parked by the Smerch missile tail in the ground, while others passed by. At 8:10 a.m., a Russian cruise missile slammed from the sky into the building's upper right corner, engulfing it in fire and carbonizing the nearby vehicles. Another missile hit the same building shortly thereafter. Debris flew into the tattered sign that asked "Is Kharkiv next?"

The timing of the Russian strike was not accidental. The regional administration headquarters was teeming with military and civilian personnel, including newly recruited Territorial Defense fighters. Governor Syniehubov and Kharkiv's other top military and civilian officials were scheduled to meet in the building that morning, something that Russian intelligence knew. The governor and most other attendees were late and survived. Dozens of others in the compound and in the cars nearby did not.

Russian missiles kept pounding Kharkiv's main Sumska Street, destroying its elegant shops, restaurants, and bars. Putin's promises of restraint to Macron hadn't lasted a day. After dark on March 1, four cruise missiles hit Kharkiv's Air Force University compound, one of them gutting a residential annex that housed retired officers and the families of active-duty officers. Almost all of the men were already on the front lines. It was mostly children, women, and the elderly buried under the rubble. In the northern neighborhoods of Kharkiv, closest to the front line, Russian artillery and rocket launchers unleashed fire on residential high-rise neighborhoods. Kharkiv, Mayor Terekhov said in a recording made from an underground shelter, had not seen such horrors since the 1940s. "It's not just war," he noted, his voice shaking. "It's the murder of us, of the Ukrainian people."

IN KYIV, THE OKHMATDYT CHILDREN'S HOSPITAL WAS JUST TWO BLOCKS from my former high school. Half-finished high-rises across the highway junction had been briefly taken over by Russian infiltrators, and the hospital was lightly damaged in the crossfire. The threat of Russian bombs and missile strikes meant that most of the patients—and their families—now stayed in the basements that had been converted to shelters. I recalled its corridors, places where I used to come for my own childhood ailments.

On March 1, the hospital's basement was a grim sight, full of listless children and their dazed, disoriented parents. Valentyn Vetrov, whose one-year-old son had undergone more than twenty surgeries to fix birth defects, had additional reasons to worry. His wife and their remaining five children were trapped on the wrong side of the front lines, in the southern city of Berdyansk, which had been occupied by Russia. The hospital's director, Volodymyr Zhovnyakh, said that the war was already murdering children beyond the direct toll. Some diabetics, especially from the suburbs close to the fighting, such as Bucha or Irpin, could no longer come to get insulin. Others no longer had access to baby formula. Like many Ukrainians, he was distraught by Western indifference as Russia rained death from the skies.

"The world is watching us, praying for us, and not doing much else. Ukraine, unfortunately, is on its own," he said.

The United States and its allies had refused Zelensky's requests to impose a no-fly zone over Ukraine, fearing a direct confrontation between NATO and Russia. But Ukrainian resistance was gradually changing the Western approach. With the Nord Stream 2 project already officially frozen by Germany, the EU on February 28 allocated 500 million euros to fund the Ukrainian Armed Forces, banned air connections with Russia, and outlawed transactions with the Russian Central Bank. Two days later, the EU and the United States disconnected Russia's biggest banks from the SWIFT international payments network, crippling the Russian financial system. The EU also banned the operations of Russian propaganda broadcasters, Sputnik and Russia Today, that operated several TV channels in European languages. Scores of multinational companies began to wind down once-lucrative Russian businesses.

The United States and its European allies also started supplying Ukraine with ever-deadlier weapons, defying Russia's threats of a catastrophic retaliation. Even Germany broke a taboo, promising antitank and antiaircraft missiles. "The Russian invasion of Ukraine marks a turning point," said Chancellor Olaf Scholz on February 26. "It threatens our entire postwar order. In this situation, it is our duty to help Ukraine."

ON THE AFTERNOON OF MARCH 1, RUSSIA'S MINISTRY OF DEFENSE ISSUED AN ominous statement. To stop the "information attacks" besmirching Russia, Moscow would use high-precision weapons to target "technological objects" of the SBU and of the 72nd Center for Information Warfare Psychological Operations in Kyiv, it said. Residents of Kyiv living near these sites and "rebroadcasting nodes" were urged to leave their homes for their own safety.

Almost no one in Kyiv had ever heard of the 72nd Center. The wording was so vague that it could apply to any part of the city. For all we knew, one of the servers could be next door.

"This looks awfully like a pretext for hitting the city center, just like in Kharkiv," Stevo said. We decided to spend the night at the fishing lodge once again. At least that would give us a night without the constant air raids and the ever-closer artillery. The lodge's owner was happy to see us again, and a generous meal awaited us on arrival.

The Russians did indeed strike Kyiv that evening, targeting the main TV tower. The missiles failed to destroy the structure, interrupting broadcasting for just a few hours. But debris and shrapnel killed five passersby, scattering on the nearby Babyn Yar, the ravine where tens of thousands of Kyiv's Jews were murdered by the Nazis between 1941 and 1943. Just the previous October, Zelensky and the presidents of Israel and Germany

had opened a new memorial there, designed by Serbian artist Marina
Abramović.

Natan Sharansky, the head of the Babyn Yar supervisory board and a
former Israeli deputy prime minister, was furious. A native of Donetsk,
Sharansky had spent nine years in Soviet prison camps for campaigning
against the ban on emigration to Israel. "Putin seeking to distort and manipulate the Holocaust to justify an illegal invasion of a sovereign country
is utterly abhorrent," he fumed. "It is symbolic that he starts attacking Kyiv
by bombing the site of Babyn Yar, the biggest of Nazi massacres."

SCATTERED ACROSS THE ROAD THE NEXT MORNING, MARCH 2, WERE DIS-
connected electrical wires, large pieces of metal, and glass from damaged
cars under the TV tower. A woman in a roadside store was busy cleaning up.
All in all, the damage was limited. Our expectation of a massive salvo destroying buildings and knocking out infrastructure across Kyiv hadn't
materialized—for now. But the mood in the city was increasingly grim—
especially so among Kyiv's large Jewish community. Unlike in most of eastern
Europe, Ukraine's Jewish community hadn't been completely wiped out by the
Holocaust because many Jews—like my own grandmother—had managed
to flee east and returned home after World War II. Millions of Ukrainians
now either have some Jewish heritage or are married to someone who does.

In the Brodsky Synagogue in the center of the city, a Ukrainian lawmaker, Oleh Voronko, stood guard with a Kalashnikov rifle that he was issued in parliament on the first day of the war. He was weary. "These days, I
sleep two hours a day, and always with a gun in my hands," he said. The
building was empty: the evacuation convoy of several buses had already left.
Voronko wasn't Jewish himself, but his wife, Albina Feerman, was. "I spend
every night in the shelter in the Metro, and on day seven of the war it has
turned out that every third person in my shelter is Jewish," she said, smiling. Feerman told me she came to Ukraine in 1998 from the Russian city of
Rostov to study, and still carried a Russian passport. Like so many other
Kyivites with family and friends in Russia, she was heartbroken by the way
people there were distancing themselves from her. Out of the twenty top
friends on her social media timeline, Feerman told me, only two had pri-

vately messaged her to express support and condemn the invasion. "The other eighteen post cats and puppies all day, and are silent," she said.

In Podil, Kyiv's once overwhelmingly Jewish neighborhood on the right bank of the Dnipro, another synagogue was a beehive of activity, with buses getting ready to head toward the Hungarian border. Galina Naletnikova, a seventy-year-old former philosophy professor, had moved to Ukraine from Moscow four decades earlier to be with her late husband, much of whose extended family had been killed in the Holocaust. She sat in the synagogue's basement, lost in thought, waiting for her evacuation bus to a destination that she didn't know. Her son had chosen to stay in Kyiv to fight. "I've told him to come visit my apartment once in a while because I've had to leave my cats behind," she said. "I don't know what will happen. It is all so absurd."

Around the corner, Vitaliy Semchenko was saying goodbyes to his wife, Kateryna, and their two children, one aged two years and another just one and a half months. A cyber defense expert, Semchenko—whose cousin lived in Israel—remained to help the city's defenders while Kateryna was taking the children abroad. Wouldn't you want him to come with you? I asked her. "No," she replied, "he is staying so that we would be able to come back."

❖

In the suburb of Irpin to the west, the bridge between Kyiv and the town had been blown up by Ukrainian forces. Civilians fleeing from Irpin and the towns beyond it—Bucha, Hostomel, Vorzel—were walking on a ramshackle pedestrian crossing toward Kyiv, balancing on a pipe and a series of precarious planks. With bright yellow tape on arms and helmets to identify them, Ukrainian troops moved the other way in small groups.

Volokhov and his fellow Flemish knights had been deployed on the Irpin front line, establishing a new reconnaissance unit that they chose to call Terra, after the home planet in the Warhammer 40,000 game. One of Volokhov's friends knew how to fly a commercial drone, and they started using it to find Russian positions and guide Ukrainian artillery strikes. Other acquaintances pitched in to buy additional drones.

A Ukrainian colonel who went by the call sign Pedro was upbeat as we met him in Irpin. "The Russians are demoralized, just sitting there without food and water," he said. "They thought they would be in Kyiv in forty-eight hours, and instead we broke their back one by one."

Yet the Russians were far from defeated. After the initial rout in Bucha, they were returning to that town, and creeping closer to Irpin, massive reinforcements arriving over the road from Belarus. Two days later, on March 4, the trickle of refugees at the bridge turned into a flood, with people trying to carry their suitcases and their pets across the river. I was surprised at how many cats and dogs everyone in Irpin, Bucha, and Hostomel seemed to have. These suburbs had attracted prosperous Kyivites who valued space and fresh air.

Tanya Rybko had spent the whole morning walking with her two children from Hostomel and was giddy at finally reaching relative safety at the bridge. A couple of days earlier, she said, a Russian sniper ambushed a Ukrainian unit outside her home, killing four men. She and her neighbors helped three injured Ukrainians, organizing an ambulance to take them away. The Russians had occupied a high-rise nearby, taking its residents hostage and firing at Ukrainian forces in a nearby factory. "We ended up in crossfire, gunshots, explosions, quite a night it was," she said. Fearing that locals would provide information to Ukrainian troops, which could be used to target them, the Russians also began confiscating people's phones.

Mohammed Amin, a Tunisian software engineer who had recently bought an apartment in Irpin, was in tears as he crossed the river with his Ukrainian wife and their son. "Everything was so good here. The Russians are just jealous of us. They feel themselves defeated and so they just hit civilian apartments, they know very well what they are hitting," he said. "And these people here," he added, pointing at Ukrainian troops at the bridge, "they are heroes, believe me."

We walked across to Irpin, past abandoned cars on the other side of the destroyed bridge, and ran into a squad of Ukrainian special forces troops preparing an ambush in a courtyard. They had a British .308 sniper rifle and British NLAW antitank missiles, with another missile stashed in a separate backup trench closer to the river. They were surprised to see us but eager to talk, beaming with pride at having been able to stand their ground. "The

Russians certainly didn't expect that we would fight, and that we would know how," said the commander, Volodymyr, insisting that we take a selfie together. "Every day, we go out to hunt and destroy them."

As we spoke, a Russian jet, flying sideways, appeared overhead above a block of high-rises nearby. We could hear strikes and see curls of smoke rising to the right and to the left of us. "The Russians tried to come here with their tanks, but didn't get far," Volodymyr said. "More are on the way, and we're getting ready to welcome them." The soldiers, he said, operated a drone with thermal cameras to help them locate their prey.

As we walked back to the bridge, a Ukrainian soldier scanned the skies with an antiaircraft missile on his shoulder. The Russian jet disappeared. He had no other targets for now. A minivan careened to a stop at the spot where the bridge ended, and Ukrainian soldiers pulled out a blindfolded Russian prisoner, handing him over to another team across the river. He obeyed the commands meekly and quietly. This was the first Russian soldier, dead or alive, that we had seen in person since the war began. Manu ran to snap photos.

We stopped at a friend's apartment in Podil on the way back. Trained as a combat medic, Alik had spent the previous days going on missions with a small Ukrainian special forces team, striking Russian tanks and supply convoys in the Hostomel area. He was back home for the night, having tea with his girlfriend and shaking his head at how surprisingly bad the Russians turned out to be. "We're in shock at how dumb their behavior is," he said. "Unbelievable." The team had lost two soldiers in nine days of war, he said, and killed more than sixty Russians.

Kuleba, the foreign minister, spoke to Zelensky by phone from western Ukraine around that time. "Dmytro, my regret is that you are not here with us now," he recalled the president telling him. "I regret that you don't see how we are beating the Russians."

⊰⊱

When we headed back to Irpin two days later, on March 6, the sides of the road were lined with yellow buses to evacuate civilians. The Russians had seized control of most of Bucha, retaking Vokzalna Street, which had been littered with the burned hulks of their armor. From there, they turned right to set up positions on Yablunska Street facing Irpin.

Our phones went dead as soon as we approached Irpin. The Russians had by now destroyed or jammed mobile-phone towers, trying to stop residents from informing Ukrainian forces of their movements. Most Ukrainians had a government services app, Diya, installed on their smartphones, which made it possible to share intelligence with the click of a button. In this new information blackout, nobody knew yet that a newly arrived Russian unit, the 64th Motor Rifle Brigade, had forced the residents of Yablunska Street into basements at gunpoint. Those who dared to venture out were shot dead by snipers.

The shelling was creeping up to the eastern entrance of Irpin, and the fleeing families ran grimly toward the buses. This was no longer a place for lingering. The Russians were getting closer and closer.

On the way back toward the destroyed bridge, I passed by a bronze-painted monument to World War II Soviet soldiers, a chapel, and an armored Humvee in which a couple of Ukrainian troops were sheltering. The supermarket by the bridge had been hit, its windows broken. Spotting Manu and Stevo, who had gone ahead, I shouted, "Hey guys," just as a shell flew above us with an ominous whistle. We all hugged the cold ground. Stevo counted the seconds from whistle to impact—seven—and we tried to backtrack through a secondary street, taking cover every few seconds. Shrapnel from an artillery shell hitting the ground sprays out in an upturned conical pattern, and so the lower you are, the less likely you are to be pierced by jagged shards of hot metal.

Along our way, a house struck by one of the shells was on fire, its pipes, roof tiles, and furniture scattered in the courtyard. A thick, acrid smoke singed my nostrils.

When we finally made it back to the main road, all the yellow buses were gone. Manu said he would drive out with another Spanish photographer who was on the scene, following Stevo and me as we hit the gas on the stretch of empty highway. We picked up a family that was trying to walk to the city along the roadside before arriving at the checkpoint amid the high-rises on the outskirts of Kyiv. Ambulances and then ordinary cars started pulling up, some of them carrying wounded soldiers and civilians. Blood pooled on the asphalt. The area of the bridge was being shelled again and again. Ten minutes had passed, then fifteen, and there was still no sign of Manu—and no way of reaching him. Was it possible that the Russians had overrun the area?

"I have to go get him," Stevo said. "Wait here."

"Let's go," I replied. "Drive as fast as you can."

"Here we go again. My life is shit." Stevo grinned stoically.

Manu was there, with his cameras, at the end of the road. Stevo made a dramatic U-turn, shouting, "Get in, you prick!" through the rolled-down window. "I've got something!" Manu shouted back.

A minute or two after I had walked past the monument to Soviet soldiers, a Russian shell had hit nearby, killing a woman, a man, and two children. The bodies lay there, covered by blankets, their carry-on suitcases nearby. Russia was deliberately shelling civilians trying to escape. *"Bastardos, bastardos de mierda,"* Manu kept swearing.

We assumed initially that this had been a family, a father and mother and child—the second child, mortally injured, had been removed from the scene by Ukrainian soldiers attempting to rescue him. But a few hours later, a woman who saw Manu's photos published online got in touch with him via Instagram. "I need to know who the man under the sheets is. Please!!!" she wrote. The clothing was familiar. It was indeed her husband, Anatoliy Berezhnoy, a Baptist volunteer who had gone into Irpin trying to help evacuate local civilians. "He was the kindest person on this entire planet. He loved God so much. He loved other people," she wrote once her worst fears were confirmed. "He couldn't join the army because of his health condition. But he wanted to help. So he did it. Unconditionally."

The dead woman, Tatiana Perebeynos, had originally escaped to Irpin from Russian-occupied Donetsk in 2014. She had been the chief accountant of a Palo Alto technology firm. A professional photo of her, smiling confidently in a green blouse, with manicured nails and an expensive-looking watch, was soon published in a California newspaper. It was hard to reconcile that image with the crumpled, bloodied corpse under a tattered blanket on pockmarked Irpin asphalt.

CHAPTER 14

RUSSIAN TANKS CATCH FIRE
REALLY WELL

U sually narrow and quiet this time of the year, the Irpin River was the last natural obstacle that separated Russian forces from Kyiv. On March 6, thwarted by resistance elsewhere, Russia's military turned its attention to the small, prosperous village of Moshchun northwest of the capital. Dotted with holiday villas, it sits amid pine forests on the eastern bank of the river.

Already on February 27, a reconnaissance unit of Russian VDV troops had attempted to establish a foothold there, crossing via a small bridge that hadn't been blown up in time. Ukrainian troops scrambled to repel the initial incursion, driving the Russians back to the river's western bank.

The newer, much larger offensive involved thousands of troops from some of Russia's most elite units, including the storied 331st VDV Airborne Regiment from Kostroma, which just a month earlier had intervened in Kazakhstan, and the 155th Marine Brigade from Russia's Far East. Moshchun's bridge had already been destroyed, and on March 6 the Russians brought along several pontoon-laying trucks to build new crossings. The first two pontoons were spotted by drones and destroyed by Ukrainian artillery. Several Russian armored vehicles with "V" markings on their sides burned on the riverbank.

But the Russians managed to set up a third pontoon farther north, where Ukraine's Soviet-vintage artillery couldn't strike accurately. Russian

troops and fighting vehicles started to cross the water. Intense Russian artillery fire, aided by Orlan drones, suppressed Ukrainian guns. The Russians, unlike the Ukrainians, had plentiful ammunition. They didn't think
twice about firing several dozen artillery shells at a small outpost with a
handful of Ukrainian soldiers.

Realizing the peril, Ukraine's high command scrambled all available
forces to Moshchun. Ukraine's 72nd Mechanized Brigade, the main force
responsible for the Kyiv front, was augmented with fighters of the Territorial Defense, Azov veterans who had formed their own special forces unit,
detachments of the GUR military intelligence, Kyiv police, and SBU. A
hodgepodge of newly enrolled members of the International Legion, foreign
volunteers who often had little or no experience, also joined the fray.

As the commander of the 72nd Brigade, Colonel Oleksandr Vdovychenko, discussed plans for Moshchun's defense, the chief of Ukraine's
Ground Forces, Colonel General Oleksandr Syrsky, wondered whether
something could be done to widen the river. The Irpin flows northward, into
the Kyiv Sea, where the water level is sixty inches higher because of the Kyiv
hydropower station dam downstream. A special system of sluices pumps Irpin's water into the reservoir. By March 7, these sluices were already behind
Russian lines. Sneaking through the forest, Ukrainian reconnaissance units
managed to reach the area and blow up the pump. Water began to flow
down from the Kyiv Sea. Every morning, Vdovychenko would order his
troops to fly a drone and check how much the river had expanded overnight. Not enough to disrupt the Russian onslaught, was the reply.

⠶

All over northern Ukraine, General Zaluzhny's strategy of a thousand
cuts—hitting Russian convoys along overextended supply lines and
ambushing poorly commanded Russian armored units—was proving successful. It generated a daily stream of videos showing decapitated tanks and
disoriented Russian prisoners being removed from burning fuel trucks.
Russian T-72 and T-80 tanks usually carry their shells in a ring within the
turret. If a tank is hit by a Javelin or another antitank weapon, this can trigger a powerful explosion that usually kills the crew and makes the turret fly

off. In military slang, this is called "lollipopping," because the turret and the attached gun look like a giant rusted lollipop when separated from the rest of the tank. By the second week of March, there were dozens, perhaps hundreds, of such lollipops scattered in the fields of Ukraine, with more popping off every day.

As a Russian tank column approached the Kyiv suburb of Brovary, Lieutenant Tetyana Chornovol, a former parliament member and investigative journalist, sped to the front line northeast of Kyiv in her red hatchback. She had antitank missiles in the trunk. After the 2014 revolution, Ukraine's military had begun formally accepting women in combat roles, and on the eve of the Russian invasion some 32,000 women were serving in the country's armed forces. Voluntary battalions created during the fight for Donbas were especially willing to remove the gender barrier.

On March 9, tanks from the Russian Army's 6th Guards Tank Regiment rolled without infantry support on the four-lane highway approaching Kyiv, oblivious to the Ukrainian soldiers such as Lieutenant Chornovol lying in wait in the courtyards on both sides of the road. A Ukrainian drone filmed the engagement.

First, Ukrainian soldiers with NLAW missiles hit the front and back vehicles. Lieutenant Chornovol fired from the Ukrainian-made Stuhna antitank system; intended for export, its command display was in Arabic. Her first missile missed; the second hit. Retreating chaotically, the Russian column became a perfect target, struck again and again by missiles and artillery. Minutes later, seventeen tanks and three other armored vehicles were ablaze. It was a rout. The Russian regiment's commander, Colonel Andrey Zakharov, died of his wounds shortly afterward.

⸎

Similar scenes unfolded in the wooded terrain to the north and northeast of the Ukrainian capital. Russian columns rushing to Kyiv on February 24 had bypassed the regional capital cities of Chernihiv and Sumy, which remained surrounded but undefeated despite heavy bombardment. In Chernihiv, the Ukrainian Army's 1st Tank Brigade, which had only returned from Donbas to its base in the area in December, immediately engaged the enemy. While the Russian breakthrough on the right bank of the Dnipro—via Chornobyl and toward Hostomel—was a surprise, Ukrainian commanders had planned for the Russian thrust to Kyiv via Chernihiv on the left bank of the river.

Valentyn Koval, a cheerful, baby-faced twenty-two-year-old from western Ukraine's Chernivtsi region, received orders to deploy to the forested area near Nizhyn, southeast of Chernihiv, for "exercises" on February 23, a day before the invasion. A lieutenant commanding a unit of Ukrainian Uragan multiple-launch rocket systems, he knew immediately that he wasn't really going for training. His brigade brought along an unusually large amount of live ammunition: 220mm rockets that, while imprecise, can deliver a devastating blow to personnel and equipment more than twenty miles away.

One of the most momentous events in modern Ukrainian history had occurred in these forests: the Battle of Kruty in January 1918. Then the fledgling Ukrainian state had also faced a Russian invasion aiming to quickly capture Kyiv. When some 6,000 Russian troops commanded by Mikhail Muravyov arrived at the Kruty railway station, they were confronted by a ragtag force of a few hundred Ukrainians, many of them Kyiv university students as young as seventeen with little training. The students fought hard, and delayed the Russians by a few days, blowing up railway tracks and bridges. The Russians hunted down the survivors, executing dozens of prisoners in a massacre that has been seared into Ukraine's national memory ever since. Pavlo Tychyna, the futurist Ukrainian poet, wrote these lines after witnessing the burial of thirty students killed in Kruty:

> Whom did Cain begrudge?
> Avenge, oh God!
> Above all, they loved
> Their beloved land.

O nce the Russian columns crossed the border, moving across the Desna River from Koval's battery, local civilians flooded the lieutenant with intelligence. Koval received a call from an old man hiding in a village along the road. "The grandpa kept saying: not now, not now, not just yet. And then he went: I see the damnedest foes, they're on the road, fire on them, son, now." That Russian tank convoy was obliterated.

Trained crews like Koval's worked without rest, jumping from one Uragan vehicle to another and driving from their forest hideouts to fire as other troops loaded up and serviced the systems that had just completed their missions.

An Uragan rocket weighs nearly 620 pounds and needs a special crane to be loaded into the launcher. Koval's battery's crane eventually broke down, just as his commanding officer arrived with a request to finish off a Russian column that had been hit but still contained scores of functioning or lightly damaged tanks and other armored vehicles. Some of Koval's crewmen had served in Donbas in 2014 and were used to nonstandard solutions—so they pulled out their leather belts. Straining their backs, eight men using belts managed to manually pull up and load the rockets. That Russian column was also turned into a smoldering wreck.

When Koval finally had a moment to check the news on his smartphone, he saw that the area where he was operating was marked as under Russian control on the maps. "The internet thought that we are occupied," Koval said. "But we were still there, fighting for our homes."

⋯

Unlike in Chernihiv, hardly any regular Ukrainian forces were based in the neighboring region of Sumy, just twenty miles from the border. As Russian columns drove past Sumy toward Okhtyrka and Kyiv, local volunteers, border guards, and SBU intelligence officers banded together in improvised self-defense groups.

Two fighters named Artyom and Dmytro with experience in Donbas, but who otherwise normally worked as executives for multinational corporations, set up one such platoon after picking up guns on the first day of the war. "The people who joined had no idea how to fight, but they knew that this is our home, and someone needed to defend the home," Dmytro told me weeks later. "Otherwise, someone else would have knocked on our door to say: you don't live here anymore." Their initial priority was attacking vulnerable Russian fuel trucks to disable the Russian military closer to the front lines.

Artyom and Dmytro started off by capturing two abandoned Russian BMPs and a fuel truck. While the truck and one of the BMPs were out of diesel, the second BMP turned out to be fully fueled. It also contained an abundance of weapons, including rocket-propelled grenades. "Our first trophy. Until then, we had just one RPG for the whole platoon," Dmytro recalled. "After that, life became a little more fun. RPGs aren't perfect, but they are way better than Molotov cocktails."

The capture of these armored vehicles marked the beginning of the Sumy insurgents' transformation into a mechanized force, as more trophy BMPs and BTRs joined the unit. Psychological warfare was key: the fighters tried hard to convince the Russians that their resistance was a formidable force that warranted diverting resources. "We knew they are listening to us on the radio, so we kept talking as if there were seven thousand of us, while in reality it was only three guys." Artyom laughed. "And they fell for it."

Quickly, the Russians realized they could be attacked from all sides. Convoys started traveling in large numbers, with 80 to 120 vehicles, for safety. Frequent breakdowns meant that these columns often had to stop to fix the straggler and to reload its cargo and passengers, making them more vulnerable to drone strikes and to Ukrainian artillery. Civilians in almost every village, Artyom said, started passing information to the Ukrainian military. The Russians responded by detaining anyone with suspicious information on their phone, often shipping these inmates to interrogation facilities within Russia.

The initial successes made more local men join the resistance. "At first, people were in awe of the Russian tanks," Artyom said. "But, as it turned out, they catch fire really well."

⁂

While the forested, undulating terrain of the country's northeast turned out to be perfect for hit-and-run guerrilla attacks, the open steppes of the Ukrainian south were ill-suited for insurgent warfare. In Kherson, Ukrainian patriots trapped behind Russian lines initially chose peaceful resistance. Thousands gathered daily on the city's main square, opposite the regional government headquarters, waving Ukrainian flags. On March 5, one particularly daring protester drove around with the new "Bayraktar" song blaring out of loudspeakers. Another jumped atop a Russian BTR in the heart of the city, planting a blue-and-yellow banner on its turret.

The Russians were under orders to exercise restraint, and initially allowed these protests to unfold—with intelligence officers carefully filming the participants to identify, and later detain, the organizers. They also permitted the city's mayor, Ihor Kolykhaev, to continue operating from the municipality building, which kept flying the Ukrainian flag.

The bulk of the Russian military continued pushing north. Advance Russian units reached the eastern entrance of Mykolaiv, a sprawling port city of nearly half a million people. There, unlike in Kherson, the regional leadership stayed on to fight. Mykolaiv's governor, a Korean-Ukrainian property developer named Vitaliy Kim, started posting funny, mocking videos describing the city's predicament and assuring its citizens that the Russians wouldn't win. "Good evening, we are from Ukraine," every video began—giving Kim a pop-star following among Ukrainians starved for optimism.

Major General Dmytro Marchenko, a stocky paratrooper originally from the area, rushed from Kyiv to organize Mykolaiv's defense. He found a city demoralized, with some residents trying to take down Ukrainian flags from the streets, convinced the city would be seized just as quickly as Kherson had fallen. Enraged, Marchenko ordered troops to prepare for a fight. Every night, he raised the drawbridge on the road toward Odesa to make sure no senior officials could escape. The Russians weren't as mighty as everyone was imagining, he kept repeating: "They are cowards, we have to smash them, we shouldn't be afraid, we are in our own home and we will fight for every house and every street." Initial skirmishes forced the Russians to retreat.

Instead of trying to quickly take the port city, Russian columns rushed farther north, reaching the town of Voznesensk sixty miles up the Southern Buh River. Such a rapid advance put the Russians in the immediate vicinity of the South Ukraine Nuclear Power Plant, one of four operating in Ukraine.

Another Russian offensive pushed toward the town of Enerhodar, home to the Zaporizhzhia Nuclear Power Plant, which sits on the southern shore of the vast Kakhovka Reservoir. A small Ukrainian National Guard unit in Enerhodar, its back to the water, was no match for the massive Russian force that rolled into the city on March 4. The plant was under Russian control within hours. A small fire erupted in part of the compound, but there was no radiation leak.

Zelensky spent that night calling world leaders, warning them of a potential nuclear disaster that would dwarf the 1986 Chornobyl catastrophe. "Europe must wake up," he implored. "No country except Russia has ever shelled nuclear power blocks. This is the first time in the history of mankind. The terrorist country is resorting to nuclear terrorism."

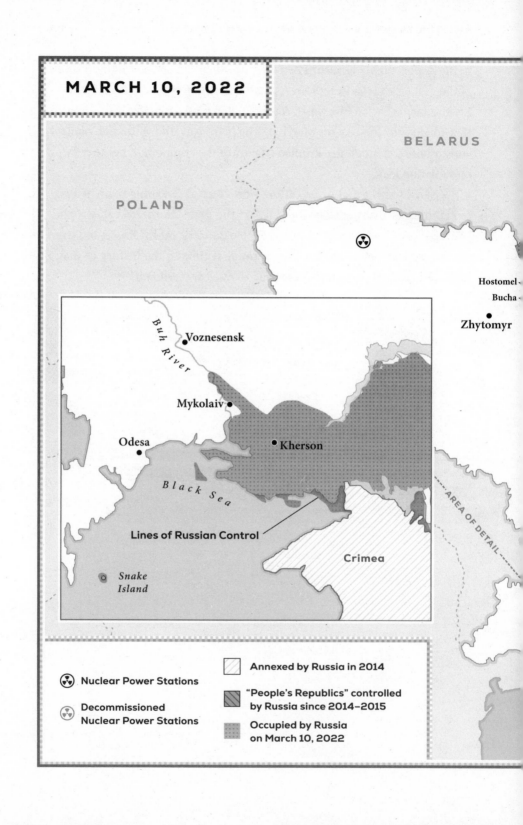

MARCH 10, 2022

BELARUS

POLAND

Hostomel
Bucha
Zhytomyr

Buh River

Voznesensk

Mykolaiv

Odesa

Kherson

Black Sea

Lines of Russian Control

AREA OF DETAIL

Snake
Island

Crimea

Nuclear Power Stations

Decommissioned
Nuclear Power Stations

Annexed by Russia in 2014

"People's Republics" controlled
by Russia since 2014–2015

Occupied by Russia
on March 10, 2022

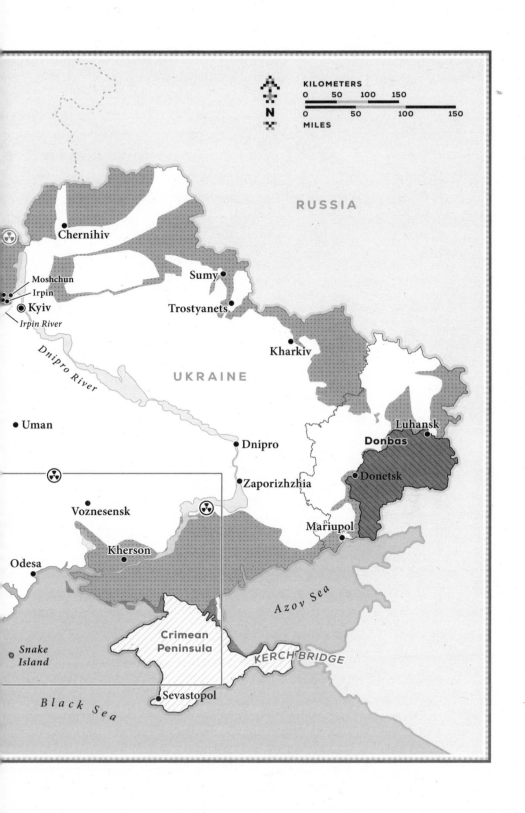

KILOMETERS
0   50   100   150

MILES
0   50   100   150

N

RUSSIA

Chernihiv

Moshchun
Irpin
Kyiv
Irpin River

Sumy

Trostyanets

Kharkiv

UKRAINE

Uman

Dnipro

Dnipro River

Luhansk

Donbas

Zaporizhzhia

Donetsk

Voznesensk

Kherson

Mariupol

Odesa

Azov Sea

Snake
Island

Crimean
Peninsula

KERCH BRIDGE

Sevastopol

Black Sea

PART 4

>:◻:<

DESTRUCTION

CHAPTER 15

A REALLY DIRTY WAR
IN KHARKIV

B y the second week of March, it became clear that Putin's initial war plan had failed. Unable to advance, Russian forces took out their fury on Ukrainian civilians—and on the civilian infrastructure they had previously spared. Kharkiv bore the brunt of the Russian war machine, but it wasn't clear how badly. No other Western news organization had been to the city since the massive Russian shelling and strikes began on March 1. That's where I wanted to go.

The direct highway between Kyiv and Kharkiv takes only about five hours to drive. But it skirted too close to Russian positions and was interrupted by destroyed bridges. Nobody knew exactly where current front lines lay, so we chose to take the long route via the city of Dnipro. The farther away we got from the Russians, the more paranoid local Territorial Defense fighters and police became at checkpoints. There was now one such roadblock in almost every village, with little coordination between them. It made the transport of weapons and other vital supplies difficult. Days after we passed through, the Ukrainian government asked for most of these checkpoints, barricades, and chicanes in the rear to be dismantled.

Frequent Russian missile strikes meant that anyone with a camera was doubly suspect—presumed to be a spotter until proven otherwise. We stopped at a gas station in the Cherkasy region, roughly halfway to Dnipro. While all the restaurants were closed in Kyiv, it turned out that gas stations

still served coffee and at least some hot food, usually in the form of ubiqui-
tous hot-dog buns stuffed with mayo, ketchup, and mustard.

Just as I picked up the coffees, a police car screeched to a halt. Officers
in full body armor jumped out, screaming and pointing their guns at us.
One pressed the barrel of his Kalashnikov rifle into my ribs, pushing me
onto the hood of the car. Another pulled Manu out. We had been reported
as Russian spies taking photos of strategic targets, they said, breathing
heavily, their voices full of satisfaction. The policemen relaxed somewhat as
they examined our press cards and flicked through our phones' photo gal-
leries. But they lowered their guns only after I managed to video call a senior interior ministry official in Kyiv who vouched for us. Unwilling to
accept complete defeat, the cops demanded to see the car's registration and
insurance. At this point, Stevo blew up, speaking English: "You're fucking
joking, aren't you? You fuckers have just stuck a gun in my face and now you
want to see my car insurance?"

"The foreigner is very upset, is he?" the policeman asked me, this time
politely.

"Yes, he is."

At that point, my phone rang. It was the regional chief of police, ordering
the cops to let us go. "Please drive safely," the patrol officer said as he saluted.

Dnipro turned out to be much livelier than Kyiv. Alcohol was still available, and the city had a few open restaurants. We settled in an overwrought
hotel, with its gaudy post-Soviet faux-Baroque interiors and a fully operational bar. The barman made us perfect Negronis, our first since the invasion. We needed them.

The next table was occupied by an extended family from Kharkiv, more
than a dozen people of three generations. We would travel to the city at sunrise, I told them. "You're weird. Everyone else is going in the other direction," the grandfather replied.

⁕

In modern war, you want low clouds, wind, and rain, so that enemy drones
can't guide artillery fire and enemy planes and helicopters can't fly. March 10
was a cold, crisp morning, with blue skies. The worst kind of weather.

It takes about two and a half hours to drive to Kharkiv from Dnipro. I arranged to see Mayor Terekhov and asked his aide where would be best to stay overnight. "What kind of question is this?" the aide replied instantly. "The subway station, of course. Nowhere else in Kharkiv is safe."

On social media, we'd seen footage of devastation from Kharkiv in the previous days. Yet nothing could have prepared me for the main Sumska Street. The city had been eviscerated. The elegant fin-de-siècle buildings with their art-nouveau and neoclassical facades—the buildings where we had gone to shop, eat, and party in January—were all gutted, their windows and roofs blown out. Giant icicles where water had burst out of broken pipes clinked eerily in the wind overhead, dropping every few minutes. Decapitated mannequins spilled out of windows.

There had been no looting. High-fashion boutiques still displayed their wares, even with the front walls missing in places. A bar that we had patronized still had its collection of liquors, but the ceiling was caved in. There were even cigarettes visible through broken glass, in a city where cigarettes had become a prized commodity because truck drivers were too scared to make deliveries.

The city center was empty except for a half-dozen men who methodically removed the rubble from the street. They were Kharkiv taxi and Uber drivers. "There isn't much work now, and someone needs to clean up the city, and to raise the morale. We can do it, so we do it," one of them said.

As I spoke to the driver, a frail, elderly woman cautiously crossed the street. She was clearly disoriented and asked for directions to the nearby branch of PrivatBank, one of the main Ukrainian banks. Her debit card had been eaten by the ATM there, she said. "Have you seen PrivatBank? Have you? I need to get the card back, for my pension," she kept repeating. But the branch was gone, only a twisted jumble of metal under the remains of the bank's green logo. Somehow, the bank's security alarm still functioned, blaring faintly through the rubble. A Nike billboard nearby proclaimed, "We planned for everything."

While much of the Kharkiv city center had been pummeled more than a week earlier, the Nikolsky shopping mall around the corner where we had bought our tents and other survival gear before the war still smoldered. A Russian missile had slammed into its roof the previous night.

Up the road, on Freedom Square, a Ukrainian soldier walked us into the remains of the regional government building where I had interviewed the governor a few weeks earlier. He pointed out a crater in the courtyard where an ambulance was vaporized after being struck by a missile. A stiff body was still lying outside, covered by branches. At the entrance, Stevo noticed charred blood spattered on formerly white walls. "Someone died a terrible death just here," he murmured. Inside, rescue teams were still digging, looking for more bodies. They weren't hoping to find anyone alive anymore. A bronze plaque that used to hang on the blown-out door of what used to be the governor's office was propped against a chipped column. A portrait of Taras Shevchenko, Ukraine's national poet, was perched on the remains of a couch. A lost blue-and-yellow bracelet was barely visible under the debris on the ground.

The soldier, who used to be a studio portrait photographer before the war, pointed at a fifth-floor apartment of a modern high-rise across the street. The building had been turned into a twisted spiral of broken metal and concrete. The apartment's outer wall had been sheared off by the blast. The soldier's friend was inside during the strike but survived unscathed. Sometimes, people were lucky like that, he said.

A woman on the square outside, by the stairs leading down into the underpass and subway station beneath, asked us for cigarettes. Manu gave her a pack and I asked why she was still in Kharkiv. "Why would I leave? I have reflected about it and decided that it's safer here," she replied. "The war is everywhere anyway, though it looks like it's finishing." For now, she added, she was living in the subway station below, instead of risking it at her apartment. Her behavior seemed odd, but so did almost everyone's. It was a city in distress.

At the ruins of the Kharkiv Air Force University, deputy commander Lieutenant Colonel Oleh Pechelulko took us around to see the damage from four Russian missiles that had hit it on March 1. The blast wave had blown out windows in apartment buildings two blocks away. The six-story building where Pechelulko's family used to reside was gutted, every window a black hole with rising soot streaks from the fire that had carbonized almost everything inside. A crane was trying to pick through the debris. Burned, upturned cars littered the road. The playground for officers' children, with its giant mural of a pink-maned lion, was nearly invisible under a mound of snow-covered bricks. Pechelulko told me he was lucky. While many of his colleagues lost spouses, children, and parents that day, his own wife had left the building shortly before the Russian strike. "Everything has burned down. Nothing is left. Not memories. Not documents. Nothing. I am continuing the war just with what I had on my back that night," he said. "All the men had gone off to fight and defend Kharkiv that night. Now, every one of them will avenge his family, his murdered children, his murdered wife. We will never forgive, but we need weapons." In another building on the compound, rescuers were still digging out the corpses of cadets. Pechelulko was a big, stocky man. His eyes welled. "Every day, bodies are being found, and we have to tell the families, the parents."

How many people like him, I wondered, would make it their lifelong mission to make Russia pay for what it had done?

TEREKHOV, THE MAYOR, HAD GIVEN ME AN APPOINTMENT INSIDE THE SUBWAY station on Kharkiv's Constitution Square, near his bombed-out municipality building. He was easy to spot, mobbed by constituents who bivouacked on the platform and inside the stopped trains. The station had heating, electrical outlets, and toilets. "Our main task now is to save the lives of our people, which is why I call on everyone to come down to shelters like this," Terekhov began. I asked him whether Kharkivites were afraid that Russian troops, still on the edge of the city, would be able to take it over in coming weeks.

"It won't happen," he replied indignantly. "Nobody wants the Russians here; we didn't invite them. In Kharkiv, we used to see Russians—and I am not exaggerating—as our brothers. Every fourth person here either hails from Russia or has family there. But not even in our worst nightmares could we imagine that they would bomb our residential areas, destroy our city's infrastructure. Our people are in shock. The mindset has reversed completely. The attitude to Russia is very negative now. There will probably be several generations before that changes."

Terekhov spoke in Russian. After he finished, I looked at the improvised library—a table full of used books—inside the subway station. The books were also mostly in Russian, with classics like Bulgakov, Chekhov, and Tolstoi alongside Ukrainian translations of Harry Potter and *The Chronicles of Narnia*. The wall nearby was decorated with the drawings of children who had been sleeping underground. "Putin go home, I love Ukraine," read one. Another, signed by seven-year-old Illarion, had a picture of a poodle wearing Ukrainian colors. "We all want peace," it read. "My Adele is also for peace and for Ukraine."

When we returned to the surface, the weather had turned, with snow falling and the city getting dark quickly. The artillery fire was louder and louder. We drove around the empty streets and decided to spend the night in the subway under Freedom Square. Stevo insisted that we park the car in a narrow courtyard, so it would be protected from shrapnel. We found a suitable area and ran with our survival backpacks to the subway's staircase. But in the underpass, the gates to the subway station were blocked, with cardboard boxes and other debris piled up at the entrance. This station wasn't serving as shelter. The only other person in the underpass was the woman to whom we had given cigarettes that morning. She stared at us blankly, lost in her own world, and didn't respond to a hello.

Trying to beat the curfew, we raced to another empty courtyard near Constitution Square, just by the Nikolsky mall. Deep underneath, the subway station was quiet, the sound of artillery barely audible. I fell asleep under a giant prewar poster advertising the Chelsea Football Club, owned at the time by Russian oligarch Roman Abramovich.

❖

Volodymyr Radchenko, the orthopedic surgeon from the Kharkiv suburbs who had escaped the Russian onslaught in the early hours of the war, was already gone from the city under constant bombardments and shelling. He and his family were making their way to Germany, part of an exodus of millions of Ukrainians, mostly women, children, and men over sixty. Younger men with three or more children were also permitted to leave.

Many had traveled in the opposite direction. Vsevolod Kozhemiako, the entrepreneur who had been skiing in Austria when the war erupted, had already returned to Kharkiv, after nearly getting shot at a Territorial Defense checkpoint. He hosted employees and friends in the basement of his corporate headquarters, trying to figure out the best way to join the war against the Russian invaders.

Across town, closer to the front line, soldiers from Ukraine's 92nd Mechanized Brigade hid from Russian bombs and shells in another subway station. Every few minutes, pickup trucks came loaded with antitank missiles. "We can only operate in small groups now. We receive information from the locals all the time, and we try to move ahead and hit the Russians little by little," Lieutenant Andriy Babak told me. "But, of course, there are also locals who help the other side, that's sadly true."

Inside the improvised base, there were a few soldiers who had been separated from their unit. They had eventually made their way to Kharkiv from behind Russian lines.

One of them, Andriy Tkachuk, told me that he and ten fellow soldiers had hiked to a nearby village after their company, deployed on the Russian border, was mauled in the first hours of the war. At first, residents fed them and let them change into civilian clothes and hide their weapons in an abandoned house. A Russian infantry fighting vehicle stopped by the house during the night, unloading a few volleys, but then moved on. After dawn, two soldiers in the group decided to try escaping on their own, while Tkachuk and eight others made their way through the forest. When they walked into the village, unarmed, local men jumped out to tackle them, fearful that the presence of Ukrainian soldiers would trigger Russian reprisals against the entire community.

"At first the villagers beat us, then they fed us and gave us water," Tkachuk recalled. "They were too afraid about what the Russians would do." Finally, after nine days of hiding, Tkachuk and the other soldiers managed to find a path through the woods to a settlement where Ukrainian police still operated. From there, police officers drove them to their brigade.

"It's much better than in the first days of the war. In the first days, it was chaos, nobody could understand anything," Lieutenant Babak told me as his phone started ringing with the Bayraktar song. "If somebody tells you they were not afraid in the first days, they are lying to you."

✦✦✦

The only pediatric neurosurgeon left in eastern Ukraine, Oleksandr Dukhovskyy, was exhausted. On March 11, the day I saw him in a Kharkiv hospital, he was supposed to be attending an international conference in Bogotá, Colombia. Just like most staff, he hadn't left the hospital since the war began, saving the lives of children and adults maimed by Russia's war machine. He talked wistfully about Caribbean vacations as he showed me the misery in his hospital's wards.

"It's a war, and it's a really dirty war." Dukhovskyy sighed. "The Russians understood that they can't manage to win in the battlefield, that the nation is united and strong against them, that nobody wants them here, and so they decided to hit peaceful civilians instead. They are not really human, these people."

He held up his phone with the pictures of a recent patient, a girl whose skull had been smashed inward by the blast wave from a Russian strike that hit her apartment: "If you are not afraid, I can show you the photos."

Dukhovskyy told me he realized that Russia was an enemy as far back as 1994, when he traveled to Moscow for a conference. At a buffet dinner with Russian surgeons, he was stunned to listen to people he had considered colleagues and friends as they mocked the Ukrainian language and asserted that Ukraine was an artificial nation that shouldn't exist. "That's when I understood that we aren't brothers and never will be," he said. "We have a different makeup."

In the ward, I watched as Stanislav Baklanov, a manager at a construction company, comforted his seven-year-old son, Vladimir. Stanislav was in Uzbekistan on a business trip when the war began. His wife had been driving with Vladimir and their daughter, trying to escape Kharkiv, on February 28, when Russian soldiers fired on them, killing her instantly, while Vladimir was brought to the hospital with life-threatening wounds. His sister was unhurt. Stanislav, who arrived in the city days later, closed the door so that his son wouldn't overhear our conversation. "He probably knows that his mama is dead, but he still keeps calling her," he said. "Best if he doesn't know. He's got too many problems of his own to deal with right now."

Down the corridor, Serhiy Kosyanov was grappling with feelings of guilt. On the afternoon of March 7, he had spent two hours in line getting gas for his family car. He had wanted to move his family out of the city, but just as he was opening the door to their apartment building downstairs, a Russian projectile flew into his living room. A shard from the explosion lodged between the base of the skull and the spine of his eight-year-old son, Dmitri. Dmitri's sister suffered burns.

"I came home just a little bit too late." Kosyanov shook his head in the ICU waiting room. His wife, Elena, held his hand. "All our pets have burned alive," she said quietly. "Two cats. One dog. One hamster."

CHAPTER 16

MARIUPOL'S NEIGHBORHOOD
OF APOCALYPSES

On the evening of March 11, we left Kharkiv. There was a snow-storm, with a chilling wind whipping down the deserted streets. Constant explosions marked the rising toll. It felt hopeless, like nuclear winter. Putin had expected the city to welcome his embraces, and he was bludgeoning it for refusing to surrender. Any Russian pretenses of caring about Russian-speakers were forgotten.

Cut off from reinforcements, and slowly strangled, Mariupol was subjected to a similar retribution. Russian propaganda usually insisted, perversely and against all evidence, that residential neighborhoods in the two cities were being bombed by Ukrainian "Nazis" rather than Russian artillery and aircraft. But some of Moscow's top propagandists were occasionally caught in a moment of honesty.

"Mariupol. The neighborhood of apocalypses. Should this destruction be shown to the entire world?" wrote Russian state TV military affairs correspondent Aleksandr Sladkov, who would later be promoted to advise Putin on military recruitment. "Let them see it in Kyiv and Lviv, in Cherkasy and Poltava, in Ternopil and Chernivtsi: if the city doesn't surrender, it gets destroyed." Moscow now practiced the Genghis Khan school of war.

Unable to reach Mariupol, we drove instead to the southern city of Zaporizhzhia, the hub for Ukrainians fleeing occupied areas in the south and east. Zaporizhzhia was less than an hour's drive from the front lines and almost all the hotels were closed. The one that we found on a quiet part of the Dnipro riverfront had a sauna and a Russian *banya* attached. The young women working at the reception desk were busily discussing how to repaint the sign to say "Ukrainian" *banya* instead.

Refugees from Mariupol were being bused to the Zaporizhzhia municipal circus building, where locals had brought mountains of used clothes and toys, and where volunteers provided food, tea, and bookings for buses and trains to western Ukraine or abroad. When we came, however, there was nobody from Mariupol. The Russians had once again shelled the agreed evacuation route. It had been days since anyone was able to escape the besieged city.

The only displaced people in the circus that day were from villages and towns east of Zaporizhzhia, some of them already occupied by Russia and others under attack. On the walls, notice boards listed the details of Mariupol refugees looking for their relatives and friends. Some had matter-of-fact annotations. "The house is destroyed," read one. "The grandmother is dead," read another.

❖

Mariupol's hundred-bed military hospital was full, and its patients included a few Russian POWs captured by Azov. Wounded soldiers and civilians had to be moved to other medical facilities across the city. Local civilians started taking care of the injured troops, bringing them food and cigarettes. Flying through volleys of Russian fire, three Ukrainian military helicopters carrying medical supplies managed to land on one of Mariupol's central squares. Yulia Paevska, the medic, helped load them up with some of the wounded for the return journey.

On March 9, a Russian warplane hit Mariupol's maternity hospital, killing and injuring several women. A photo taken by the AP's Evgeniy Maloletka of Marianna Vyshemirska, a bloodied patient of the maternity ward making her way through the gray rubble, shocked the world. Yet again, Moscow denied the obvious. Seizing on the fact that Vyshemirska was an

Instagram model before the war, Russian diplomats around the world prof-
fered conspiracy theories that the bombing didn't really happen, and that
the photos had been staged by Ukrainian forces to make Russia look bad.
The maternity hospital, Russian foreign minister Sergei Lavrov insisted,
was nonoperational anyway and was used by "the neo-Nazi Azov Battalion." Twitter moderators had to delete a post with this claim by the Russian
embassy in London.

The same day, two groups of Russian troops, operating under the cover
of fog, tried to penetrate Mariupol from the north. They ran into an Azov
ambush and fled, leaving the bodies of their comrades behind. Exhausted
but pumped up with adrenaline, dirt-streaked Azov soldiers brought a
bloodied shoulder insignia bearing one star to Kyrylo Berkal's command
post for Sector C. "Look, we've killed a major," one of the men boasted as he
grabbed an energy drink. Picking up the trophy, Berkal instantly realized
that the star was too big, and that the shoulder strap missed a major's two
vertical bars. He almost choked as he whipped out his phone to check Russian rank insignia. "What major? It's a major general!" he shouted. "How
the hell did he turn up here?"

The Russians had just lost Major General Oleg Mityayev, the commander of the 150th Division, the core force targeting Mariupol. His vehicle
contained valuable code books that allowed Ukrainian fighters to decipher
Russian radio communications in the following days. "That moment, I
imagined that it will be like in cartoons, once you cut off the head and kill
the main villain, his army melts away," Berkal recalled. "Unfortunately, that
didn't happen."

Berkal didn't know it yet, but Mityayev was the second Russian general
killed in Mariupol. A sniper shot had already felled Major General Andrey
Sukhovetskiy, deputy commander of Russia's 41st Combined Arms Army.

By now, Azov had run out of artillery shells. Punching through a weaker
area of the front line, Russian forces managed to enter Mariupol from the
west. House-to-house urban combat began, with Ukrainian fighters aiming
to stop the Russian onslaught using snipers and mobile antitank teams that
moved from high-rise to high-rise, escaping via elevator shafts. Mariupol's
civilians were caught in the middle.

✦✦✦

In the first weeks of the war, a new vocabulary had taken hold in Ukraine. Few Ukrainians used the word "Russians" to describe Russian soldiers. It just didn't have all the negative emotional connotations that Ukrainians now associated with the hated invaders who were turning their cities into rubble.

The word "Russia" comes from the Kyiv Rus principality, a state established in the ninth century by Viking princes who sailed down the Dnipro on their way to seek Byzantium's riches. Modern Ukrainians consider it as their country's rightful heritage. So do the Russians, a claim that turns the very presence of a separate and independent Ukraine into an existential threat to Russia's foundational narrative.

Putin and Zelensky share the same first name, that of Kyiv's Grand Prince Volodymyr, or Vladimir in Russian, who had brought Christianity to the Rus. My own parents named me after Volodymyr's son, Grand Prince of Rus Yaroslav the Wise, whose sarcophagus occupies pride of place in Kyiv's St. Sophia Cathedral. (My mother often fretted that I would be mocked for my name if I didn't do well in school.)

Putin saw these common roots as proof that Ukrainians and Russians are one people—who should all be ruled by him. To many Ukrainians, Moscow, an uninhabited swamp when princes Volodymyr or Yaroslav were alive, had misappropriated their history—and with it, the right to the very name Russia. After the war began in 2022, tens of thousands of Ukrainians even signed a formal request for Zelensky to rename Russia as Muscovy in the Ukrainian language, a petition that he asked his prime minister to examine.

Established nearly a century after Prince Yaroslav's death, Moscow rose to prominence because of the Mongol invasion that devastated much of eastern Europe in the thirteenth century. As Muscovy grew in power thanks to its princes' special status as tax collectors for the Mongols, most of today's Ukraine fell under Polish and Lithuanian rule, retaining cultural connections to the rest of Europe and a far greater degree of personal freedom— something that, Ukrainian historians say, explains the difference in national character, and modern Ukraine's rejection of authoritarianism.

As Ukrainians resisted Russian rule over the centuries, they called their enemies *moskals*—a distortion of Muscovite—rather than Russians. Another widespread slur name than emerged centuries ago is *katsap*, which comes from the Turkic word for butcher, by itself a testament to Ukraine's tragic history.

But after February 24, 2022, the most popular denomination for Russian invaders was borrowed from J. R. R. Tolkien's *The Lord of the Rings*. In Ukrainian official statements and in military reports, they were now called "orcs," after Tolkien's humanoid monsters.

Some Russian soldiers and military propagandists took this Tolkien reference in stride, starting to refer to Ukrainians as "elves." But most simply followed Putin's rhetoric that Moscow was continuing the battles of World War II and referred to Ukrainian soldiers as "Naziks" or, absurdly, "Germans." As for the Ukrainian state, Russian propagandists starting calling it "Country 404," for the computer error code, or "Swine Reich."

❖

In occupied Kherson, the brief period of Russian restraint was coming to an end. Russian troops started dispersing protests with force and detaining their participants. Moscow also made the first steps to create a collaborationist administration that would govern these lands, with local quislings coming into the open.

It all began on March 15, with a small rally by the monument to fallen Soviet soldiers. Ostensibly, the occasion was the commemoration of the seventy-eighth anniversary of Kherson's liberation from Nazi Germany. Neither Russian nor Ukrainian banners were on display. Instead, the organizers carried the red Soviet "Victory Flag" as a hundred or so attendees, mostly women beyond middle age, laid red tulips and chanted, "*Spasibo dedu za pobedu*"—the Putin-era Russian rhyme that translates as "Thank you, Grandfather, for Victory."

The main speaker was Kirill Stremousov, a well-known pro-Russian activist who had gained notoriety during the COVID pandemic for leading antivaccine protests. Before the war, Stremousov used to organize the "Russian Run"—a race that usually gathered a few dozen young men who jogged through Kherson, waving the Russian tricolor or the black, yellow, and white banner of the Russian Empire. The SBU, penetrated by Russian agents, never disturbed him.

Stremousov had a degree of international fame. In 2017, a YouTube video of him wildly spinning his four-month-old daughter by her leg became so viral that it even made it to Britain's *Sun* tabloid. "How Could He? Outrage as sick dad swings baby around his head like a ragdoll and claims he can 'hear her bones popping,'" went the headline. A proud vegetarian and yoga practitioner who had hitchhiked his way across Latin America, Stremousov imagined himself Kherson's own Che Guevara.

"Kherson is a free city," he proclaimed at the March 15 rally. "Historic justice has returned to our city." He even delivered part of his speech in fluent Ukrainian, reciting a 1960s poem that condemned Ukrainian nationalists who had sided with Nazi Germany during World War II.

The second speaker was Volodymyr Saldo, Kherson's mayor from 2002 to 2012 and formerly one of the most powerful men in southern Ukraine. The 2014 Maidan revolution had turned him into a marginal figure. Saldo had failed in subsequent attempts to get reelected to parliament or to return to the mayor's office, fighting off continuous accusations of corruption and links with organized crime.

In contrast to Stremousov's rhetorical flourish, bland-faced Saldo made just a few restrained remarks at the rally. His assistant initially claimed he had been forced to attend. But there was no going back. Kherson's former mayor had cast his lot with Moscow, and would soon become head of the Russian occupation administration.

⊰◈⊱

The challenge in the early weeks of the war was that nobody knew exactly where Russian-occupied territories began and ended. Open-source intelligence analysts started to publish their own approximations online, basing conclusions on geolocated photos and videos of Russian troops from social media. So did Western governments. None of these maps were accurate: the British ministry of defense kept saying that Kharkiv was encircled even as we freely traveled in and out.

On the maps, Russia was marked in control of the town of Voznesensk, a red arrow striking deep into central Ukraine some fifty miles northwest of Mykolaiv, our next destination. This forced us to take a circuitous detour that tripled the usual driving time, from six hours to eighteen. Other roads, it turned out, were closed along the way as the Ukrainian military prepared defenses, making our trip through rutted byways even longer. Roadside billboards instructed locals which parts of Russian tanks should be targeted with Molotov cocktails. These improvised weapons were now rebranded as "Bandera smoothies," after the initially German-backed leader of anti-Soviet Ukrainian nationalists in the 1940s, Stepan Bandera.

At one gas station somewhere in central Ukraine I was excited to find steaming *varenyky* dumplings on display alongside the only food usually available at the time, the omnipresent hot dogs. Stevo, a vegetarian, had been subsisting on a diet of hot-dog buns filled with just mayo and ketchup. Our hopes were dashed: the dumplings were not for sale. They were served only to uniformed troops—for free.

By night, we had reached only as far as Uman, my grandmother's hometown. There, a kosher hotel, which usually caters to Ultra-Orthodox pilgrims visiting the nearby grave of the venerated Rabbi Nachman, was still open. Now all the other guests were refugees from Russian-occupied parts of Ukraine. As we plotted the next day's moves, I stumbled across the local Telegram channel of Voznesensk and was surprised to read that the Russian troops had in fact been pushed out of the city.

"Change of plans," I told Stevo and Manu as we gathered for dinner in my room, all its signage in Hebrew. "We're going to Voznesensk."

CHAPTER 17

RUSSIA'S ROUT
IN VOZNESENSK

Stevo blasted Leonard Cohen's "The Partisan" as we sped through the flatlands of the Ukrainian south on the sunny morning of March 15. Voznesensk's mayor, Yevheni Velichko, had told me at dawn that the way to the city was safe. The road took us past the shiny domes of the South Ukraine Nuclear Power Plant, which was reflected, spaceship-like, in the cooling ponds.

At the northern entrance to Voznesensk we came across grimy, tired Ukrainian troops towing a trophy Russian BTR personnel carrier. This was the first time I saw a captured Russian fighting vehicle, the "Z" sign on its turret freshly painted over in white. The deadly machine was about to be turned around against its former masters. "We've fucked them over, we did it," one of the soldiers said, as he gave me a high-five.

Voznesensk's thirty-two-year-old mayor was dressed in body armor and was accompanied by stern guards with assault rifles at the ready. Like many other Ukrainian elected officials, Velichko—a former real estate developer—had taken things into his own hands when the Russians approached. Some local businesspeople had provided machinery to dig fortifications to cut off secondary roads and block side streets, he said. Others had brought granite from their quarries. Another entrepreneur, with a textile factory of his own, had made ammunition pouches for local Territorial Defense fighters.

"The army fights and we do everything else by ourselves here," Velichko told me when we met at the remains of the bridge across the Mertvovod River bisecting the city. Antitank mines were still laid out across the road, in front of a statue of the Virgin Mary dressed in intense blue colors.

On March 2, a Russian armored column had appeared on the other side of the bridge, its tanks hitting the base of the local Territorial Defense and heavy mortars starting to rain on Voznesensk's apartment blocks. Separately, Russian VDV air assault troops were dropped in nearby forests, closing in through the countryside.

Velichko's crews had dug up the riverbanks, making it impossible for Russian fighting vehicles to ford the Mertvovod. Soldiers from the Ukrainian Army's 80th Air Assault Brigade had booby-trapped the highway bridge over the river, planning to blow it up once the first tanks rumbled across. Intense shelling by Russian tanks, however, severed the Ukrainians' remote-detonation wire, foiling the plan. A Ukrainian volunteer fighter had to run under fire, triggering the bridge's charge manually just as the Russian column approached. "The enemy ended up trapped in the streets, with nowhere to turn," recalled the brigade's commander, Colonel Ihor Skybiuk. Ukrainian soldiers had also destroyed the railway bridge leading to Odesa across the Southern Buh River, and another main bridge near the city.

Stuck beyond the Mertvovod, the Russians focused at first on the rural area of Rakove in southern Voznesensk, taking over villagers' homes on a ridge overlooking the city. Natalia Horchuk, a twenty-five-year-old mother of three, told me Russian soldiers startled her by appearing in her garden on the morning of March 2, telling her to leave for her own safety as they parked four tanks and infantry vehicles between the houses. "Do you have anywhere to go?" they asked her. "This place will be hit."

"We can hide in the cellar," she offered.

"The cellar won't help you." Like most other residents of the street, she and her family fled on foot to the next village. Hours later the battle began.

Russian tanks also hid under the awning of the Shell gas station at the southern entrance to the city, trying to suck out its diesel after running ahead of their own supply convoys. Others moved to a forested strip adjoining a large wheat field near the main road. Local defenders were led by a reconnaissance officer named Vadym, a Donbas war veteran who was in contact with the 80th Brigade artillery units.

The Russians had managed to find a back road to the city because a local Kremlin sympathizer had showed them the way, Velichko, the mayor, told me. But such traitors were an exception. Vadym's and Velichko's phones soon overflowed with intelligence tips passed by the villagers about the Russians' precise locations. Ukrainian teams set up ambushes and relayed coordinates to Ukrainian artillery. Shells started to fly.

The Russians, Skybiuk recalled later, didn't have time to deploy their own artillery before their positions were hit by Ukrainian howitzers and mortars. "We opened massive fire at them just as they were preparing to engage. It was an epic picture: smashed artillery systems, overturned Grads." The Russians did try to attack the Ukrainian artillery units by dropping paratroopers from the VDV's 11th Air Assault Brigade in the Ukrainian rear, but the effort failed because of poor coordination between Russian units. Artillery crews of the Ukrainian 80th Brigade engaged the Russian paratroopers with small arms and machine guns, holding them at bay until Ukrainian infantry arrived.

AS DARKNESS FELL, MYKOLA, A FIGHTER WITH THE VOZNESENSK TERRITOrial Defense who owned a local company that transported gravel and sand, hid in bushes near the wheat field where several Russian tanks and a mortar unit in Ural trucks had set up positions. Just hours earlier, other local defenders had been cut down by a machine gun from the Russian BTR in a compound across the field. As a cold rain poured from the sky, Mykola kept sending target coordinates to a Ukrainian artillery unit via a social-messaging app. So did others. "Everyone here helped at the time," Mykola told me as he was picking up leftover Russian ammunition on the edge of the wheat field. "Everyone shared the information."

Using this intelligence, small teams of Ukrainian soldiers armed with antitank missiles also attacked Russian tanks and fighting vehicles. By the morning of March 3, the Russians were routed, their vehicles burning, their positions devastated. Some thirty of the forty-three tanks, trucks, and armored vehicles that entered Voznesensk the previous day had been destroyed or captured by the Ukrainians. At daybreak, most of the Russian survivors fled, taking some—but not all—of their casualties with them.

Not everyone managed to escape. Vadym told me he captured several Russians. One Russian reconnaissance senior lieutenant had ordered a younger soldier to swap uniforms, so that he could pass for a private. That ruse didn't last long: Vadym had found the unit's personnel list in the column's command vehicle.

"The Russians had orders to come in, seize, and await further instructions. But they had no orders for what to do if they are defeated. They didn't expect us to be strong," Vadym said. "If they had taken Voznesensk, they would have cut off the entire south of Ukraine. But we didn't let them."

An entire Russian battalion tactical group was destroyed in that battle. Most of the Russian soldiers in Voznesensk came from Crimea, serving in the 126th Coastal Defense Brigade based in the annexed peninsula. Before 2014, many of them had been Ukrainian citizens. Ukraine lost forty-three of its own soldiers and Territorial Defense volunteers to defend Voznesensk, Mayor Velichko said later.

⚜

We stopped for a moment in the local clinic where Vadym's mother worked. European Union posters still hung on the wall from before the war. The roof had been destroyed by a Russian shell. The Russians never reached that far, staying on the next street up the ridge. As Vadym showed me the homes that had been occupied by the Russians, he carefully shone his laser light to make sure there were no tripwires. Green Russian Army ration bags and bloodied bandages were scattered everywhere, drawers pulled out by Russian soldiers who had searched for valuables.

One local man, Vasyliy, had been detained by the Russians for possessing binoculars, and was falsely accused of being an artillery spotter. "They had put him in a cellar, and told him they will execute him in the morning," Vadym said. "But in the morning the orcs didn't have time to execute him. They were too busy fleeing."

Anatoly Hedulian, seventy-one, had just returned to his home as we visited the area. The Russians had stolen his bread and other food at gun-point before expelling him and his wife, who could barely walk. His house had been ransacked. "My leather jacket is gone. My sweaters are all gone. Everything is gone," he lamented. "But thanks God the Russians are also gone."

They were not all gone. In the railway station, a generator had been hooked up to a freezer car with several bodies of Russian soldiers picked up across Voznesensk. They were stacked one atop another in transparent plastic bags, rigid in their dark-green uniforms, cut down in the prime of youth.

In nearby forests many more still were lying, some eaten by animals, others buried by villagers in shallow graves, said Mykhailo Sokurenko, the town's funeral director. He took us to Voznesensk's outskirts in a van with the sign "Cargo 200"—a Soviet-era code number for a military fatality.

"Sometimes, I wish I could put these bodies on a plane and drop them all onto Moscow, so they realize what is happening here," he said, cursing as we drove off.

In a field just outside Voznesensk, he watched as men dug out yet another Russian soldier. Nearby, the remains of a Russian Mi-24 helicopter were strewn across dozens of yards, a missile pod with unfired missiles still untouched, the cabin lying far from the tail, inscribed with the Russian word for "danger." The Russians, Vadym said, kept buzzing Voznesensk with helicopters for days after their defeat, seeking to pick up some soldiers—likely officers—who had hidden in the forests after the main Russian force retreated. Then they stopped.

CHAPTER 18

"THE CITY IS BEING LEVELED"

On the day we arrived in Voznesensk, March 15, more than thirty thousand people finally managed to escape besieged Mariupol, streaming out in a long column of battered, often windowless buses and cars that crossed fifteen Russian-manned checkpoints on the way to Ukrainian-controlled Zaporizhzhia. Ukrainian defenses inside Mariupol were collapsing amid fierce urban combat.

The column of refugees included the three journalists from the AP—Evgeniy Maloletka, Mstyslav Chernov, and Vasilisa Stepanenko—who had documented Russia's destruction of Mariupol. By then, Russian tanks had reached the edge of the hospital where the journalists were sheltered, a facility overflowing with the wounded and the dying. Ukrainian soldiers with blue masking tape on their uniforms had burst into the hospital the previous day and urged the AP team to escape Mariupol with the planned convoy. Otherwise, the soldiers warned, the Russians would capture the reporters and force them to claim that they had doctored their photographs and reports. The world needed to know the truth.

The March 15 convoy was so big that Russian soldiers didn't have time to search all the cars. They didn't find the memory cards with the evidence of Russian atrocities that Stepanenko was hiding on her body.

Yulia Paevska, the Ukrainian medic, was also trying to leave Mariupol that day. She wasn't as lucky. The Russians had compiled lists of wanted people, and her name was on it. At one of the checkpoints, she was searched and taken away. Kremlin propaganda trumpeted that the Russian military had detained the chief medical officer of Azov, the "bloody Tayra" who supposedly killed the parents of local civilians and tried to use their kidnapped children to escape from Mariupol. In the detention camp, jailers refused to provide Paevska, who had had her thyroid removed, with vital medication.

THE NEXT DAY, ON MARCH 16, RUSSIA BOMBED MARIUPOL'S REGIONAL DRAMA theater, a white neoclassical building whose basement prop room served as one of the city's main bomb shelters. The theater's set designer had painted the Russian word for "CHILDREN" in large white letters on the plaza in front of the entrance. As many as 1,000 civilians were believed to be in the building when Russian bombs hit at around 10 a.m. Most of these people didn't survive as the building collapsed. Moscow blamed the killings on Ukrainians. It would later bulldoze the site, leaving unburied corpses to decompose underneath.

"The city is being leveled," Svyatoslav Palamar, the deputy commander of Azov, said in a recording that day.

For Russia, taking Mariupol and destroying Azov—which the Kremlin portrayed as the power behind the throne in Ukraine—had become a key priority in the war, something that warranted diverting tens of thousands of troops from other front lines. Mariupol had also turned into a personal challenge for the Chechen strongman Kadyrov, who dispatched his private army to help storm the city.

THE CHECHENS ARE NOT A NATURAL ALLY FOR THE RUSSIANS. THE RUSSIAN Empire waged war for nearly five decades to subdue the Chechen homeland in the Northern Caucasus. Stalin exiled the Chechens in their entirety in 1944, accusing them of collaboration with the Nazis. The mountainous republic, restored in 1957, proclaimed independence following the collapse of the Soviet Union. Kadyrov's father, Akhmat, Chechnya's highest-ranking Islamic cleric, declared a jihad holy war on Russia when Russian troops tried to retake his homeland in 1994. Ramzan Kadyrov once boasted that he killed his first Russian at the age of sixteen. Chechnya's then leader, Dzhokhar Dudaev, a former Soviet general who was assassinated by Moscow in 1996, admired Ukraine, and was admired by many Ukrainians in return. Streets in several Ukrainian cities are still named after him.

When war erupted in Chechnya again in 1999–2000, Akhmat Kadyrov sided with Moscow and eventually became president. He lasted in that job less than seven months before being killed by separatist insurgents in a bombing during the Victory Day celebrations on May 9, 2004. Shaken but embraced by Putin, Ramzan took over the reins of power. In exchange for personal loyalty to Putin, he was allowed to build an independent Chechnya in all but name, with his own military force, Islamist rules that included a de facto ban on alcohol, and authority to hunt down critics across Russia. When I visited the region in 2016, my female assistant wasn't allowed to enter the Chechen parliament building because her dress didn't fully cover her ankles.

Once Putin invaded Ukraine, Kadyrov dispatched his most trusted adviser, Adam Delimkhanov, another former jihadi insurgent and now a gray-bearded senior member of the Russian parliament, to command Chechen units in Mariupol.

A few days after the carnage in the drama theater, Delimkhanov assembled fleeing Mariupol residents at an exit from the city to tell them that they shouldn't be too concerned about the horrors his men were inflicting on their hometown. Everything had been destroyed in Chechnya during the wars there, he said, but thanks to the glorious efforts of Akhmat and Ramzan Kadyrov, "we have not just rebuilt our republic, but we have made it into one of the most beautiful in Russia . . . You won't have any problems." Clad in black fatigues, Delimkhanov made the Ukrainian refugees chant "Akhmat-Strength," the motto of the Chechen regime, and promised humanitarian aid from Chechnya. The aid that his troops delivered had come, in fact, from looted Ukrainian warehouses, as attested by Ukrainian-language labels on flour sacks and bottles of cooking oil.

Marianna Vyshemirska, the former Instagram model who had been injured in the bombing of the maternity ward, was one of those Mariupol residents who had escaped to relative safety in Russian-held areas at the time.

Once under Russian control, she was paraded on TV denying that a Russian plane had ever hit the hospital.

With the AP's journalists gone, there was only one international witness of Russian atrocities left in the city: Lithuanian documentary filmmaker Mantas Kvedaravičius. On March 27, he was stopped at a Russian checkpoint in Mariupol and led away. His bullet-ridden body was found on a pile of garbage six days later.

⊰⊱

On March 15, elite troops from Russia's 106th VDV Airborne Division began the biggest push yet on Moshchun, northwest of Kyiv. The previous Russian forces that had seized a foothold on the east bank of the Irpin River near the village were badly depleted, with the commander of the VDV's 331st Regiment, Colonel Sergey Sukharev, among the hundreds of casualties.

At least five Russian artillery batteries pounded Moshchun for much of the day, flattening remaining homes. Then several hundred Russian VDV soldiers poured into the ruins, overrunning Ukrainian defenders. Russian jamming equipment disrupted communications, and Colonel Vdovychenko, the commander of Ukraine's 72nd Brigade, lost contact with his troops in the village and surrounding areas.

"We thought, this is it," he recalled later.

That day, General Valeriy Zaluzhny, Ukraine's top commander, and General Oleksandr Syrsky, the head of Ground Forces, who had been appointed to oversee the defense of Kyiv, arrived on the Moshchun front line. Vdovychenko was honest with the two generals. Ukrainian soldiers, outgunned and outnumbered, were barely holding on to the last few streets of the village. "We won't be able to keep Moshchun, we have to retreat," Vdovychenko recalled telling Zaluzhny.

"If we surrender Moshchun, we will open the way to Kyiv," the general replied. There would be no retreat.

As the battle went on the next day, and the day after, water kept flowing into the Irpin from the Kyiv Sea reservoir. This was the moment when the flooding suddenly accelerated, and the plain between Moshchun and the rest of the Russian forces quickly turned into muddy marshland, and then into a shallow lake. The Irpin River, normally just a dozen or so yards wide, now spanned more than a mile. Pontoon crossings were of little use. Trapped, Russian forces in Moshchun were no longer able to get easily resupplied with ammunition and food, or to evacuate their wounded. After five days of fighting, those who could began to retreat. Many never made it out.

"The elite of everything they had died here," Vdovychenko said. "Our people stood up for their capital, and so did nature. If the Irpin River hadn't flooded the way it did, I don't know what the fate of Kyiv would have been."

CHAPTER 19

THE TULIPS OF MYKOLAIV

The first thing I noticed in Mykolaiv was the tires. Of all colors and sizes, some spray-painted in Ukrainian colors, they were piled up at intersections, ready to be burned as an early-warning system should Russian soldiers be spotted. The Russians had briefly entered Mykolaiv's southeastern neighborhoods in the first days of March, but by March 16 they had been forced back halfway to Kherson. Governor Kim had proudly parked outside his office a trophy Russian Tigr armored vehicle, now daubed with the markings of the Mykolaiv Patrol Police.

The war was only three weeks old, but Kim—virtually unknown before the war—was by now one of Ukraine's most famous men. His trademark greeting—"Good evening, we are from Ukraine"—had been remixed into a pop song. He told me to meet him in the regional government building, a nine-story tower on a riverside plaza that was now cordoned off with barbed wire and tank traps. As I waited at the checkpoint, a convoy of Ukrainian Uragan rocket launchers rolled by.

An aide led me and Manu to Kim's office upstairs. The building was teeming with personnel, military and civilian. Just days after seeing the devastation of the bloodstained regional government building in Kharkiv, I couldn't stop thinking that a Russian missile strike on this compound was only a matter of time. Manu agreed. "Let's not stay here too long," he muttered.

Kim was jovial. "Our city is alive once again," he told me. "The situation is much worse in many other cities, so we can't really complain. The front line is being pushed farther and farther away. We are sustaining casualties, but the orcs are sustaining several times our casualties."

He advised me against leaving the city to visit recently liberated villages on the way to Kherson. "It's not your standard war. The orcs are confused. They have no communications, they are disoriented, and they shoot at any civilian car they see, afraid that someone will pop out with a rocket-propelled grenade."

JUST A FEW BLOCKS AWAY, AMBULANCES MARKED "CARGO 200" KEPT BRING-ing the bodies of Ukrainian soldiers to Mykolaiv's military morgue. When we arrived there, we saw yet another van carrying disfigured corpses from the front line with chunks of singed flesh sheared off by artillery. "I am sorry for my emotions, but our city is still standing thanks to our guys on the front lines, guys like these," said the attendant, Volodymyr Afanasiev, as he pointed to the pile of cadavers. "Now we can go to a shop that is full of goods or buy a cup of tea. We are free to walk the streets. All of this because our guys have managed to shove the Russians away."

Since the start of the war, the Ukrainian military had adopted the policy of not disclosing casualty statistics. Judging by Mykolaiv's packed morgue, they were very high.

I noticed a man and three women standing some distance away and asked what they were waiting for. They turned out to be relatives of Ukrainian sailors presumed to have been killed in a Russian missile attack on the Navy base in nearby Ochakiv on the first day of the war. Olha Tochanska told me she had been coming to the morgue almost every day since then, asking to see unidentified bodies. There were eleven of them as of now, she had been told, but the morgue staff refused to let her in.

"I want to find my husband, I need to see him," she implored. "How much longer can we wait?"

"Her husband was my son's commanding officer," chimed in Yaroslav Ferenz. "They tell us that we can't see the bodies because they are too burned. But I don't care. I need to see. I will be able to recognize my son just by looking at one fingernail."

I couldn't keep standing amid the bodies and went back to the car as Manu took his photos. Stevo never left the vehicle. The morgue had brought back bad memories, and he started telling me how, decades earlier, he had pulled a dead comrade from the battlefield. He thought at the time that the friend was alive because his leg twitched. In fact, it was just another bullet hitting the corpse.

The center of Mykolaiv was somehow relatively intact. Artillery sounded remote, and the area had experienced nothing like the wholesale destruction that had been wrought upon central Kharkiv. Coffee shops were open on Mykolaiv's main promenade, serving frappuccinos. Shoppers crowded the main market. Even in the outlying districts closer to the front line, supermarkets operated normally, supplied with bread, dairy, and fruit. Stylish young women sat in front of flower shops that brimmed with the colors of fresh roses and tulips. "It's not that we are no longer afraid, but we are getting used to this," said one of them, twenty-three-year-old Yulia Fistik. "Business is good. There are lots of soldiers in town, and they all buy flowers."

Hours later, on March 17, a Russian missile salvo hit the barracks of a Marine brigade in Mykolaiv, killing or injuring well over a hundred service members in their sleep. On March 29, another Russian missile struck the regional government building just before 9 a.m., taking out an entire nine-story section in the middle. By the time rescuers finished pulling bodies out of the rubble, thirty-seven people were confirmed dead, including Governor Kim's secretary. The governor himself survived because that morning he had overslept.

⸭

My editors called me as we drove through Mykolaiv. I had spent two months crisscrossing Ukraine and management wanted the three of us to take a break. I wanted to stay but didn't have much of a choice. After a daylong drive across the country we ended up in Lviv, a different universe where restaurants served Georgian food and bars were filled with Western volunteers for the International Legion. The next morning, we hit the Ukrainian-Polish border. The crossing point in Medyka wasn't crowded anymore but still displayed the debris from the flood of humanity that had

passed across in the previous weeks: discarded water bottles, broken um-
brellas, lost gloves.

The Ukrainian woman in front of us in the passport line spoke melodic
Ukrainian to a boy and a girl, both younger than ten, who held her hands.
The children spoke back in Russian—a sign that, like many people in
Russian-speaking parts of Ukraine, she had just made a conscious choice to
switch languages. The boy was her son, and the girl was the daughter of her
partner. The Ukrainian border guard didn't let them through. The woman
needed written permission from one of the girl's parents to cross. "What do
you want me to do? Her dad is a soldier somewhere on the front line, and
her mother fled to Spain when the war began, and we have no idea where
she is now," the woman said, exasperated. "Do you have any idea what we
are trying to escape?"

The border guard was unmoved. "These are the laws, nothing that I can
do," she said. People behind us pushed ahead, and I stepped to the counter.

On the Polish side, there were mounds of stuffed animals to be picked
up by arriving Ukrainian children, and a tent city of assorted humanitarian groups offering free tea, food, train tickets, SIM cards, and lodging.

The history of relations between Ukraine and Poland, both modern
and ancient, is complicated. There were moments of shared glory like the
Miracle on the Vistula of August 1920, when Polish troops and remnants of
the army of independent Ukraine dealt a devastating defeat to a much larger
Soviet Russian force near Warsaw, ensuring the survival of an independent
Poland. What is now western Ukraine ended up as part of Poland, which at
times tried to assimilate or marginalize its large Ukrainian minority, curb-
ing the rights that Ukrainian institutions had enjoyed in cities such as Lviv
or Ternopil under Austro-Hungarian rule.

In the 1930s, the radical Organization of Ukrainian Nationalists started
assassinating Polish officials and moderate Ukrainians, deepening the division between the two peoples. During World War II, an estimated one hundred thousand Poles, mostly civilians, died in ethnic massacres perpetrated
by Ukrainian insurgents in western Ukraine's Volyn region. Though Stepan
Bandera, the initially German-supported leader of OUN, was in a Nazi concentration camp at the time, his glorification in modern Ukraine, a tribute

to OUN's subsequent resistance against Soviet rule, has long been an affront to Polish sensibilities, poisoning relations between the two neighbors.

But in Ukraine's direst hour, the controversies of the past were put aside. Poles—like no other nation—opened their homes and their hearts to the millions of Ukrainians who flooded their country. I knew that my Polish friends and acquaintances were collecting money for Ukrainian relief, buying cars and medical supplies that could be sent to the Ukrainian Army, and trying their best to help Ukrainian refugees find jobs and education opportunities. Nevertheless, it was still a shock to see Ukrainian flags flying from building after building in Cracow, from municipal buses and from the windshields of cars. Poland's history over the past three centuries was dominated by Russia's attempts to suppress its freedom and its very existence as a separate nation. To most Poles, Ukraine's fight was their own as well.

The Polish-language poster on a coffee shop in central Cracow summed up the feeling. "Ukrainian soldiers are defending your nation," it read.

A Ukrainian woman stands by a burning house that had been hit by a Russian shell in Yatskivka in the northern Donetsk region, October 2022.

Ukrainian civilians escape from the Kyiv suburbs of Irpin
and Bucha as Russian forces advance, March 2022.

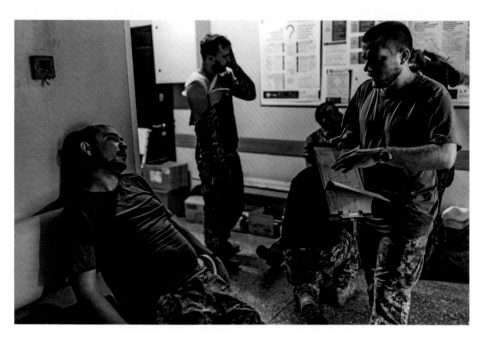

Wounded Ukrainian soldiers in a field hospital
in the eastern city of Bakhmut, August 2022.

A Ukrainian municipal official looks at the newly discovered body
of a Russian soldier in Voznesensk, southern Ukraine, March 2022.

Kyiv Opera and Ballet Theater prima ballerina Anastasiya Shevchenko
prepares for a show in Kyiv, July 2022.

Soldiers of Ukraine's Carpathian Sich battalion leave on
a reconnaissance mission near Izyum, May 2022.

Residents of Severodonetsk in the basement of a funeral parlor that
became their shelter because of constant Russian shelling, May 2022.

Ukrainian medics pull out an injured soldier at
a field hospital in Bakhmut, August 2022.

A Ukrainian soldier runs down the stairs of the bombed regional government
headquarters building on Kharkiv's central Freedom Square, March 2022.

Ukrainian soldiers jump to take cover as they come under
Russian fire on the western outskirts of Kyiv, March 2022.

The bodies of Anatoliy Berezhnoy, Tatiana Perebeynos, and her child
minutes after they were killed by Russian shelling while trying
to escape Irpin, west of Kyiv, March 2022.

New recruits of Ukraine's 36th Marine Brigade
training in the Mykolaiv region, July 2022.

Vsevolod Kozhemiako, commander of the Khartiya unit, in the village
of Ruska Lozova as it comes under Russian tank fire, April 2022.

Ukrainian soldiers help a man with a blown-off foot who was found near a destroyed Russian military convoy in Lyman, Donetsk region, October 2022.

Ukrainian rescue teams remove the charred bodies of two civilians who had been killed in a Russian Grad rocket attack on Kharkiv, April 2022.

PART 5

VICTORY IN THE NORTH

CHAPTER 20

THE ISTANBUL SURPRISE

On March 29, Russian and Ukrainian delegations gathered around a long table covered by a crisp white tablecloth in Istanbul's Dolmabahçe Palace, on the banks of the Bosporus. Expectations for this round of peace talks were high. At the head of the table, Turkish president Recep Tayyip Erdoğan delivered the opening speech. "It is up to the sides to stop this tragedy. Achieving a cease-fire and peace as soon as possible is to the benefit of everyone," he intoned. "The world is waiting for good news."

The meeting in Istanbul was the continuation of discussions that Kyiv and Moscow had begun in Belarus during the early, desperate days of the war. Putin's adviser, former culture minister Vladimir Medinsky, remained at the head of the Russian delegation. The Ukrainian team at the talks was led by David Arakhamia, the majority leader of Zelensky's party in parliament. As it happened, Medinsky had been born in Ukraine, while Arakhamia, an information-technology businessman of Georgian blood, was a native of Russia who had moved to Ukraine in his childhood.

"That's an antiseptic," Arakhamia told Medinsky as he pointed at a bottle of alcohol gel on the table between them. "Ah, I thought it's vodka," the Russian delegate joked. Kuleba, the Ukrainian foreign minister, had just publicly advised Ukrainian negotiators not to accept any beverages from the Russians, and not to touch any surfaces.

THE NEGOTIATING PROCESS HAD BEEN SURROUNDED BY MYSTERIOUS MIS-
haps since the beginning. On March 2, as the Ukrainian delegation prepared
to return to Belarus for the second round of talks, one of the negotiators,
Denis Kireyev, was pulled out of his car in central Kyiv by members of the
SBU intelligence service. When his bloodied body was found a few blocks
away later that day, officials in SBU, an agency that had been thoroughly infiltrated by Russian spies, claimed that Kireyev was a traitor who had been
shot while resisting arrest. Ukraine's rival GUR military intelligence service, where Kireyev had served undercover while pursuing a career in bank-
ing and business, was outraged. Three days later, GUR posted a photo of
Kireyev, describing him as a hero who had died in the line of duty.

GUR chief Kyrylo Budanov explained months later that Kireyev's mission had been to play for time, using his personal ties to two members of the
Russian delegation, so that the Ukrainian military could consolidate positions. "The situation was close to critical . . . There were some people who
weren't very interested in Ukraine winning. First of all, people on the
Ukrainian side," Budanov said. He added that he had discussed the assassination with the SBU chief at the time, Ivan Bakanov, but received no explanations. It was Budanov's last meeting with Bakanov, who vanished from
public view in early March, though he continued to meet with visiting intelligence officials from the West.

Bakanov was Zelensky's childhood friend from Kryvyi Rih, one of the
few people who had the president's trust. The two men had grown up in the
same building. Bakanov used to run Zelensky's TV production company and
headed his 2019 election campaign. Yet under his management, SBU turned
out to be full of Russian assets whose influence caused catastrophic setbacks
in the battlefield, particularly in Kherson. The rot went all the way to the top.
Bakanov's former deputy, Andriy Naumov, the head of SBU's powerful coun-
terintelligence branch tasked with rooting out Russian spies, was also a traitor,
according to Ukrainian prosecutors. He fled Ukraine to Serbia on February 23, a few hours before the war began, and was later caught at a border checkpoint with North Macedonia trying to smuggle out a bag with gems and
several hundred thousand dollars in cash. He remains in Serbian custody.

In July, Zelensky fired Bakanov under an article of the military statutes that involves negligence causing fatalities and other grave consequences. Bakanov disappeared from public view soon afterward, resurfacing a year later as a provincial lawyer in the Poltava region.

Another drama unfolded in Kyiv just after Kireyev was killed. Concluding that Medinsky, a relatively junior official, lacked direct access to Putin, the Ukrainians had enlisted the services of Russian oligarch Roman Abramovich, who secretly visited Kyiv and met with Zelensky. On March 3, Abramovich and one of the top Ukrainian negotiators, Crimean Tatar lawmaker Rustem Umerov, developed unusual symptoms in Kyiv: red eyes, constant tearing, peeling skin on the face and the hands. Abramovich even briefly lost his eyesight. The symptoms resolved by themselves after a few days, and by the time the two men had left Ukraine it was too late for a medical examination. Was it an attempt by Russian hard-liners to torpedo the talks, and to intimidate Abramovich?

Ahead of the March 29 meeting in Istanbul, the Ukrainians seemed open to the idea of adopting neutrality and abandoning their aspiration to join NATO, ostensibly one of Russia's main reasons for launching the war. While Ukraine, alongside Georgia, had been promised at the alliance's 2008 summit in Bucharest that the two nations "will become members of NATO," no practical steps to begin negotiations had followed.

Ukraine, Zelensky indicated in the first weeks after the Russian invasion, would be ready to forgo its NATO dream in exchange for binding security guarantees, by the West and Russia alike. Ukrainian negotiators also showed flexibility on Russian demands for Ukraine to reduce its military, and on committing to freeze the issue of Crimea for the foreseeable future. None of this, of course, was enough to stop the Russian onslaught on the ground and the Russian bombs and missiles that kept raining down on Ukrainian cities. What Moscow wanted was a complete surrender.

In their first meeting since the war began, Kuleba sat down with his Russian counterpart, Sergei Lavrov, in the Turkish resort town of Antalya on March 10.

"I asked Lavrov a simple question behind closed doors in Antalya: Minister, what do you want? That is all I wanted to know," Kuleba told me. Lavrov, a once-respected diplomat who has headed Russia's foreign ministry since 2004, didn't reply.

"He went with his classic stories about neo-Nazi Russophobic Ukraine and all this crap," Kuleba recalled. "Before this meeting, I was hesitant whether he believes or plays the game. But after walking out of the meeting, I had the impression that he does believe in it. This is the defensive function of his mind. He made his choice, he decided to play until the final whistle. They have all convinced themselves that it's true, because that's the only way you can continue with it."

From the very beginning, Ukraine decided to participate in these negotiations with Russia to gain time and to secure small breakthroughs, such as humanitarian corridors for the evacuation of refugees from Mariupol, Kuleba said.

"If a country of enormous size and what seemed to be undefeatable military power attacks you, of course you try to stop it by all means available, and you engage in negotiations. But these were not real negotiations," the Ukrainian foreign minister added. "We had no illusions about the genuine intentions of Russia. From day one and until Istanbul, Russia was not acting in good faith."

IN THE NINETEEN DAYS BETWEEN KULEBA'S MEETING WITH LAVROV AND the Istanbul talks, however, the battlefield situation shifted dramatically in Ukraine's favor. On March 21, the last Russian forces abandoned Moshchun, leaving their dead and the wrecks of their vehicles in the ruins of the village. Elsewhere in the Kyiv area, the Russians suffered from incessant attacks on their supply lines by small, nimble Ukrainian units. Stuck on the western bank of the Irpin River, the Russians had lost their most combat-ready forces and now faced the risk of Ukrainian troops flanking them through the forests farther west.

In occupied parts of Chernihiv and Sumy, the Russians also began to lose ground, one small town after another. On March 26, Ukraine's 93rd

Brigade successfully stormed the strategic city of Trostyanets just twenty miles from the Russian border, opening the highway and breaking the siege of the regional capital, Sumy. As the Russian survivors fled Trostyanets, they left behind charred hulks of tanks and self-propelled howitzers, and graffiti proclaiming "Zelensky Pederast" on the few buildings still standing on the town's main square.

In the following days, Ukrainian troops pushed north of the main highway between the capital and Zhytomyr, threatening the rear of the main Russian force that was deployed on the western approaches to Kyiv. One day before the negotiators gathered in Istanbul, advancing Ukrainian troops ousted the Russians from the neighborhoods they controlled in the contested city of Irpin, near Bucha. The momentum of the war had clearly changed.

Ordinary Russians had no idea. In TV reportage that aired that week, one of Russia's leading *voenkors*, Yevgeny Poddubny, trumpeted an imminent victory. "The Ukrainian capital is de facto blockaded by the firepower of the Russian formation," he reported breathlessly from the Hostomel airfield, which the Russians would abandon days later. "Air assault troops are breaking open the defenses in Irpin, the satellite town of Kyiv. Formations of the Kyiv regime suffer serious casualties, the Armed Forces of Ukraine no longer have enough fuel and ammunition."

❖

At the Istanbul talks, the mandate of the Ukrainian team was to push for a Russian withdrawal to pre–February 24 lines while showing apparent flexibility on many key issues, with actual decisions deferred to a planned meeting between Zelensky and Putin. Kyiv's negotiators weren't empowered to make any binding commitments. Russia's major demand, in addition to neutrality, was to cap Ukraine's ability to defend itself in the future. According to draft documents later publicly shown by Putin, at that stage Moscow wanted Ukraine's armed forces cut down to 85,000 troops, with only 342 tanks and 519 artillery pieces—an increase from Russia's initial offer in Belarus, but still far from Ukrainian wishes. While agreeing to the principle of partial demilitarization, the Ukrainian negotiators countered in Istanbul with the proposal for an army of 250,000 troops, roughly its pre-war level, with 800 tanks and 1,900 artillery pieces, according to the draft documents.

Just before the conference started, Russia's defense minister, Sergei Shoigu, made a striking announcement from Moscow. The main goals of the "special military operation" had been generally fulfilled, he said. "The military capacity of the Ukrainian Armed Forces has been significantly diminished, which allows us to concentrate the main attention and the main efforts on reaching the principal goal: the liberation of Donbas," he said.

Hours later, Medinsky appeared at a press conference in Istanbul with even more astonishing news. The talks held that day had achieved significant progress, he announced, and Moscow had decided to take steps to deescalate the conflict. He then stepped aside and Colonel General Alexander Fomin, the Russian deputy minister of defense, approached the microphone. Dressed in a smart navy blue suit instead of his general's uniform, Fomin no longer repeated the crude threats he had made at the negotiations' first round in Belarus.

The Russian military, Fomin told stunned reporters, had decided to "drastically, by orders of magnitude, decrease military activity in the Kyiv and Chernihiv direction." The decision, he explained, was made because of the progress in talks on Ukraine's future neutral, nonnuclear status, and "to increase mutual trust and create necessary conditions for further negotiations."

It took a few days for the full meaning of these words to sink in, but what Fomin was announcing was nothing short of the full withdrawal of battered, overextended Russian troops from northern Ukraine. The Russians were not just pulling back from Kyiv but also abandoning the entirety of the occupied parts of the Chernihiv and Sumy regions.

Ukrainian negotiators such as Mykhailo Podolyak praised progress in remarks the same day but said that any accords would be subjected to referendum. The two delegations agreed to keep talking as they left Turkey, taking the outcome of their discussions to their presidents in Kyiv and Moscow.

WHAT HAPPENED BEHIND CLOSED DOORS IN ISTANBUL ON MARCH 29 AND shortly afterward is a subject of intense disagreement between Russian and

Ukrainian leaders. According to Putin, Ukrainian negotiators in Istanbul had accepted most of Russia's demands. "The agreements were practically reached," he lamented four months later. "Our troops left the center of Ukraine, Kyiv, to create conditions" for further talks to finalize that accord, he said.

Ukraine vehemently disputes that account. Neither side made binding commitments in Istanbul, Kuleba told me. "There was no deal," he said. "Under the friendly pressure of President Erdoğan, both sides agreed to proceed to engage in serious discussions about how the end of the war may look like. Of course, we tried to engage them in a conversation. But to engage in a conversation and to commit yourself to something are completely different things."

As for the Russian pullback, Ukrainian—and American—officials say Putin had no choice but to withdraw by late March because of Ukrainian military successes on the ground. Igor Girkin, the former defense minister of the Donetsk "people's republic," agreed. "If leaving the seized territory has become inevitable, it's best to do it before your troops are routed by the adversary," he said shortly after the Istanbul announcements. "We will still need these troops—the war will be long."

Other Russian war hawks were heartbroken. "I am not a politician and not a general, I don't see the full picture," Aleksandr Kots, one of Russia's main *voenkors* who would later become a Putin adviser, wrote on Telegram as it became clear that Russian troops were leaving the Kyiv region. "I have been to Hostomel and shook the hands of true Russian heroes. Nobody can take away their feat of arms. Nobody can devalue it. They couldn't be taken in battle. And it's already part of History."

As he published these words, Ukrainian troops were already entering the Hostomel airfield, which Russia was never able to use as its beachhead to capture Kyiv, and the neighboring town of Bucha. What the Ukrainians discovered there rendered any Istanbul understandings moot.

CHAPTER 21

BLUDGEONED IN BUCHA

Like other northwestern suburbs in Kyiv's green belt across the Irpin River, Bucha was a relaxed town of single-family homes and five-story housing blocks set amid pine trees, playgrounds, and parks. It had a handful of resorts, with swimming pools for the guests, and an equestrian club. Many of its 37,000 prewar residents had moved there from more cramped apartments inside the capital, and almost everyone seemed to own multiple pets.

As Ukrainian forces advanced into Bucha from Irpin on March 29, past a neoclassical Stalin-era concert hall flanked by statues of a worker and a proletarian mother that had somehow survived the surrounding destruction, they stumbled upon a horrifying sight. Dozens of bodies lay rotting under the rain on Yablunska Street at the entrance to Bucha, and in surrounding areas. One man had been shot as he tried to ferry some food, a bag of potatoes and an empty bottle of Coke still lying at his feet. An elderly woman was sprawled next to her bicycle down the road. A tiger-patterned jacket covered the head of a man who had gone to walk his dog. Some corpses were missing limbs, likely eaten by dogs, while others had brains spilling from cracked skulls. Civilian cars, some crushed by tanks, some peppered by heavy machine-gun fire, remained on roadsides, many with the stiff corpses of their passengers still strapped in by their seat belts.

As the Ukrainian soldiers probed further, they found several men, many of them stripped naked to their waists, executed and lying on the ground in the courtyard of 144 Yablunska Street. Later, a surveillance video emerged of Russian troops taking these men, likely suspected of being informants for the Ukrainian military, to the execution site. On sidewalks, in ditches, and in improvised graves, there were other corpses with their hands tied. Some bore the signs of torture: poked-out eyes, cut-off fingers. My *Journal* colleague Brett Forrest was the first Western reporter to enter Bucha that day. Signs of death were everywhere: the torso and head of a woman in a garage where the Russians had likely tried to steal fuel, a man shot in the head in an auto body shop, limbs and heads protruding from an open pit covered by a thin layer of sand. After Brett's car punctured a tire on one of the many pieces of shrapnel on the road and had to stop, a local man emerged from his home. There, too, a body of someone recently killed by the Russians was slowly decomposing.

More than 450 civilians had been killed in Bucha during the month the town was under Russian occupation. Atrocities had been occurring throughout occupied Ukraine, especially in Mariupol. But in Bucha, the Russian soldiers fled so fast on March 29 that they hadn't had the time to conceal the scale of the slaughter.

As the footage from Bucha spread on social media, Zelensky—like most Ukrainians—was overwhelmed with fury. "The essence of evil has come to our land—murderers, torturers, rapists, and looters who call themselves an army," he said in an address to Ukrainians. "They have killed consciously, and with pleasure."

Leaving Kyiv for the first time since the war began, Zelensky walked through Bucha on April 4, past the burned-out remains of Russian tanks, BMPs, and BTRs. "Volodymyr, thank you so much for staying with the people, for not fleeing," a middle-aged woman shouted as the Ukrainian president came to a food distribution point established by the military. Then she asked Zelensky for help to feed the multitude of Bucha's homeless cats and dogs. "It's in the nature of our people that they treat animals like humans," Zelensky said later that day. "While the Russian soldiers treated humans worse than animals."

Even though the Ukrainian and Russian negotiators remained in touch, fine-tuning the documents drafted in Istanbul the previous week, Zelensky signaled that day that the atrocities uncovered in Bucha had changed every-thing. "What has happened here is genocide," he said, stern-faced, during his visit to the town. "It is very hard to keep talking when you see what has happened here."

❖

There was no contrition in Moscow after the horrors of Bucha came to light. Even though hundreds of independent journalists visited the town in the days after its liberation, witnessing the evidence firsthand, Russian officials insisted that the bodies in Bucha were not in fact dead, seizing on a video that appeared to show one of them twitching because of the raindrops distorting the image.

"It's a clear provocation," thundered Foreign Minister Lavrov. Not a single Ukrainian civilian had been harmed in Bucha, declared Russia's ministry of defense. Putin commended the 64th Brigade that committed the Bucha atrocities for its bravery and gave it the honor of being an elite Guards unit.

"I know history well. I know that a Russian soldier is organically, genet-ically incapable to do what he is accused of doing," Vladimir Medinsky added, saying that the Ukrainians must have staged the atrocities in that town because Bucha rhymes with the English word "butcher."

CHAPTER 22

HOWITZER TIME

As Russian forces retreated from northern Ukraine, they were harassed by Ukrainian troops along the way, with rearguard units ambushed on the narrow, forested roads. The countryside around Kyiv, Chernihiv, and Sumy was dotted with burned or abandoned Russian armor, fields littered with leftover Russian ammunition, discarded uniforms, and empty green-and-white ration packs. The cream of Russia's army had been destroyed in Putin's failed blitzkrieg. As the survivors drove to Belarus, they carted off TVs, washing machines, iPhones, even toilet bowls. A leaked security camera feed from a post office in a Belarusian border town showed the Russians shipping all these stolen Ukrainian possessions to their families in faraway Russian towns.

Only one Western ambassador, Poland's Bartosz Cichocki, had remained in Kyiv through the Russian attempt to besiege the Ukrainian capital, while other embassies either relocated to western Ukraine or shut down altogether. But now, with the Russians pushed back, foreign dignitaries started to return, a recognition that Ukraine was going to survive—and could even win, against all odds.

On March 15, the prime ministers of Poland, Slovenia, and the Czech Republic were the first foreign leaders to visit Zelensky after the invasion, braving the height of the fighting in the capital's suburbs. British prime minister Boris Johnson arrived in a city transformed on April 9. The Russians were gone, artillery could no longer be heard, and the capital had become sufficiently safe for Johnson to stroll with Zelensky on Khreshchatyk Avenue.

"In the last few weeks, the world has found new heroes, and those heroes are the people of Ukraine," Johnson said at a joint appearance. On his previous trip to Kyiv just before the invasion, Johnson had shared with Zelensky the British intelligence assessment that Russia believed it could seize Kyiv within hours. "How wrong they were! The Ukrainians have shown the courage of a lion, and you, Volodymyr, have given the roar to that lion."

In private, Johnson delivered another message for Zelensky. Less than two weeks had elapsed since the Istanbul talks and, despite Zelensky's outrage in Bucha, the two negotiating teams still pursued contacts online. "I was a bit worried at that stage," Johnson told me. "I could not see for the life of me what the deal could be, and I thought that any deal with Putin was going to be pretty sordid. Any deal would be some victory for him: if you give him anything, he'll just keep it, bank it, and then prepare for his next assault."

This opinion wasn't shared in some other Western capitals, where a quick end to the war was considered a priority. Johnson said he hadn't coordinated this message with the Biden administration, and senior American officials told me they had not been consulted. Yet, as the British prime minister sat down with Zelensky in Kyiv, he delivered his pitch. "Nobody can be more Ukrainian than Ukrainians, it is not for me to tell you what your war objectives can be, but as far as I am concerned, Putin must fail and Ukraine must be entitled to retain full sovereignty and independence," he recalled telling the Ukrainian president. "We're not directly fighting, you are. It's the Ukrainians who are fighting and dying. But we would back Ukraine a thousand percent."

Zelensky didn't need much convincing. The conversation quickly shifted to the concrete ways—such as the provision of military supplies—in which the United Kingdom could assist the Ukrainian Armed Forces. Online talks between Ukrainian and Russian teams fizzled away.

In the months to come, Ukrainian and Russian representatives continued to meet on a variety of issues, such as trading prisoners or reopening Ukrainian ports to grain exports. But the Ukrainians were no longer inclined to discuss any limitations to their sovereignty with Moscow. Zelensky's new position was to demand a full withdrawal of Russian troops from all Ukrainian lands conquered since 2014, including Crimea, and the prosecution of Russian officials suspected of war crimes.

"In Istanbul, we still didn't understand the type of war that Russia was waging, its genocidal intent," Mykhailo Podolyak explained. "Once we returned from Istanbul, and the Russians left the Kyiv region, we saw the beastly crimes that they had committed there. And we understood that Russia will try to annihilate Ukraine no matter what. Negotiations are pointless for them."

In Moscow, Putin was certain that Washington had forced Zelensky's hand to abandon the talks as it aimed to exhaust Russia in a protracted war. Senior Russian officials kept angrily raising this point in meetings with their American counterparts. "Utter bullshit," a senior Biden administration official told me. "I know for a fact the United States didn't pull the plug on that. We were watching it carefully."

❖

The same week Johnson visited Kyiv, the European Union's Ursula von der Leyen brought to Zelensky the first document for Ukraine's formal application to the EU. Kyiv would gain official candidate status—something it had been denied for decades—two and a half months later. "We are with you as you dream of Europe," she said as she handed over the envelope to the Ukrainian president. "This is where your path towards the European Union begins."

Ukraine was no longer alone. Given no chance to survive at the outset of the war, it had been essentially abandoned by the West. But Ukraine had shown its resilience, and its war had begun to become the West's own—a conflict in which preventing a Ukrainian defeat by all means short of direct confrontation with Russia turned into a stated foreign policy priority for the United States and its NATO allies. To avoid such a defeat, Ukraine needed heavy weapons, and lots of them.

Western-supplied Javelin and NLAW antitank missiles were helpful in February and March, particularly to the mobile teams raiding Russian supply lines near Kyiv. But Ukraine repelled Russia's initial onslaught largely thanks to its thousands of Soviet-designed howitzers, tanks, rocket launchers, and air-defense missiles. By April, after the most intense combat seen in Europe in nearly eight decades, Ukraine was running critically low on ammunition for all that equipment. With Soviet-caliber shells hard to find outside Russia, the only sustainable solution was to switch to NATO-standard heavy weapons. Mindful of Putin's hints of nuclear retaliation should the West interfere with his invasion, the White House initially hesitated to ship such high-profile symbols of NATO involvement.

The first breakthrough came on April 13. That day, President Biden approved the delivery of 155mm howitzers to Ukraine, the first pieces of NATO-standard artillery sent to Ukraine. It was a small amount—only eighteen M777 guns were included in the first batch—but Biden's decision, made after concluding that Putin's threats were empty, was a watershed moment. In the following weeks and months, the United States and its NATO allies would supply more and more sophisticated weapons to Kyiv, breaking one self-imposed taboo after another. The trickle was slow, sometimes painfully so, with every delay measured in Ukrainian lives. But as Western commitments grew, so did the stakes.

This engagement was driven not just by a calculated realpolitik, but by an emotional outrage over Russian atrocities that spread through democratic societies, in part as a result of Zelensky using every available occasion to speak directly to Western audiences, from rock festivals to university commencements. "In diplomacy, morality is part of the public narrative, but rarely part of the real decision-making process," Foreign Minister Kuleba told me. Ukraine's example, he added, was a rare exception: "Sympathy based on moral arguments was a game changer. Some governments acted the way they did not merely based on their practical considerations, but under enormous pressure of their public opinion."

❖

For years before the invasion, Kyiv focused on developing an indigenous long-range antiship missile, the Neptune, to protect Odesa and other coastal cities from a Russian amphibious landing. Yet none were believed to be fully operational. Assuming itself to be safe, the flagship of Russia's Black Sea Fleet, the cruiser *Moskva*, sailed in April near Snake Island—and within the range of the Neptune. The famous reply of a Ukrainian border guard trooper on the first day of the war—"Russian warship, go fuck yourself"— had come in response to surrender demands from *Moskva*'s command post. The Ukrainians had their chance for revenge.

Skimming the water, two Neptune missiles hit *Moskva* on April 13, causing a fire to erupt on board. By the next day, the damaged cruiser sank—the biggest warship to go down since World War II. Embarrassed to acknowledge Ukraine's prowess, Russia's ministry of defense officially blamed it on an accident, and initially claimed that the entire crew of more than 500 men had been rescued. It later admitted that dozens of sailors had died or been lost at sea.

Russia's hubris was to blame. "Cruiser *Moskva* was like these huge convoys that had moved into the Kyiv region," General Zaluzhny recalled later. "A failure to fear resistance, an inability to imagine that someone can hit and destroy the second-strongest army in the world—it had drawn to Kyiv these convoys that we ended up burning down, and it drew this rusty bucket into the range of our weapons. We had to take advantage of such an opportunity."

This wasn't the only piece of bad news for Putin. The same day, Zelensky announced the arrest of Viktor Medvedchuk, the fugitive pro-Russian politician. Disguised in a Ukrainian soldier's uniform, Medvedchuk had been recognized at a random Territorial Defense checkpoint in Transcarpathia, near the Hungarian border. In a speech, Zelensky offered to exchange him for Ukrainian prisoners of war held by Russia.

US defense secretary Lloyd Austin and secretary of state Tony Blinken took the train to Kyiv the following week to discuss Ukraine's needs and to announce the reopening of the American embassy that had shut down in February. "We want to see Russia weakened to the degree that it can't do the kinds of things that it has done in invading Ukraine," Austin said, a bold expansion of Washington's declared policy goals. Days later, on April 26, he convened at the US Ramstein Air Base in Germany the first of many regular meetings where the United States and its partners would pledge more and more weapons for Ukraine.

Blinken sounded exuberant after this visit to Kyiv. "We don't know how the rest of the war will unfold, but we do know that a sovereign, independent Ukraine will be around a lot longer than Vladimir Putin is on the

scene," he said. "Russia has already failed and Ukraine has already succeeded."

UKRAINIAN OFFICIALS WERE MORE DOWNCAST. LARGE PARTS OF SOUTHERN
and eastern Ukraine remained under Russian occupation. More important,
they believed, Putin hadn't really given up on his original goal of eliminat-
ing their country. The retreat from Kyiv signaled a change in tactics, not
strategy.

A lengthy article published by Russia's RIA state news agency in April
outlined Moscow's intentions. "Denazification will inevitably be a de-
Ukrainization," it said. The very name Ukraine would be abolished because
"Ukrainism is an artificial anti-Russian construct without its own civiliza-
tional content." Practically, this de-Ukrainization was meant to be conducted by the physical liquidation of Ukrainian elites, whose reeducation
was deemed impossible, the article explained. As for the remaining Ukrainians, they "must suffer the hardships of the war and internalize the experience as a historic lesson and atonement for their crime." The Ukrainian
crime, of course, consisted of refusing to self-identify as Russians.

Former president Dmitry Medvedev, who headed Putin's party and
served as deputy head of Russia's national security council, outlined this
program of genocide in a slightly more couched language. The Ukrainian
state, he wrote, would suffer the same fate as the Nazi Third Reich. As for
the goals of the "special military operation," a critical one was to "change
the bloody mindset, full of fraudulent myths, of the people who are Ukrainian today."

The troops that Moscow pulled out of northern Ukraine were heading
back into the fight, in and around Donbas. The bloodiest days of the war
were about to begin. "The battle for Donbas will remind you of World War II,
with large operations, thousands of tanks, armored vehicles, planes, artillery," Kuleba warned a gathering of NATO foreign ministers on April 7.
"Either you help us now," he added, "or your help will come too late, and
many people will die."

CHAPTER 23

AZOVSTAL

uring the first week of April, after bloody street battles that destroyed hundreds of buildings and killed thousands of Mariupol civilians, Russian forces finally managed to seize most of the city. The two main formations of Ukrainian defenders had been separated from each other and pushed into isolated pockets. The long agony of the besieged metropolis began—horrors perpetrated out of sight, with medieval brutality.

Most fighters of the Azov Regiment that Russia sought to wipe out were still holed up in the Azovstal steelworks compound on the southeastern shore of Mariupol. Owned by Ukrainian billionaire Rinat Akhmetov, Azovstal was one of the city's main employers before the invasion, with 10,000 workers.

Surviving doctors and nurses of the 555th Military Hospital that had been bombed by Russia set up an improvised operating room in one of the Azovstal bunkers. Other bunkers were used as shelters by some 800 Ukrainian civilians hiding from constant bombardments. Anna Zaitseva and her child, Svyatoslav, were still there, on the brink of starvation, as her husband fought the Russians on the other side of the compound. Another Azov soldier had found a treasured possession in his uniform—a crumpled, mangled piece of chocolate—and gave it to her son. It was the most precious gift. All the games that the children played in the bunker by then involved dreams of food. They handed each other drawings with imagined delicacies: a bottle of Coke, a hamburger, a piece of cake.

The second main Ukrainian force in Mariupol, the 36th Marine Brigade, had been pushed by the Russian advance into another industrial area three miles northwest of Azovstal, the Azovmash machinery plant and the nearby Illich Steel and Iron Works. The brigade had a long and painful history with the Russians: it was formed in 2014 by the members of Crimean-based Ukrainian naval infantry units who refused to serve under Russian colors after Moscow annexed the peninsula. Azov's Kyrylo Berkal, the former Phuket tour operator who commanded Sector C of Mariupol's defense, was quartered with a handful of Azov fighters at the Illich plant.

The closest Ukrainian-held territory was nearly fifty miles away and hopes for a Ukrainian breakthrough to relieve Mariupol were fading fast. While Ukrainian victories in the north had broken the sieges of Chernihiv and Sumy, the huge concentration of Russian forces in Mariupol would have made any such attempt there suicidal. By then, Russia had deployed at least a dozen battalion tactical groups inside Mariupol—more than one-tenth of its entire force arrayed in Ukraine. The second-largest city of Donbas and a critical node of Russia's new land bridge to Crimea was a prize that Putin wasn't willing to let go.

UNABLE TO RESUPPLY MARIUPOL DEFENDERS BY LAND, UKRAINE'S GUR MILitary intelligence in late March launched seven daring helicopter missions into Azovstal. Two Mi-8 choppers from Ukraine's 16th Aviation Brigade, piloted by grizzled veterans of peacekeeping missions in Africa, flew into the besieged city as Mi-24 helicopter gunships accompanied them to provide fire support and protection from Russian air defenses.

A Georgian lieutenant colonel who joined Azov in 2014, Georgi Kuparashvili, was evacuated in the early morning during the first of these flights. He had sustained serious injuries to his abdomen in a firefight with the Russians and had already undergone an emergency surgery in an Azovstal bunker but needed proper care to survive. Denys Prokopenko, the Azov commander, urged him to board the chopper: "You either die here in a bunker, or you die trying," he recalled. He decided to try.

The shelling of the Azovstal area was so intense that Kuparashvili doubted until the last moment that the choppers, which had doubled back over the Azov Sea to avoid detection, would be able to land at the plant. A military officer knowledgeable about Russian air defenses, he didn't have high hopes about the onward journey. "These people had come to Azovstal, risking their lives, and so I had to trust them and to trust my commander," Kuparashvili told me. "But, personally, I really didn't believe that I could make it out."

The most important cargo that these choppers unloaded were boxes containing Starlink satellite terminals, which enabled internet access despite Russian efforts to shut down phone networks and jam satellite signals. They were particularly precious in Mariupol, where most phone connections had long been cut off. The choppers also brought in antitank missiles, other ammunition to replenish the defenders' dwindling stocks, boxes of medication, and a few dozen extra fighters.

The odds of success were low not just because of Russian air defenses but also because Ukraine's own infantry might shoot down the choppers over the front line, assuming them to be Russian. These missions were so clandestine that the regular Ukrainian forces hadn't been informed about them. "We understood that it was likely a one-way flight," one of the pilots, Yevheni, later recalled. Another of the sixteen injured Azov fighters evacuated on the March 21 flight described the trip as a "roller coaster on steroids." Trying to avoid being spotted, the choppers hugged the ground, following the contours of every valley and hill. That day, they all made it back.

But the Russians eventually caught on. On March 31, two Mi-8 helicopters on another resupply and rescue mission took off from Azovstal, after loitering just ten minutes on the ground. The Russians instantly attacked them with portable antiaircraft missiles, machine-gun fire from BMPs and BTRs, and fire from Navy ships off the coast. "Rockets were flying like sparrows," recalled Yevheni, who flew a fire support mission on an Mi-24. One of the Ukrainian Mi-8 choppers, its engine damaged, managed to limp all the way across the front line. The second was shot down: one of the missiles aiming at it had been deflected from its course by flares, but another had slammed into its left side. While most people in that chopper died, one of

the two survivors included a GUR lieutenant from Odesa. He was repeatedly interrogated, including on camera, about these missions. Russian TV
triumphantly showed the debris strewn over a field outside Mariupol.

The secret was out. GUR tried two more such helicopter runs to Mariupol in the following days. One was a success but the next, the seventh in
total, turned into a disaster. Another Mi-8 was shot down over the sea, and
an Mi-24 on a rescue mission was downed too. There would be no more
such attempts.

⁂

Azov's commanders said from the very beginning that they would fight
to the end. The Marines of the 36th Brigade, by contrast, were confused. The orders they had received from the Marine Corps headquarters
were ambiguous. Troops defending Mariupol could either attempt to break
through, try to join Azov in Azovstal, stay put, or—if there was no other
choice—surrender.

Instead of deciding, the brigade's commander, Colonel Volodymyr Baraniuk, just relayed these options to his subordinates. Berkal was shocked.
"This is not something you can do in the middle of combat," he recalled. "It
just created chaos in their heads. The brigade simply imploded."

On April 4, as Berkal woke up in the early morning to inspect positions
of the 501st Marine Battalion south and west of the Illich plant, he realized
that there was nobody there. The battalion's command post had been abandoned too. Without telling anyone, the entire battalion had surrendered to
the Russians. It was a stroke of luck that the Russians were slow to move into
the breach. Berkal managed to scramble enough troops that morning to
patch up Ukrainian defenses.

Morale among the remaining Marines plummeted quickly as casualties mounted. More than one hundred Marines had been killed and some
four hundred injured by then. A hopeless but seductive idea of trying to
break out and fight their way to Ukrainian-controlled territory in Zaporizhzhia took hold.

On April 12, as discipline began to unravel, Baraniuk agreed to the
plan. He ordered the brigade's tanks and fighting vehicles to be painted with

the Russian "Z" symbols to deceive the enemy and set out at the head of the convoy. He had not bothered to warn Ukrainian forces in Azovstal that he was leaving, Azov's commander, Prokopenko, complained bitterly.

Not all the Marines followed Baraniuk. Azov's Berkal and Captain Ser-hiy Volynski, the deputy commander of one of the Marine battalions, chose to remain in Mariupol. Some 150 Marines under Volynski's command and 54 men from Berkal's combined unit boarded ten trucks and three armored vehicles, each painted with a "Z," and started to roll toward the Azovstal plant. Russian attention in those moments was focused on the main Marine column trying to escape the city, in the opposite direction. As Mariupol was enveloped by morning fog, Berkal's convoy drove through the Russian checkpoint. He was expecting a hail of bullets at any moment. But the sleepy Russian troops just waved them through. "They either thought we are Russian, or the guys at the checkpoint understood everything, but got scared we'd kill them," Berkal recalled. "It was one of the miracles of Mariupol."

Minutes later, he was inside Azovstal, reunited with his comrades from the Azov Regiment.

Led by Baraniuk, the much bigger column of Marines didn't get far. Ambushed by the Russians and hit by artillery and airstrikes, almost all these Marines were either killed or taken prisoner. It was a rout. Only a handful of survivors, walking through forests and fields in civilian garb, managed to get across the front line.

MOSCOW INITIALLY CLAIMED THAT BARANIUK, TOO, HAD DIED THAT DAY. Then, a few weeks later, Russia paraded the captive colonel, who didn't seem to be injured, on television. In an interview with his captors, Baraniuk accused Azov of exposing the Marines' flank when they had retreated to Azovstal and said that his brigade had been betrayed by the high command in Kyiv. "They had promised certain help. But that help never arrived," the colonel complained in his filmed interrogation. "That's in a way what had pushed us to try to link up with our units."

Azov's commanders were furious. The regiment's chief, Prokopenko, thundered that Baraniuk's unilateral decision had "caused catastrophic, irreversible consequences" to Ukraine's ability to defend Mariupol. The 36th

Brigade had possessed enough weapons and ammunition to continue holding the Illich plant, and its abandonment of the area meant that all the Russian forces in Mariupol now concentrated on Azovstal. "Don't make heroes
out of deserters and the fighters who voluntarily opted to surrender. They
have chosen the path of shame," Prokopenko urged.

Russian forces by then were already inside parts of Azovstal. On April 21,
Kadyrov's chief representative on the Mariupol front line, Adam Delimkhanov, recorded a video in front of Azovstal's burning entrance, flanked
by a few dozen bearded fighters waving the flags of Chechnya, Russia, and
the Donetsk "people's republic."

"We can say that the operation to destroy and cleanse Mariupol has
been completed today," he said triumphantly. Then, raising their rifles, the
fighters started chanting "Akhmat-Strength" and the Muslim profession of
faith, "Allahu Akbar."

The same day, April 21, defense minister Shoigu reported to Putin that
the Ukrainian enclave in Azovstal was firmly isolated and could be captured in three or four days. "I consider the proposed storming of the industrial zone to be inexpedient and order to cancel it," Putin replied. Instead,
he instructed Shoigu to make the siege of Azovstal so tight "that not even a
fly can fly through." Russia's priority now was to save the lives of its soldiers,
the Russian president said. As for the Ukrainian defenders, he added, anyone choosing to surrender would be guaranteed safety and treatment in ac-
cordance with international law.

There was, of course, no letup in the bombing of Azovstal. But Russian
troops indeed no longer risked their lives to try to capture the compound.

※

In the following days, Ukraine, with the help of the International Committee of the Red Cross and the UN, managed to negotiate a deal allowing
Ukrainian civilians to leave Azovstal. The bunker where Zaitseva and her
son and parents had been sheltering was hit by a Russian bomb on April 25.
The two exits had been blocked by debris and her mother's arm was broken
by the shock wave. Still, they managed to climb out through a hole made by
a collapsed wall. "Look, this is the sky, this is the grass, this is the sun that

you see for the first time," Zaitseva told her toddler. It was winter when he had last been outdoors.

On April 30, the Russians ceased fire for a few hours and Azov soldiers told Zaitseva and other civilians to be ready to leave. Her husband, Kirill, injured by then, was staying behind. The civilians boarded tattered white buses, all their windows shot out by shrapnel, and drove to a link-up point outside Azovstal. There, they were transferred to other buses, in the presence of the Red Cross and the UN—and the Russian military. Instead of being taken across the front line and to freedom, they were driven first to a Russian filtration camp for lengthy interrogations. Moscow was suspicious that Azov fighters could be hiding among the civilians.

Female Russian soldiers told Zaitseva and other women to strip naked, examining their tattoos and scars, and invasively searching their bodies. Then the Russians screened every refugee's phone, recovering deleted photographs and copying contacts. A Russian officer offered to hold Svyatoslav while Zaitseva was filling in paperwork. "Never," she replied angrily. "You've been bombing him for two months, and now you want to hold him?" She eventually made it to Ukrainian-controlled Zaporizhzhia and called her husband in Mariupol. The connection was bad, but they managed to exchange a few words. It was one of their last conversations.

FOR THE UKRAINIAN SOLDIERS REMAINING AT AZOVSTAL, THE SITUATION was increasingly hopeless. They had become heroes to many Ukrainians, the modern-day Spartans who resisted against all odds. Public buildings all over Kyiv were decorated with giant banners praising their courage. But by early May, they had run out of options. In Kyiv, with the support of Erdoğan, Zelensky tried to negotiate an "extraction" deal under which the fighters would be transferred from Mariupol to Turkey or another third country for the duration of the conflict. But Russia wanted an unambiguous Ukrainian defeat in Mariupol and replied that it wasn't interested in anything short of a full surrender, which the Ukrainian troops at Azovstal refused to accept without an explicit order from Kyiv.

Lacking fresh water, troops discovered a stock of pickled cucumbers, drinking the brine to stay hydrated. There were other random food items and wet wipes in bombed warehouses to keep them going. The one thing in catastrophically short supply, in addition to ammunition, was medicine. "At that time, getting wounded was like in the Middle Ages—it meant almost certain death. It was better to be shot dead right away, at least you died without suffering," Berkal recalled. "The most horrible thing was to visit the field hospital, where your comrades were rotting alive."

On May 8, Zelensky acknowledged reality. "Unblocking the city of Mariupol with arms is impossible," he said. "It is impossible today. These are not thoughts, these are the conclusions of our military leadership."

With that in mind, and after obtaining guarantees from the International Committee of the Red Cross, the Ukrainian government ordered the defenders of Azovstal to lay down their arms. On May 16, as the first batch of wounded Azov soldiers was being taken to hospitals under Russian control, Azov commander Prokopenko, himself injured, announced the bitter decision. "The defenders of Mariupol have executed their orders, despite all the hardships, tying up the overwhelming enemy forces for eighty-two days and allowing the Ukrainian Army to regroup, to prepare more personnel, and to receive a large quantity of weapons from partners," he said. "In order to save lives, the Mariupol garrison is fulfilling the approved decision of the higher military command, and hopes for the support of the Ukrainian people."

For the next four days, Ukrainian troops kept walking out of Azovstal, many of them limping on improvised crutches or carried by their comrades. They were frisked by Russian soldiers, stripped to examine their tattoos, and put on buses that took them to prison camps. A total of 2,439 Ukrainian troops surrendered at Azovstal, according to Russia's ministry of defense. Zaitseva saw her husband among the prisoners on the footage filmed by Russian TV. Prokopenko, the Azov commander, and Volynski, the acting commander of the 36th Marine Brigade, were the last to leave the ruins of Azovstal, on May 20. Berkal also walked out that day.

While other top Azov commanders were immediately taken to Moscow, Berkal, because of his prewar job as head of the training academy, was mistaken for a regular National Guard major and sent together with the bulk of Ukrainian POWs to the internment camp of Olenivka, in the Donetsk "people's republic."

Denis Pushilin, that statelet's head, announced after the surrender that he would organize an "international tribunal" to put the Azov captives on trial. In his supposedly independent "republic," unlike in Russia proper, legislation foresaw capital punishment. Two weeks later, a court in Donetsk sentenced to death two captured Britons and one Moroccan who had come to Ukraine before the invasion and served in Mariupol with the 36th Marine Brigade. In Moscow, other Russian officials mulled different ideas. Some of the prisoners of Azovstal, they said after the city's fall, could be traded for Medvedchuk, Putin's man in Ukraine.

Meanwhile, Russia no longer needed to maintain combat troops in the city. A dozen battalion tactical groups had been freed for the massive offensive that Moscow planned in the rest of Donbas. The apartment building with the mural of the Mariupol girl who had lost her leg in the Russian attack of 2015 was one of the few that survived the siege relatively undamaged. The city's new overlords wasted no time in painting over the image.

MAY 1, 2022

BELARUS

POLAND

RUSSIA

Kupyansk

Oskil River

Balakliya

**Lines of
Russian Control**

Slovyansk   Bilohorivka
          Siversk   Severodonetsk
Kramatorsk Soledar   Lysychansk
     Bakhmut
        Popasna

L U H A N S K

D O N E T S K

Annexed by Russia in 2014

"People's Republics" controlled
by Russia since 2014–2015

Freed from Russian
occupation

Occupied by Russia
on May 1, 2022

KILOMETERS

0   50   100   150

N

0   50   100   150
MILES

RUSSIA

Chernihiv

Sumy

Kyiv

UKRAINE

Kharkiv

Dnipro River

Izyum

Luhansk

Donbas

AREA OF DETAIL

Dnipro

Donetsk

Zaporizhzhia

Voznesensk

Mariupol

Mykolaiv

Melitopol

Berdyansk

Kherson

Odesa

Azov Sea

Snake
Island

Crimean
Peninsula

KERCH BRIDGE

Sevastopol

Black Sea

PART 6

DONBAS

CHAPTER 24

"THERE IS NO MORE TIME FOR THINKING"

Manu and I walked backed across the Polish-Ukrainian border in mid-April. It was much faster to cross on foot than in a vehicle. A line of trucks seeking entry to Ukraine snaked for miles, most of them carrying used cars that were now allowed to be imported duty-free, for the needs of the army.

Across the border, another long line had formed by the gas station. Russia had been strategically bombing the country's refineries, causing a fuel crisis. It would take only a few weeks for Ukraine to organize alternative fuel supplies from Poland, Romania, and elsewhere. But for now, the car that we had picked up in Ukraine stank because of several spare jerricans in the back.

Stevo had to remain in Poland. Our new travel companion, Ben, was a long-haired veteran of the British Army's Parachute Regiment who, before joining us in Ukraine, worked on an antipoaching project in the Democratic Republic of Congo. I was tempted to see how Kyiv, with the Russian troops gone, had come back to life. But the focus of the war had now shifted to Donbas, and that's where we headed, driving for an entire day, with pit stops for Americanos and hot dogs at gas stations along the way.

In Dnipro, our hotel was packed with people we hadn't seen before: real and aspiring members of the International Legion, some staying in the presidential suite, and all getting increasingly drunk in the bar as the night progressed. Only a handful of them had seen action near Kyiv in March, thrown to the Moshchun and Irpin front lines with Kalashnikovs and little instruction in Ukraine's darkest hour. They no longer had weapons, and all complained that they didn't know when, or whether, they would get to fight again. Some of the Americans and Brits claimed to be veterans who had participated in combat in Afghanistan, but when Ben, who had served a few tours in Afghanistan's Helmand province, started asking questions, it became clear that their stories were embellished, if not outright fabricated. "Lots of frauds here," he announced. "Boys looking for adventure."

On March 13, the Russian military had struck the International Legion's main base at the training grounds of Yavoriv near Lviv with a salvo of cruise missiles, killing several dozen mostly Ukrainian soldiers. Since then, the Russian ministry of defense was making nearly daily announcements about killing dozens and hundreds of "foreign mercenaries" in various Ukrainian towns. "I hope they don't bomb our hotel tonight," I told Ben. "That would be quite unfortunate."

THE ROAD EAST OF DNIPRO, TOWARD DONBAS, WAS PACKED WITH MILITARY traffic as camouflage-painted trucks, artillery pieces, and tank carriers headed toward the front line. The news was discouraging. Reinforced by troops redeployed from northern Ukraine, Russian forces had managed to punch through Ukrainian defenses in the town of Izyum just north of the Donetsk region. The day we arrived in Donbas, the Russians also took the town of Kreminna, moving through thick pine forests into the northern tip of the Donetsk region, alongside the Siversky Donets River. They were now on the outskirts of Severodonetsk-Lysychansk, the main urban area of Ukrainian-controlled Luhansk.

Russia's new war plan, Ukrainian commanders were telling me, was what they believed had made the most sense for Russia to attempt from the very beginning: a giant pincer move from Izyum in the north and Mariupol in the south, aiming to encircle and then eliminate the best Ukrainian formations. Such a rout of the Ukrainian army in Donbas could then allow the Russians to go for Dnipro, Kharkiv, and eventually Kyiv and Odesa.

Governors of the Ukrainian-controlled parts of the Donetsk and Luhansk regions understood the looming danger and called on all civilians to leave, to avoid ending up stranded in besieged cities like the people of Mariupol. Evacuations by rail had to stop after Russia fired a missile at the train station of Kramatorsk, the capital of the Ukrainian-controlled Donetsk region, on April 8, killing some sixty civilians. Instead, authorities organized fleets of buses, going house to house and urging residents to pack up and go.

"There is no more time for thinking. Leave! Thousands of residents of Kreminna didn't get out in time, and have now become hostages of the Russians," Serhiy Haidai, the governor of Luhansk, urged in a video appeal. "Save your lives so as not to become cheap labor for the Russians, or not to be mobilized into occupation forces." When I first met Haidai in January over coffee in the lobby of a Kyiv hotel, he was clean-shaven and polished. We talked about his mother, who like me had become an Italian citizen. He had since grown a beard, and appeared in camouflage colors, wearing body armor.

Haidai's counterpart for Donetsk, Governor Pavlo Kyrylenko, told me he expected the toughest battles to erupt north of Slovyansk, the hugely symbolic city where Igor Girkin's Russian proxies sparked the war of Donbas in 2014. As many as fifty Russian battalion tactical groups were massed north of the city. "We have no choice but to fight," he said. "If we don't achieve a victory here, Putin will not stop at us and will keep going further, toward Kyiv and onward to threaten the countries of the European Union."

I had visited Slovyansk in January, walking through a local history museum that hosted a large exhibit of "New Russia" paraphernalia and military gear dedicated to the eighty-four days that the city spent under Russian rule in 2014. Cosplaying World War II, Girkin had reenacted Stalin's wartime legislation, signing execution orders on the spot. Roughly a hundred residents died at the time, mostly civilians caught in crossfire. "Everyone is afraid, God forbid, that it will happen again. People prefer not to talk too much because who knows what will come next here," curator Oleksandr Gayevoy had told me. The museum was closed now, like pretty much everything else.

Unlike many other industrial cities in Donbas, made up of grids of drab Soviet panel blocks, central Slovyansk boasted pretty late-nineteenth-century mansions, and its main streets housed fancy restaurants and coffee

bars before the invasion. The Ukrainian government had pumped considerable money into the parts of Donbas it retained after 2014, to contrast with
the economic collapse of the areas under Russian rule.

Over dinner at a Bavarian-style beer hall in January, I had met a Ukrainian officer, Ihor, who had come to Slovyansk in 2014 and remained determined to live in the city. He agreed to meet me again on April 18, by the only
supermarket that stayed open. The city was nearly empty, storefronts shuttered, streets deserted, with artillery fire thumping in the distance. There was
nobody on the vast square outside the municipal administration, a concrete
building where returning Ukrainian forces had hoisted anew the blue-and-
yellow flag in 2014, in an iconic image of the Ukrainian state's first military
victory since 1920.

Most of the people driving up to the supermarket were soldiers, dirt-
speckled and tired, loading pickup trucks and minivans with necessities
and then speeding back to their frontline positions. Inside, most shelves
were already bare. Suppliers, the checkout assistant told me, were now too
scared to drive to Slovyansk.

When Ihor arrived, he was agitated. An ambulance crew had gone
missing, likely killed or captured by the Russians. He showed me the photos of the wrecked ambulance on his phone. Things were bad, and the Russians were getting closer. "It will be very tough," he said.

Yuri Mikish, a Slovyansk entrepreneur and volunteer whom I also met
in January, joined us the following day. He was tired: he had just driven
from the Polish border in a pickup truck that he planned to hand over to a
Ukrainian unit, bringing several boxes of supplies for other Ukrainian formations. He and his friends were also organizing evacuations for local civilians. There was room and board for them in western Ukraine or in the
EU, he said. "All they have to do now is to say yes," he said, sighing.

Some did. I met Lida, a bakery worker, as she was walking with her
partner, Denys, to the Slovyansk bus station. "We had kept hoping that this
would bypass us, that somehow we would manage to stay on," she said. "But
now, it's clear it's time to go. It has become too loud here." Denys told me he
would have liked to follow Lida out of Slovyansk, but his ex-wife was determined to stay and wouldn't let him take their thirteen-year-old daughter
along. "I'm trying to convince her and call her every day, but without re-

sult." He shook his head. Everyone choosing to remain as the Russians approached had their own reasons.

THE PSYCHOLOGY BEHIND THE DECISION TO STAY OR TO GO IS COMPLI-cated and doesn't depend on the intensity of immediate danger. Some people are too old, too sick, or too fatalistic to move, even as shells fall nearby and as their windows are blown out. Others, like Denys, have family they don't want to abandon. Some are just too attached to the comforts of their apartments, to their household possessions, and can't imagine going to a remote, unfamiliar city—even if doing so would likely save their and their children's lives. This lack of imagination, or outright self-delusion, rattled me at times. But such an inclination to minimize danger, and to believe oneself to be somehow protected, is natural. War correspondents do it all the time.

"Our citizens have a tendency to stick around until the situation becomes really hot. But when it is really hot, it's already too late. Yet they just don't want to understand," the Kramatorsk district chief of criminal police, Captain Ihor Trebach, told me in the police station's basement interrogation room, the building's safest area, which he had converted into his office.

There was, of course, also another category in Donbas: people who came to be known as *zhduny*, or the waiting ones. Back in 2014, in Slovyansk and elsewhere, a significant part of the population had embraced Putin's "Russian world" idea. While many had become disillusioned after eight years of Russian rule in occupied Donbas, in this part of Ukraine—unlike in areas around Kyiv or Chernihiv—Moscow had numerous sympathizers. "There are so many families here that have broken up because one part supported Ukraine and another backed the Russian aggression," Maryna Oliynyk, the head of the culture department at the Slovyansk military administration, told me before the full-scale invasion. She herself no longer spoke to her uncle and cousin, who, despite living in another Ukrainian-controlled town in Donbas, binged Russian TV and considered Putin a genius.

Once open war began, few of these *zhduny* openly acknowledged their sympathies. When asked about the conflict, they usually replied that they were not involved in politics. Yearning for Russian rule, many of them stayed behind even under the worst bombardments, waiting for the Russians to come. Somehow, against all evidence, they often believed that their high-rises were being shelled by the Ukrainians, not by the Russians. Many *zhduny* died before the Russian military could arrive, as did their children. After all, Russian shells didn't inquire about their victims' political beliefs.

The power of Russian propaganda exceeded that of the Russian Army.

CHAPTER 25

WAGNER'S "FLOWER

OF POPASNA"

Yevgeny Prigozhin, a former convict who later became a restaurateur and Putin's favorite caterer, was a man of many talents. In 2006, the bald, puffy-eyed entrepreneur grinned obsequiously as he served wine to President George W. Bush at a dinner with Putin. Twelve years later, the United States issued a federal arrest warrant for the activities of Prigozhin's internet troll farm that the FBI had determined interfered in the 2016 US elections. By then, Prigozhin's attention had switched from fine dining to his private army, the Wagner military company. Made up of highly trained Russian veterans, Wagner saw some action in Donbas in 2014 and 2015, but after that it focused mostly on lucrative mercenary engagements in places like Syria, Libya, Mali, and the Central African Republic. Its business model was to extend military protection to embattled governments in exchange for privileged access to natural resources.

When hundreds of Wagner troops, backed up by tanks and artillery, moved to attack a small group of US special operations forces and US Marines in Syria in 2018, Defense Secretary Jim Mattis reached out to Sergei Shoigu, his counterpart in Moscow. "The Russian high command in Syria assured us it was not their people," he later testified to Congress. The Pentagon's immediate direction to the US military in Syria, he added, was for the Wagner unit to be "annihilated." Wagner's men had been told by Russian commanders in Syria that Russian aircraft and air defenses would protect them. But, as the US unleashed all its might, from Himars and artillery strikes to Apache helicopters and AC-130 gunship planes, this turned out to be a lie. Hundreds of Wagner troops were killed or maimed. "We were simply betrayed," Kirill Romanovsky, a journalist who accompanied Wagner and worked for a Prigozhin-owned news agency, wrote in his memoirs. "When we began the assault, we didn't know that the only aircraft above us was American, and that the air-defense guys were all hiding under girls' skirts." Prigozhin was furious with the Americans and with the Russian military's top brass alike. But he kept quiet. He insisted in public that he had nothing whatsoever to do with Wagner.

In early 2022, well after the full-scale invasion of Ukraine, Prigozhin even filed a libel lawsuit in London over a series of tweets that named him as the owner of the mercenary company. Russia's foreign minister, Sergei Lavrov, played along. Wagner, he said in an interview on Italian TV at the time, had no connection to the Russian state, and certainly wasn't deployed in Ukraine.

The reality was very different. By late April 2022, Wagner had expanded to become a critical—and perhaps the most successful—part of the Russian war effort. While Russia is a far more populous country than Ukraine, its military was facing a dangerous manpower shortage by then. The bulk of its professional infantry had been committed to the war in Ukraine, and suffered serious losses near Kyiv, Chernihiv, and Sumy. Political calculations at home precluded Putin from sending draftees or announcing a mobilization for the time being. Such a step, after all, would have belied his frequent claims that the "special military operation" was unfolding strictly on schedule. "There will be no mobilization of reservists. The objectives will be reached solely by the professional troops," Putin had pledged in March.

Forced mobilizations, of course, had been carried out since early February in the Russian-controlled Donetsk and Luhansk "people's republics." These roundups shored up ranks for a while—but the two Donbas statelets, already depopulated before the war, had begun to run out of able-bodied men.

Wagner flew its soldiers from Africa to Donbas on March 19, after "the special military operation veered off course," according to Prigozhin:

"Fully equipped, right off the wheels, we joined combat and went to the hardest place."

Wagner offered lucrative pay and could count on experienced veterans who, unlike most regular Russian officers, had seen actual combat. It also possessed the money for proper equipment, hiring retired Russian and Belarusian pilots to fly its own combat jets and helicopters. But the core group that arrived from Africa was nowhere near sufficient for its objectives.

So, as Wagner sought large numbers of recruits in April and May, it dramatically lowered its standards, taking people with criminal records, chronic diseases, and moderate levels of fitness. These exceptions didn't apply for the mercenaries sent to its overseas operations. There, Wagner had to maintain the brand.

Much of the front line on the eastern edge of Ukrainian-controlled Donbas, along the cease-fire line of 2015, had barely budged since February, thanks to the extensive fortifications that Kyiv had built during the previous eight years. One critical exception was near the town of Popasna in the region of Luhansk.

There, Wagner troops in late April started breaking through Ukrainian lines as artillery leveled one neighborhood after another, turning the city into a vast field of rubble. Ukrainian defenders noted the difference. "It's not your usual Russian infantry. They know reconnaissance, and you can see it from how they walk and how they move. They also know how to call in artillery and air support," Captain Oleksandr Buntov, commander of a Ukrainian reconnaissance unit engaged in close combat with Wagner in Popasna, told me. "They bleed just like everyone else, they fall like everyone else, but you do feel their level of preparation."

Oleksiy Danilov, the Ukrainian national security adviser, also took notice. "These professional killers are being used wherever the Russian military doesn't have the capacity," he said at the time. "They work in coordinated groups, it's not their first war. It's harder to fight against them than against regular Russian troops."

The ruins of Popasna fell on May 7. After taking the city, Wagner and the regular Russian forces that followed suit fanned out in what Russian commanders called the "Flower of Popasna" offensive, threatening from the south the vital lifeline leading to the main cities in the Ukrainian-controlled Luhansk region, Lysychansk and Severodonetsk. Colonel General Aleksandr Lapin, the commander of Russia's Central Military District, had a separate plan to attack from the north, encircling Ukrainian forces in the agglomeration and breaking out toward Slovyansk. His plan, unlike Wagner's, didn't unfold as expected.

CHAPTER 26

THE BILOHORIVKA CROSSING

The village of Bilohorivka and the nearby chalk quarry lie on the southern shore of the Siversky Donets River, which curves amid thick forests, with an occasional waterfront resort and fishing lodge on its banks. There are few roads in this rural area, and no bridges across the Siversky Donets for several miles in either direction.

After taking Kreminna in mid-April, Russian troops under Lapin's command seized the woodlands on the northern bank of the river and filled the area with a formidable force comprising well over a hundred tanks, infantry fighting vehicles, and howitzers, as well as river craft and pontoon bridges. In the second echelon in the rear, an even bigger contingent was preparing to follow through the breach in the Ukrainian defenses. On May 4, Russian warplanes and artillery started laying massive fire on Bilohorivka and other Ukrainian villages south of the river. A direct hit struck Bilohorivka's school, where most of the remaining villagers had sheltered. Dozens were killed.

The Russians were in a hurry. Putin was due to make an important speech at a military parade on May 9, the annual commemoration of Soviet victory against the Nazis and the most important holiday in the modern Russian calendar. After the April withdrawals from Kyiv and northern Ukraine, the Russian president needed a clear victory. If Lapin's forces could cross the Siversky Donets and push south, cutting off the road, as many as 10,000 Ukrainian troops in the Severodonetsk and Lysychansk pocket would be encircled, and the entirety of the Luhansk region would fall under Russian rule.

The Ukrainian force on the southern bank of the river was led by Ihor Skybiuk, a no-nonsense colonel with a shaved head and a mischievous smile. The commander of the 80th Air Assault Brigade already had one major victory over the Russians under his belt: the spectacular rout in Voznesensk two months earlier.

The barrages unleashed by the Russians on Bilohorivka, from howitzers, Uragan multiple-launch rocket systems, and mortars, were the most intense Skybiuk had experienced so far. "There was a complete wall of fire. Our positions were being hit through the entire depth, from the front to the rear," he recalled later. Complicating things for Ukrainian reconnaissance, the Russians set the forests north of the river on fire, with thick smoke obstructing drone operations.

On May 8, the Russians made the first of their nine attempts to cross the river, deploying pontoon bridges and river craft to hold them in place. Skybiuk's forces were limited: with Russians attacking all around the Donbas front line at the same time, the Ukrainian military had no reinforcements to spare.

The Russians had partial success at first, ferrying some twenty tanks to a wooded area south of the Siversky Donets. As the tanks and supporting infantry began to spread out, controlling a foothold of around one square mile, the Ukrainians hit back. "We met them basically with empty hands. But we had no right to retreat," Skybiuk recalled. Tank hunters with Javelins and other antitank missiles moved to stop the onslaught but had a hard time finding their targets, which hid amid the foliage. That is when the commander of one of the Ukrainian BTRs, which was usually used to evacuate the wounded, offered to become bait, maneuvering in plain sight of the Russians. As a Russian tank moved to aim, it was spotted by the Ukrainian antitank missile team. Seconds later, it was ablaze.

The pontoons had to be destroyed, fast. The 80th Brigade's Major Oleksandr Yurkovsky climbed the chalk mine's mountainlike waste heap under

barrages of fire and started to guide Ukrainian artillery rounds. Other officers found a hiding spot in the mine's bunker, built to protect staff during
explosive work.

The brigade's battery of D-30 howitzers consisted of Russian guns taken
as trophies in the Mykolaiv region in March. They zeroed in on the crossing. Ukrainian shells smashed the pontoons, obliterating the Russian column massed on the northern side and cutting off the beachhead from
resupplies.

The Russians didn't give up. The next day, they brought in new pontoons and tried to reestablish the crossing at the same spot and elsewhere
along the river. What they didn't know was that the Ukrainians had also
brought in the new, American-supplied M777 howitzers, which could fire
with much greater precision than Soviet-vintage artillery. Nearly ninety of
these guns had arrived in Ukraine by that week, just as Ukraine's own
Soviet-standard artillery began to run out of ammunition. It was the first
massive encounter between American artillery and Russian armor. It didn't
go well for the Russians.

"I have to admit that they weren't cowards, but we saw them and hit
them, and then saw them and hit them again," Skybiuk recalled, unable to
contain his grin. By the time the Russians gave up on trying to cross the
river, on May 13, they had lost well over a hundred tanks, artillery pieces,
and fighting vehicles in the Bilohorivka area, as well as hundreds of men.
The landscape of destruction, with decapitated tanks, rotting bodies, and
sunk pontoons, was recorded by Ukrainian drones. This was one of the most
devastating defeats that Russia's military had suffered in Ukraine so far. It
was "a pogrom, frightful because of its losses and senselessness," Igor Girkin, the former minister of defense of the Donetsk "people's republic," said
of the outcome of the battle days later.

The Russian dead included Colonel Denis Kozlov, the commander of
the 12th Engineer Brigade, who was killed on May 11 in one of the final Russian attempts to set up a crossing over the Siversky Donets. He had just arrived at the front: two days earlier, Kozlov had led the celebrations in the
town of Chishmy in the Urals, where his brigade was usually located, promising a quick and imminent Russian victory.

⁘

I saw the battle for Bilohorivka only from a distance, plumes of artillery impact springing up to the left, as Manu, Ben, and I sped along the road to Severodonetsk on May 9. With clear blue skies and yellow flowers covering the fields, the landscape outside looked like the Ukrainian flag. The previous day, Governor Haidai had tried to discourage me from going. The Russian artillery had the road under fire control, and even the new armored pickup truck that we had just secured would offer little protection against shelling, he texted me. We decided to try anyway.

Just before the cell phone signal disappeared, I received a text message broadcast to all numbers in the area, targeting Russian soldiers attempting to cross the river. "If you want to survive, surrender! Don't become cannon fodder! You have only one life!" it read, providing contact details.

Earlier in the day, Putin had delivered his Victory Day speech as Russia's vaunted weapons rolled through Red Square. Russian commentators had feverishly speculated about major decisions that Putin would announce for the occasion: a declaration of outright war on Ukraine instead of the "special military operation," perhaps a mobilization of Russian civilians to address Russia's acute manpower shortage, maybe even a nuclear ultimatum to the West.

Putin disappointed the hawks. He repeated his usual parallels between Ukraine and Nazi Germany, sounding deflated—and defensive. "Russia has made a preventive strike against the aggression," he said. "This was a forced, timely, and only correct decision. A decision of a sovereign, strong, independent nation."

CHAPTER 27

LIFE AND DEATH IN SEVERODONETSK

Ever since 2014, Severodonetsk had served as the administrative capital of the Ukrainian-controlled areas of Luhansk. By May 9, it was the only remaining Ukrainian foothold across the Siversky Donets River. Russian forces had closed in from all sides, and two bridges over the river provided the only connection to the city. On the western side of the bridges, the twin city of Lysychansk, roughly the same size, sprawled atop a hill, with its oil refinery, one of Ukraine's largest, in the valley below.

I had tried to make appointments with Ukrainian officials in the area, but the mobile phone network no longer operated. Governor Haidai had already pulled back. The roadsides were lined with burned-out vehicles, military and civilian, hit by Russian shelling, some still smoking. "Drive really, really fast," I told Ben. He didn't need encouragement, swerving around craters in the asphalt. As we crossed the border between Donetsk and Luhansk, we flew past the Lysychansk refinery on our right. Repeatedly hit by the Russians, it was still ablaze. A thick cloud of black smoke rising from the facility covered much of the sky, obscuring the sun.

In Lysychansk, the streets were mostly deserted, stores shuttered, signs of destruction everywhere: disabled, shrapnel-peppered buses on the main road, severed power lines twisting like snakes amid the detritus. The town's police station served as the hub of what remained of government presence in the ever-shrinking pocket of Ukrainian control in the region. It was connected to the outside world by a Starlink terminal. We hopped on the Wi-Fi, too, to check our messages.

The most senior official left in Ukrainian-controlled Luhansk, the regional chief of national police, Oleh Hryhorov, was surprised that we had made it. "How are things?" I asked him in his bunker.

"Should I tell you in a simple language or a literary one?" he inquired.

"Simple, please."

"We're screwed. Completely."

Hryhorov was in no mood to sugarcoat. "We can now say that we are tactically encircled," he said. His checkpoint on the road into town had been destroyed by Russian shelling earlier in the day, with two policemen injured—one reason why we managed to enter Lysychansk unobstructed. "We are in an appendage that is all within reach of Russian artillery," he said. Only some 15,000 people, one-tenth of the prewar population, remained in Severodonetsk, hiding in basements. The proportion was similar in Lysychansk.

"Everybody who wanted to leave here has left. There are those who await the Russian world, there are those who don't care under which flag to live, and there are open collaborators who correct Russian fire," he added. About a dozen such Russian agents had been detained.

Nobody knew how many people had been killed by the Russian shelling because nobody was checking destroyed homes, he said. Mountains of garbage had piled up near buildings that remained inhabited. Their residents had been without running water or electricity for months. Shops had closed weeks earlier: nobody dared to bring in supplies, except for some courageous volunteers.

"We have no workers anymore. The municipal services basically no longer operate because all the specialists, all the professionals, are gone," added Oleksandr Senkevich, the head of transport and logistics for Lysychansk before the war and now one of the few officials remaining in Hryhorov's bunker to help run the community.

I asked Hryhorov whether we would be able to cross to Severodonetsk. Not on our own, he said, but we could go with some of his troopers. He had traveled there himself the previous day to deliver to the hospital the one thing it needed most: body bags.

—

HRYHOROV'S SPECIAL POLICE FORCES, IN FULL MILITARY GEAR, TRAVELED
in boxy armored vehicles that used to transport cash for PrivatBank. Hundreds of these vans had been repurposed for the war.

We drove to the farthest bridge from the front line, high above the
Siversky Donets's steep, emerald-green banks, and into the maze of Severodonetsk apartment blocks, past the rusted, eviscerated remains of another
PrivatBank armored van that clearly hadn't protected its passengers. We
started with the hospital, now taken over by the Ukrainian military. It was
less than a mile from the front line, and mortars and artillery shells flew
over our heads. Hryhorov's policemen nervously knelt by a wall, aiming to
minimize potential shrapnel exposure.

The hospital and surrounding buildings were full of Ukrainian soldiers, most without obvious signs of injury. Many were in their fifties, and
most seemed shell-shocked and disoriented. They no longer paid attention
to explosions around them and made no effort to seek cover. The place
smelled of defeat. How is the situation? I asked. "*Pyzda*," replied one of the
men with a Ukrainian expletive. "We are all fucked."

"They're bludgeoning us," said another.

Low on shells, the Ukrainian artillery was barely able to respond, overwhelmed by the Russian firepower.

A few blocks to the rear, I noticed a group of civilians in a courtyard. A
funeral parlor, Pantheon, had become a bomb shelter, housing twenty-six
people, four dogs, and a cat in its basement. The parlor's owner had escaped
to western Ukraine, but the manager, Natalia Lashko, decided to stay and
take care of the neighbors, those alive and those who kept dying. She told
me she did the same in 2014, when Ukrainian forces fought to retake Severodonetsk from Russian proxies.

Women were cooking food in the parlor after each funeral, using water
that was brought from a stream near a burial plot. Coffins and wooden
crosses lined the walls. The residents included several children, excited to
meet a new person for the first time in weeks. "We are afraid, very afraid,
but we still hope for the best," said Oksana, one of the mothers. She said she
worked at the local power substation and didn't leave because she felt that

she would be needed in her hometown. "Someone must rebuild it all when combat ends."

"Do you have any idea how the war is going?" I asked her.

Like everyone else in the shelter, she had no clue. There was no television, no internet, no mobile phone service, not even electricity to charge a radio. "We don't know anything about what happened to our own relatives in the same city, let alone the news in the world," she said. "Nobody ever leaves this place, we just wake up all together and fall asleep all together."

"When will peace come?" Lashko interjected.

"I don't really know," I replied.

"The only news that we want," she said, "is for the war to end so we could finally go to our homes."

Shells started hitting closer and closer, and the funeral parlor's residents who had ventured outside for some fresh air streamed back in. It was time to go. The policemen accompanying us, who had patiently waited outside, were relieved. So was I as we crossed the bridge back into Lysychansk. The river was deep and fast, and it felt safer to be on the right side.

On the way out, we ran into a thirty-year-old man, Roman. He had managed to escape to Lysychansk from Bilohorivka, the village where the Russians were busy trying to ford the Siversky Donets. His neighbors died when the Russians dropped a bomb on the village school, and he himself reached Lysychansk on foot, with no possessions. "There are no roads, no houses, nothing left there anymore." He shook his head. "An inferno."

As we sped past the turnoff to Bilohorivka half an hour later, three trucks towing M777 howitzers passed us in the other direction. They were among the American guns that would sink Russian pontoon crossing attempts over the next three days.

❖

Donbas is often imagined as a blighted, post-industrial wasteland of abandoned mines and factories set amid crumbling Soviet housing blocks. There is some truth to that, but much of the region is also made up of pretty, orchard-fringed villages that dot rolling hills, fields of sunflowers, and ancient forests of almost magical beauty. Unlike the cities, the villages

are mostly Ukrainian-speaking, especially in the northern parts of the Donetsk and Luhansk regions.

As we drove from Lysychansk, I couldn't stop marveling at the land-
scapes around us, so deceptively peaceful just a few dozen miles from the
front line. Pheasants kept running across the road. Village homes were
painted in bright blue, red, or green. We passed a truck ferrying fat, pink
pigs that seemed to be enjoying the landscape as they were being driven to
a slaughterhouse.

CHAPTER 28

"TIDY UP AFTER YOURSELF, YOU'RE NOT A MUSCOVITE"

An old trading post whose name means "raisin," the city of Izyum sits on a narrow bend of the Siversky Donets. The city center, with its fin-de-siècle traders' mansions, lies south of the river, as does the Kremyanets hill overlooking the surrounding countryside of pine forests and wheat and sunflower fields. A Soviet-era monument atop the hill marks the bloody battles that occurred there during World War II. A short distance away tower several *babas*—giant ancestral statues crafted of stone by the Turkic Polovets nomads who roamed the steppes of eastern Ukraine a millennium ago.

Every Ukrainian and Russian schoolchild studies a saga that both nations consider the founding masterpiece of their literature, *The Tale of Ihor's Campaign*. It narrates the failed expedition against the Polovets tribes by one of the rulers of ancient Rus, Prince Ihor of Novhorod Siversky in northern Ukraine. Following the bad omen of a solar eclipse, his forces were surrounded and massacred by the Polovets in 1185, one day after an initial victory not far from Izyum, in the lands known today as Donbas. "The black earth under the hooves was sown with bones, drenched with blood," goes the tale, written in the Old Rus language that later branched off into literary Ukrainian, Russian, and Belarusian. "There, the wine of blood has run out. There, the feast has ended for the brave men of Rus . . . The grass wilts with pity, the trees bow with grief."

Plenty of blood drenched the ground of Izyum in 2022.

———

THE RUSSIANS HAD PLANNED FOR IZYUM TO BE THE MAIN SPRINGBOARD for capturing Donbas. Despite fierce resistance, advancing Russian forces managed to overrun the northern side of the city in the first days of March, crossing the Siversky Donets to seize the city center weeks later. As retreating Ukrainians scrambled to create a new line of defense in villages farther south, units freed up by the Russian pullback from Kyiv rushed to the rescue. One of the first to arrive was a volunteer battalion named Carpathian Sich.

Created as a volunteer company when conflict over Donbas erupted in 2014, Carpathian Sich was founded and led by Oleh Kutsyn, a politician affiliated with the right-wing Svoboda party of Ukrainian nationalists, which had been popular, particularly in western Ukraine, before the 2014 revolution, but was no longer a major political force. Back in 1989, when Ukraine was still under Soviet rule, Kutsyn became famous for raising the then-banned blue-and-yellow Ukrainian flag over his hometown of Tyachiv.

The battalion had named itself after the military force of Carpathian Rus, a self-proclaimed Ukrainian state that briefly existed in 1939, as Hungary seized from dismembered Czechoslovakia the Transcarpathian region, where Tyachiv is located.

Disbanded once large-scale fighting in Donbas ended as a result of the Minsk-2 agreements, Carpathian Sich remained dormant until the February 24 Russian invasion, its veterans pursuing civilian careers. Hours after Russian troops crossed the border, however, the force's core leaders—Kutsyn, the commander, and Rusyn, the deputy commander—rushed to Kyiv from Transcarpathia, reactivating old networks and bringing veteran comrades together. The reestablished unit grew to battalion size after action in Irpin and other Kyiv suburbs. In addition to new Ukrainian recruits, it also opened its ranks to foreign volunteers who didn't want to deal with the bureaucracy of Ukraine's new International Legion.

Kutsyn was busy in Kyiv that week and told me to link up with Rusyn instead. Stevo had just returned to Ukraine and was spoiling for action. He, Manu, and I drove past convoys of troops to the railway junction of Barvinkove on May 21. Rows of decoy howitzers made with pipes and branches were arranged along the way to fool Russian drones that constantly surveilled the area. We parked our pickup truck on the town's main square, reversing onto a lawn and under a tree to avoid being noticed from the air. The local Instragram photo spot, a large red-and-white installation reading "I ♥ Barvinkove," remained intact amid the damage of recent Russian airstrikes.

Rusyn insisted on feeding us a hearty Ukrainian breakfast at the battalion's rear base, and then showed us the maps. The enemy on the other side, he said, was Russia's storied 4th Kantemirov Tank Guards Division, with their modern T-80 tanks that used sophisticated thermal scopes and optics imported from France despite EU sanctions. "These are highly trained units, with precision weapons. You can feel it's a proper professional army," he said. "It's much tougher down here than it used to be in Irpin." War in the open terrain, without the protection offered by city blocks, he said, was more advantageous to Russia, which used its aviation to strike Ukrainian positions and to deploy cluster munitions and phosphorus bombs that burned right through metal. Only recently had Ukraine pulled enough air defenses to the area to stop Russian bombers and helicopters from flying overhead with impunity.

At first, Rusyn told me, the Russians attempted the same approach, a massive frontal attack, that they had tried so disastrously near Kyiv. "They thought that everyone will be scared, run away, and their tank columns will simply overrun us," he said. After losing several tanks, the Russians learned their lesson. "They realized that these tactics don't work," he said. "They no longer move in big columns that can be destroyed in bulk. We still kill them, but it's not as easy."

⁘

Carpathian Sich's main forward base was in an abandoned school complex in the village of Virnopillia, twelve miles southwest of Izyum. By now it was a ghost village of wrecked, abandoned homes and destroyed farming equipment, with no civilians in sight. The dirt road leading there was under Russian fire control, and we drove at breakneck speed. White "pencils," remainders of Russian cluster-munition rockets, were stuck diagonally in the fields around. The military driver, with a patch proclaiming

"Ukraine—Fortress Europe" on his shoulder, shifted gears and pulled the pickup truck's handbrake with a stunt driver's flourish, playing the "Ride of the Valkyries" on the sound system. There were clearly fans of Wagner on both sides of this front line.

Clouds of smoke bloomed above Virnopillia. Yet another Russian artillery barrage targeted the school. We pulled off the road, into thick bushes, and waited for half an hour. Then, driving even faster than before, the driver dropped us off, turned around, and sped away. The life expectancy of a car left in Virnopillia was counted in hours.

"Hurry up, jump in there, don't linger," one of the soldiers told me, pointing to a concrete gap that led to the basement. A shell had struck just by the entrance the previous day, severing the leg of one of the troopers, he said. Using flashlights, we ran inside.

Shelling resumed a few minutes later. The basement, with several interconnected rooms and dark corridors, was teeming with troops. Some slept, on a break between missions, with Javelin, NLAW, and Stinger missiles stacked by their mats. Most gathered in one large room, lounging on rows of seats taken from an event hall that no longer existed. Plasma screens broadcast footage of the outpost and surrounding areas, captured by a camera placed on a mast a few hundred yards away and relayed by Starlink to the headquarters in Barvinkove. It was a strange feeling, watching in real time on a blue screen as shells lobbed into us, rattling the ceiling so hard that pieces of plaster kept falling onto our heads. The soldiers paid no attention. A dog that lived with them wasn't as well adjusted and squealed nervously every time an explosion was particularly loud. The kitchen area had coffee, cookies, and jam, under a sign reading "Tidy up after yourself, you're not a Muscovite."

The base's commander, Semèn, explained that his men operated a network of outposts from which they watched and probed Russian positions. "We are not a passive victim hiding in a burrow and just waiting for the enemy to come and get us. We carry out offensive operations and try to destroy the enemy, during the day and during the night," he said. "It's a very complicated game. We keep trying to study their routes, their numbers. Then we choose their vulnerable points and hit them."

The daily Ukrainian strikes, either by armed drones, artillery, or antitank missiles, were slowly eroding the Russians, and had already forced them to slow down attempts to attack, he said. "They don't have enough men, they don't have the morale, and they keep losing the armor that they cannot replace. It's hard for them. They are not idiots and they don't want to die, either."

Semèn had the same opinion of the overall Russian strategy as Igor Girkin, the former Russian FSB colonel, against whose forces he had fought in Donbas eight years earlier. Putin invaded Ukraine with an army that was catastrophically short on manpower, equipment, and ammunition, Semèn explained: "They had forty-eight hours to take Kyiv and win. After that, once we set up our defenses, it became impossible for them to pursue real offensive operations."

He offered us an opportunity to accompany a reconnaissance squad on a mission into no-man's-land once the Russian barrages subsided.

❖

The reconnaissance mission's commander, Marian, was one of the old-timers who used to serve as a tank officer in the regular Ukrainian Army. As we waited for a pause in the shelling, he explained why the artillery barrages were so heavy just now. "The Russians are very angry today because yesterday we killed two of their tanks," he said. "Every soldier here, ask anyone, their biggest dream is to destroy a Muscovite tank."

These T-80 tanks were burned down using cheap commercial drones rigged with mortar shells. "I am blown away by how creative and inventive the Ukrainians are, destroying multimillion-dollar tanks with something that they assemble in a garage," said Juris Jurašs, a former member of Latvia's parliament overseeing Carpathian Sich's drone operations.

Shortly after the Russian invasion, Jurašs had helped push through legislation allowing Latvians to fight for Ukraine. Then he resigned his parliament seat and joined Carpathian Sich. "Like most normal people I had a huge shock when the war began, and a desire to help Ukrainians because it's such a giant injustice," he explained in the Virnopillia basement, his voice drowned out by booms above us, as he checked his weapon. Before his political career, Jurašs oversaw enforcement operations for Latvia's anticorruption watchdog. Its primary targets were oligarchs using Russian money to subvert Latvia's democracy, he said: "This is the continuation of the war that I used to wage at home."

Wearing a ghillie suit and carrying a sniper rifle, another member of the team, Oleh, led us out once the shelling paused. "I hope this war ends before winter," he muttered. "I really hate fighting when it's cold." He ran a funeral parlor in Kyiv before the invasion. Now he was in the business of finding Russian soldiers to kill. "The Russians have unlimited ammunition, and so they fire anywhere they please. We only strike at confirmed targets, when we obtain precise coordinates, either by drone or reconnaissance," he explained. This was going to be one such reconnaissance mission.

We ran past the twisted ruins of blown-up cars and trudged up the hill along a strip of forest. Russian positions were to the right of us, on the other side of the trees. To the left was a field of emerald-green grass pockmarked with hundreds of black craters.

Halfway to our destination, Oleh turned right and into the forest, hacking at the broken branches and overgrown brush. It would be harder for a drone to spot us there. It seemed like a jungle scene from the Vietnam War. Everyone watched their step, looking for mines and tripwires. Panting, we reached a small hill where an observation point had been dug out, its roof propped up by the empty container of an NLAW missile.

"Careful here," Marian told me. "There is a Russian foot."

Russian reconnaissance teams also ventured here at times, and one of them was recently ambushed by his men. A Ukrainian rocket-propelled grenade had severed a Russian soldier's foot, abandoned here as his comrades pulled the rest of him back, leaving a trail of blood. Clad in a black sock, the foot stood strangely erect, like a broken fragment of a Roman statue. The explosive wave must have pulled away the boot, Marian reckoned.

We waited as Oleh peered through binoculars, making notes on his tablet loaded with Kropyva, the Ukrainian military's mapping software used to calculate artillery coordinates. He had spotted a Russian BMP in the next tree line. The Russians were really close. I noticed a bloodied helmet under a tree. It had markings in English. "This was one of ours," Marian said. "The Russians ambushed our squad here a few days ago."

"Oh," I replied, growing stiff.

"Stay low," Oleh whispered. "You don't want them to see us."

As we crouched, Marian pondered the course of the war. He had already been injured in his leg by a piece of shrapnel from a Russian tank shell. He hailed from Stryi, a town in western Ukraine that had been a hotspot of insurgent resistance against Soviet rule in the 1940s and 1950s. "Our war with Muscovy has lasted hundreds of years," he mused. There was only one way to guarantee that the future generations of Ukrainians live in freedom, he believed: "Our ultimate goal is to make sure that there is no such state called Russian Federation."

"We're good to go," Oleh whispered loudly. "Stayed here long enough." We walked back through the forest for a minute or so, then the shelling began. We had been noticed. With a loud whistle, rounds flew over our heads. We dove to the ground, Stevo counting the seconds between boom and impact, and taking a video on his phone. Not every outgoing boom was followed by an explosion: several of the shells malfunctioned. The rounds that did explode missed us by dozens of yards, some of the shrapnel clipping treetops above. "Not close enough," Stevo quipped in the video after one of these hits. Russian artillery, thankfully, was imprecise.

Rising after the barrage ended, we resumed hacking through the forest. At every clearing Marian swung his gun to the left, in case of a Russian ambush. None appeared that day.

Back in the school basement, Oleh gathered with other commanders around his tablet, relaying the Russian BMP's location to an artillery unit. The strike would come within minutes.

Coordination with artillery, air defense, and other forces—nearly absent when Carpathian Sich first arrived on this front line—was making all the difference now, Jurašs told me as he waited for the pickup to take us back to Barvinkove. "At first, it was pretty much tanks against assault rifles here. It's a big deal to overcome your fear when you understand the difference between your and your enemy's capabilities, and still hold the line," the Latvian politician turned fighter said. "Now, it's like day and night. Reinforcements are coming left and right. The Western weapons are doing their job. Morale rises once you realize your own strength."

I asked Jurašs about the battalion's losses. They were high, especially at first, he said. "You're in the car together in the morning, joking, sharing a breakfast, and then he's gone just like that. This is very hard," he said. "But morale doesn't fall after that. A desire to avenge the boys motivates us to fight."

At the main base in Barvinkove, I said my goodbyes to Rusyn, the deputy battalion commander. I told him I hoped to meet the commander, Kutsyn, the next time I visited, perhaps by then in Izyum. "Yes, in Izyum." Rusyn laughed. "Or maybe, why not, in Moscow?"

On the way out, we stopped at a roadside coffeehouse. Just a dozen miles away from the devastation of Virnopillia, it seemed to belong to another universe, with its soft music, neon lights, and spotless bathroom. The barista made us Lavazza cappuccinos. Adrenaline still coursing through our veins, Stevo showed her a video he had shot earlier in the day, with shells falling around. She wasn't impressed. "Is that it?" She pursed her lips at the end. "Happens all the time around here."

Manu was disconcerted by the far-right tattoos we spotted on the forearms of a few soldiers of Carpathian Sich. One had proudly rolled up his sleeve to show a Nazi-style eagle, with a Ukrainian *tryzub* instead of a swastika in its claws. Manu had Jimi Hendrix tattooed on one shoulder and Spanish flamenco musician Camarón de la Isla on the other. "In normal life, we would be enemies with these people. I have a black man and a gypsy tattooed on my body," he mused. "But this is not normal life. Like it or not, these guys are defending our way of life, our freedom."

Manu and I didn't get to meet the commander of Carpathian Sich. Four weeks later, Kutsyn was killed by a Russian shell.

CHAPTER 29

UNLEASH THE KRAKEN

Russia's renewed focus on Donbas meant that Ukrainian forces could probe undermanned Russian positions near Kharkiv. The need was dire. More than two months of daily shelling by tanks, artillery, and multiple-launch rocket systems had turned the sprawling Saltivka residential neighborhood of high-rises on Kharkiv's northern edge into an uninhabitable wasteland. Virtually every building was singed with soot from fires and defaced with shrapnel. Trees and electric utility poles had collapsed onto disfigured cars. There was no electricity or water. The few remaining residents cooked on open fires when they emerged from basements during pauses in Russian attacks. Most were old and disoriented, surviving on food brought by the military or gutsy volunteers. Unexploded ordnance was strewn on the streets, and puncturing a tire on jagged shrapnel was unavoidable.

In central Kharkiv, too, the thuds of explosions were constant, some far away and others close enough to rattle windows. In late April, we stayed in the city for a few days. At the one hotel that had reopened, I pushed my bed to the corner away from the window at night, sleeping wedged between the wall and an unfastened flak jacket to shield me from glass shards or worse. Most buildings around us had already been hit. A surprisingly well-stocked supermarket, on the basement floor of an otherwise shuttered shopping mall, operated around the corner.

Death in the city was random. On a drive in northern Kharkiv, we passed a hatchback sedan ablaze. It had been hit by a Russian Grad rocket minutes earlier and was sending up dark, acrid smoke. We hadn't realized that a man and a woman were burning inside. Half an hour later, on our way back, the fire had been doused. Three ambulance workers in red overalls were trying to extract the remains. Maksym, a bystander who told me that he had survived because he jumped into a ditch as he heard the Grads fly, took it upon himself to direct the paramedics. "The skull, don't forget the skull!" he shouted. Then, wearing latex gloves, he picked up two other body parts, impossible to identify, and carefully deposited them into an open black plastic bag. By then, Mayor Terekhov told me, some two thousand Kharkiv apartment buildings had been damaged by Russian shelling. Hundreds, maybe thousands, of civilians had been killed. Nobody knew for sure how many.

"A genocide is under way here. Kharkiv is a Russian-speaking city, and people here used to be rather loyal to the Russian Federation," he said. "But now the situation has turned 180 degrees. The east of Ukraine has become more radically anti-Russian than the west of the country. There is a reason. It's one thing to see the horrors that they inflict on TV, and it's another to live them in real life."

To reduce casualties and protect the city, Ukrainian forces needed to push the Russians as far as possible from Kharkiv's edge, Terekhov said, out of range of Grads and field artillery. Already in early April, Ukrainian forces launched local offensives east of the city, taking the villages of Mala Rohan and Vilkhivka. In late April, a new Ukrainian breakthrough forced the Russians to abandon a large strip of countryside to the northeast of Kharkiv. Much of that fighting was done by the Territorial Defense and new volunteer formations like Kraken that had absorbed veterans of the war in Donbas. Discipline and training varied. Members of one such group, the Slobozhanshchyna battalion that operated under the vague supervision of the SBU, filmed themselves shooting into the legs of captured Russian soldiers in Mala Rohan, causing an international scandal and loud complaints from Moscow. The unit suffered heavy losses that day, including the death of its commander. It wasn't allowed to the front line afterward.

⋯✦⋯

Kraken was secretive about its operations, except to say that it worked under the authority of the GUR military intelligence service. In the last days of April, its troops, wearing a triangular patch with the giant sea monster, stormed the village of Ruska Lozova on Kharkiv's northern edge. A prosperous community of 5,000 people before the war, Ruska Lozova fell in a matter of hours. Russian survivors retreated to the next town up the road and into nearby forests. "The most important thing was the surprise of the attack," Kraken's deputy commander, Lieutenant Colonel Vito, told me in Kharkiv's Freedom Square two days later. "The enemy resisted, and they were liquidated." His unit had taken three prisoners in the town, he said. It was an important victory, removing one of the last pockets of Russian presence within Grad range of Kharkiv. What Vito didn't tell me that day was that Major General Kyrylo Budanov, the head of GUR, had donned body armor and picked up a gun to participate personally in Kraken's assault.

As we spoke, a car pulled up next to us on Freedom Square. Serhiy Shumov, a Ruska Lozova resident, had just brought some neighbors from the village and asked the soldiers if they knew where to house them in Kharkiv. The Russians were mercilessly pounding the village now. Under Russian rule, Shumov told me, there had been no cell phone service, no electricity, and hardly any food supplies, with locals living off pickles and preserves in their basements. "Everyone was just scavenging for whatever they could find." He pointed at his waist. He used to weigh 212 pounds before the war, he said, and was down to 165 pounds now.

While collaboration was rare around Kyiv and other parts of northern Ukraine, the mayor of Ruska Lozova had openly sided with the Russians, just like several other mayors and officials in occupied parts of Kharkiv and Donbas, Shumov said. "Understand, the Russian soldiers are good people, work with them," the mayor had told a local gathering soon after the takeover. Maybe half the village supported the Russians, he estimated. As fighting intensified, many of his neighbors followed the Russian military's advice to relocate to Russia. "We will soon liberate Kharkiv city," a bearded Russian commander, likely from Chechnya, had told the locals in March.

"Please, in the meantime, go to Russia because these Ukrainian Nazis will shoot at you and burn your cars."

Widespread collaboration meant that those known for loyalty to Ukraine, such as Shumov's father-in-law, disappeared off Ruska Lozova's streets. By the time Kraken stormed the village, most pro-Russian residents had escaped north. As for the remainder, "people cried of happiness when they saw our soldiers," Shumov said. His sons, thirteen-year-old twins, were the first to spot Ukrainian troops, in their pixelated uniforms, moving through their home street.

Most escapees from Ruska Lozova were temporarily housed in a cavernous dorm in the southern, relatively safe part of Kharkiv. Vera Nikitichna, seventy, stood vigilant outside when I came by, looking with forlorn hope at every car that pulled in. When Ukrainian soldiers had appeared, urging her and her eighty-year-old husband to jump into a van with them and leave, he refused, saying that he wanted to finish planting potatoes. The couple became separated in the commotion. Neighbors who escaped Ruska Lozova the next day told her that the area had been repeatedly bombarded afterward. "My husband probably thinks that I'm dead and is still looking for my body." She sighed. They didn't have any children or close relatives.

"We used to live peacefully, didn't touch anyone," she added, resigned. "And now we have become penniless and homeless in our old age, when we're of no use to anyone."

⁂

Ukrainian soldiers turned us away at the checkpoint on the road to Ruska Lozova. Officially, access to it and other liberated villages near Kharkiv was banned for anyone except soldiers and residents officially registered there. These villagers were carefully screened on the way back to Kharkiv, with soldiers checking their phones for calls to Russian numbers or photos of military importance. Anyone found with a history of Russian contacts was detained on the spot and sent to the SBU for further investigation.

I didn't give up on trying to visit and kept calling everyone I knew in the military. The next day, an officer with the Kharkiv Territorial Defense took us to a bombed gas station half a mile before the checkpoint. "A very important man has agreed to take you to Ruska Lozova," he said. "It's up to him if he wants to tell you his name."

A spray-painted SUV pulled up minutes later. A lean forty-nine-year-old in an enhanced helmet usually worn by special forces and an Afghan-style checkered scarf jumped out, introducing himself as Vsevolod. "Sit in the front, don't smile, and pretend like you belong," he told me. This time, we rolled through the military checkpoint without a hitch, speeding on a highway littered with the remains of Russian armor. A damaged Grad truck with a "Z" sign on its cabin stood on the roadside, perhaps the same one that had fired the rockets that killed the couple in the hatchback. Inside Ruska Lozova, we swerved into the courtyard of a home, seeking shelter in the basement.

Vsevolod Kozhemiako, the entrepreneur who had rushed home from the Austrian Alps in the first days of the war, was now a military commander, running the brand-new Khartiya battalion that he had raised as part of the Territorial Defense. During the war of 2014 and 2015, he had frequently visited Donbas front lines, bringing assistance to Ukrainian soldiers. In the following years, he hired many Donbas veterans for his Agrotrade farming business, which counted 2,000 employees before the invasion.

After returning to Kharkiv in the first week of the war, Kozhemiako decided that it would be easier to create his own force than to find a role in the existing Ukrainian military. Donbas veterans, many of them his employees, formed Khartiya's core. "There are many people who want to defend Ukraine, but don't want to enter formal structures because they fear they will have an idiot as a commander. With me, they know me and trust me," he explained.

As the unit was all-volunteer, its soldiers unpaid by the state, Kozhemiako was picking up the tab with the help of fellow Kharkiv businessmen. Khartiya entered Ruska Lozova shortly after its liberation, replacing Kraken, and was now tasked with repelling Russian attempts to counterattack. It was the unit's first combat mission. Russian tanks, hidden in a forest strip a mile and a half away, regularly shelled Khartiya's positions, but so far had made no attempts to retake the town.

"Our discipline is severe, maybe even stricter than in some army units. You can't relax when you are at war," Kozhemiako said, after scolding one of his men for taking off his helmet. An amateur pianist who spoke in short sentences peppered with curses, Kozhemiako admitted that he had little tolerance for the regular army's ways. "We have a joke that the Russians will never understand the corporate governance of our army because we our- selves don't understand it," he said. "My business is built in a Western way. The company is smaller, and decisions are made quickly by one man."

Many of his company's properties—grain elevators, warehouses, land— were located in parts of the Kharkiv region occupied by Russia. Some of his managers had stayed behind, cooperating with the occupiers. Elsewhere, neighbors who collaborated with the Russians had helped themselves to his grain. "One day, we will back, for sure," he said.

IN THE NORTHERN AREAS OF RUSKA LOZOVA, WITHIN SIGHT OF RUSSIAN tanks, the only way to move was on foot. We sprinted between houses that provided cover, jumping over fences and heaps of accumulated trash. Artyom, a major with Ukraine's National Guard who worked with Kozhemiako's men, showed me the Russian positions from his observation point in one of the villas. The Russians appeared to have pulled back their best forces and with- drawn the jamming equipment that used to obstruct Ukrainian drone op- erations, likely because they needed to reinforce their offensive in Izyum, he told me. Most of those left on this stretch of the front line were mobilized troops from the Luhansk "people's republic."

Ukrainian soldiers offered me a tour of the town's highlights. The house of Ruska Lozova's fugitive mayor had a large bookshelf decorated with Af- rican statues. The books provided an indication of his political leanings: there were two volumes of a Stalin biography, a biography of Putin, a thick volume called *Russia, a Great Destiny* under an icon of the Virgin Mary of Kazan, a collection of Nietzsche's writings, and a book by historian Lev Gumilev, the father of the Eurasianist ideology favored by Russian imperi- alists.

"He had time to pack up and leave on his own terms," one of the soldiers told me.

The regular Russian troops didn't have such a luxury. One villa seemed to be the depository of the loot that they hadn't been able to take as they fled the Kraken's rapid advance. Two fridges stood in the courtyard, one of them still with a collection of the owner's butterfly and puppy magnets on the door. A giant boar's head, removed from someone's wall, was propped up on a soft leather chair. Female-shaped mannequins with lacy black underwear were piled up in one room next to a stack of boxed kitchen appliances and a box of Puma running shoes. Russian ration packs were everywhere, and a mountain of cigarette butts had formed atop an ashtray.

"Slowly but surely, we are pushing them back," Artyom told me as I left.

◈

While Ruska Lozova and other recently liberated villages were deserted because of incessant Russian shelling, Ukrainian advances meant that life slowly began to return to Kharkiv itself in May. One by one, restaurants, coffee bars, and smaller hotels resumed business in the safer parts of the city. Restaurateur Stanislav Lubimsky, who had spent the previous months cooking for soldiers and for residents living in the subway, reopened his Neapolitan pizzeria in central Kharkiv. "Springtime has come, the weather is nice, the sun is shining, and people want to eat out again now that things have calmed down in the city," he told me as we stopped by for lunch. "Let's hope everything continues like this, towards victory."

People also started to return to villages that had been liberated weeks earlier but now, thanks to the latest Ukrainian advances, were finally far enough from the front lines. In Mala Rohan, still dotted with rusting Russian tanks and the wreckage of a Russian helicopter, repair crews were busy restoring the power cables and the gas pipeline when I visited. Down the street, Mykola Kotov began fixing the damage to his family home. It wasn't as badly off as some of the neighboring houses, several of which had completely collapsed. One villa, hit by a shell, had crumpled atop a blue SUV that, for some reason, had Irish license plates.

Kotov's house was structurally intact, though he had to replace part of the roof, install new windows, and fill the shrapnel marks on the facade with stucco.

Russian artillery and multiple-launch rocket batteries had been deployed just outside the house through March, firing at downtown Kharkiv, he said. One day, one of the Russian soldiers had come by to ask for cigarettes.

"We have come here to defend you," the Russian soldier said.

"From whom?" Kotov's wife asked them.

"From the Nazis whom Zelensky has sent to attack you."

Kotov didn't tell the Russian that he was a retired Ukrainian officer, or that one of his sons was serving in the Ukrainian Army.

Kotov's house was built by his grandmother in 1943, from the ruins of a family home destroyed when Mala Rohan was liberated from the Nazis that year. Now that another set of foreign invaders was gone, Kotov told me he was determined to eliminate all traces of their presence. "The Russians have been expelled," he said. "We are back home. I was born here and I was raised here. We're going to rebuild once again."

Chapter 30

KYIV LIVES

After weeks in the gritty, bombed-out cities and villages of eastern Ukraine, Kyiv was a shock to the senses. The last time I had set foot in the city, under the gray skies of March, the Ukrainian capital was deserted and surrounded by Russian troops on three sides.

On a warm, sunny spring day in the last week of May, I crisscrossed the crowded Kyiv downtown on an electric scooter, which could be unlocked by anyone with a smartphone. Checkpoints had been dismantled. Antitank barriers on Khreshchatyk had been removed too—not gone altogether, but lined up on the sides, allowing traffic to flow freely.

Many, if not most, of the Kyivites who had escaped in the first weeks of the war had returned home by then. Glamorous young couples sipped cocktails in sidewalk cafés. The restaurant in my hotel served several kinds of sashimi, evidence of the fact that the Russians had failed to disrupt Ukraine's logistics infrastructure. I met Zelensky's spokesman, Sergii Nykyforov, for a Sunday drink in ZygZag, one of Kyiv's bars most popular with artists and journalists. That day, in late May, was the first time he had found a moment to throw out his wilted Christmas tree, Nykyforov told me. People in government finally had a moment to come up for air.

The large square outside St. Michael's Cathedral, which had served as a field hospital for protesters during the 2014 uprising, was packed with destroyed Russian armor. These T-72s and T-80s were the only Russian tanks that had made it to Kyiv. For many Kyivites, visiting the site was a cathartic experience. Families brought young children to play on the tanks, howitzers, and BMPs that had come here to kill Ukrainians, but had ended up destroyed and captured. A young woman walked around the exhibition, mesmerized, as her pug strained against its leash. When the dog stopped to pee on the treads of a tank, people nearby cheered and clapped. Many Ukrainians had felt helpless as the war began. Being able to see and touch so much evidence of Russian humiliation restored their confidence. Russia wasn't omnipotent after all.

There hadn't been any Russian missile attacks on Kyiv for weeks, and nobody paid attention to occasional air-raid sirens. Unlike Kharkiv or Mykolaiv, let alone the shattered cities of Donbas, central Kyiv was unscathed for now. With the immediate danger to Kyiv removed, things seemed to fall into a pattern familiar from the Donbas war of 2014: a bloody meatgrinder in faraway eastern regions and a discordant veneer of peace in the prosperous capital.

The illusion of normality vanished after dark, as the 11 p.m. curfew kicked in. The city used to party through the night, every night. Now only police cars, with their flashing blue lights, and military convoys roamed the streets.

JUST OUTSIDE KYIV, IN IRPIN AND BUCHA, NOTHING WAS NORMAL. IT WAS A strange sensation, crossing what used to be a deadly front line. Manu and I stopped by the monument to Soviet soldiers at the bridge of Irpin, where a Russian shell had killed the Baptist volunteer, Anatoliy Berezhnoy; the accountant, Tatiana Perebeynos; and her two children on March 6. The place of their death was unmarked, as if nothing had happened there.

A temporary bridge was now open to cars, and we drove through Irpin, into Bucha and then Hostomel. Corpses had been removed long ago, and repair work was under way in the buildings that had sustained light damage. Some city blocks were nothing more than scorched ruins. On the road near Hostomel, we passed a mountain of rusted, shrapnel-pierced cars. There were hundreds of them, collected by authorities as they cleared the city after the Russian withdrawal. The owners of many of these vehicles were still being dug out of mass graves, their causes of death examined and documented by forensic experts from Ukraine and abroad.

❖

Back in Kyiv, I had an appointment with Major General Budanov, the head of the GUR military intelligence and one of the architects of the Ukrainian resistance, on May 18. The spy agency's location reminded me of a villain's lair in a James Bond movie. It was tucked on a narrow peninsula on the Dnipro, with boat access for a rapid escape. The Russians had fired a cruise missile trying to kill Budanov in April but missed, destroying several empty cars in the GUR parking lot instead.

Lean and quick-witted, with impatience in his voice, Budanov was only thirty-six. A former special forces operator known for daring missions, he had been injured in earlier fighting for Donbas and spent a long time recovering at Walter Reed Medical Center in Washington, DC.

A large painting in Budanov's office showed an owl carrying a captured bat in its claws. GUR's emblem is an owl. The symbol of its nemesis, Russia's GRU military intelligence, is a bat. A book on the Mossad, a bust of Taras Shevchenko, Ukraine's national poet, and combat patches with the letter "Z," which he told me had been taken off dead Russian soldiers, were laid out on his desk.

Ukraine was thankful for the weapons already provided by the West, he told me, but to win the war it needed much more: multiple-launch rocket systems that Washington was still reluctant to supply, large-caliber artillery, tactical missile systems with a range of over one hundred miles, and strike aviation. "We're waiting. A large-scale offensive without these weapons will be very difficult," he said.

Budanov had no patience for American concerns that such weapons deliveries would prompt Russia to somehow escalate the conflict. "We are waging war on our own territory," he said. "If someone thinks we must have restrictions on some types of weapons, I would like to remind them that Russia uses here absolutely all the types of weapons in its possession, from cruise missiles launched by submarines to strategic bombers. The entire spectrum of Russian arms has been employed here, except nuclear weapons, so far."

He told me he didn't foresee the war ending anytime soon. "Putin is in an absolute dead end," he said. "He cannot stop the war and cannot win it. He cannot win for objective reasons. And to stop it, he must acknowledge that Russia is not at all the kind of a strong and great power that he wanted to portray . . . This could lead to irreversible dynamics inside Russia itself. If they finally realize that the czar is not as great and mighty as he pretends to be, it's a step toward the destruction of today's Russia."

On the way out, I noticed a large-scale map of Snake Island on an adjoining desk. The April sinking of the cruiser *Moskva*, which had served as Russia's most powerful floating antiaircraft platform, with sixty-four S-300 missile launchers, had rendered the Russian garrison on the island suddenly vulnerable.

Russia's military hardware on the island still allowed Moscow to control all of Ukraine's merchant shipping lanes, and to monitor military activity throughout southern Ukraine, as well as NATO movements on the coast of Romania, Budanov explained. "Snake Island is strategically important, militarily and economically," he said. "The Russians, like the Ukrainians, will fight for it to the end."

Fragmentary videos of Ukrainian drone strikes on the island had already come out on social media. Budanov didn't tell me, however, that his men had just attempted one of the most daring operations of the entire war.

Snake Island is tiny: only fifty-two arid acres, with a handful of buildings, a lighthouse built on the foundations of an ancient Greek temple, a museum, a helicopter landing pad, and a rusty pier. Special forces troops from GUR and the elite Alpha Group of the SBU had built a detailed mock-up of the island in April, spending weeks to practice an assault.

Ukrainian jets had destroyed the Russian Pantsir air-defense battery on the island. What the Ukrainians hadn't realized was that the Russians had brought in a replacement Tor air defense system, disassembled and hidden, on a patrol boat. Ukrainian helicopter landing attempts in early May had to be aborted twice because Russian antiaircraft missiles flew their way from the island.

Finally, once the Tor was taken out, the Ukrainian mission to reclaim Snake Island began on May 7. GUR and SBU operators landed on the rocky edge of the island, battling their way through a minefield and fortifications built by Romanian troops during World War II. Several Ukrainian Navy patrol boats provided fire support. It was tough. "We counted on an element of surprise," recalled Yevheni Khmara, commander of the Alpha group of SBU. "But the enemy had good cover, and was ready for our assault."

The Ukrainians enjoyed initial success, even raising the blue-and-yellow flag on the island and destroying the Russian radar station there. But the resistance proved too strong. The lead Ukrainian patrol boat that carried reinforcements was hit by a Russian missile, and sank shortly thereafter with its captain and some of the crew. On the island itself, Ukrainian forces quickly took numerous casualties. "The Russians acted rather professionally," Budanov acknowledged a year later. "Initially, we controlled about 50 percent of the island. But, objectively, at that moment, we didn't have enough forces on the island to push them all the way out."

As losses mounted, Ukrainian commanders on the ground decided to abort the mission. Landing under fire, a Ukrainian helicopter picked up the wounded and the dead while Ukrainian Border Guard patrol boats dispatched from Odesa helped rescue the other survivors, including those who had been on the sunk Navy patrol boat.

By then, Russia scrambled fighter jets from Crimea in pursuit. One of them, flying low toward the Ukrainian coast, spotted an Mi-14 helicopter carrying the commander of Ukrainian Navy aviation, Colonel Ihor Bedzay, who was overseeing rescue efforts just off the shore. His chopper was shot down, killing all five people aboard.

The score was evened hours later as Russia sent a helicopter with special forces to Snake Island, to bolster its garrison and to pick up the dead and the wounded. A Ukrainian Bayraktar drone hovering in the area destroyed the chopper just as the troops began to disembark. Many of Russia's elite troops were killed. The Ukrainians also managed to hit two Russian patrol boats that headed to the island. On May 9, acting on accurate intelligence, Russia struck with missiles the helicopter unit in the Odesa region that had taken part in the raid. The chopper that had evacuated Ukrainian troops from the island was destroyed on the ground, its three crew members injured. Ukrainian commanders went back to the drawing board. They needed a different plan.

⊷

Amonumental white building at the end of Khreshchatyk, originally built as the Lenin Museum in the waning days of Soviet rule and re-branded as Ukrainian House after independence, hosted a somber ceremony on May 17. Leonid Kravchuk, the first president of independent Ukraine, had died at the age of eighty-eight, the last of the three signatories of the Belovezha accords that abolished the USSR.

Neither Russia nor Belarus had any former presidents, except for Dmitry Medvedev, the inconsequential stand-in who had allowed Putin to circumvent term limits. Ukraine, with its boisterous democracy, was another matter. Unlike their eastern neighbors, Ukrainians were allergic to lifetime rulers. Only once in three decades of independence did they reelect an incumbent: Kravchuk's successor, Leonid Kuchma, in 1999—the man who refused to use force to crush the 2004 revolution.

Kuchma and two other former Ukrainian presidents, his successor, Viktor Yushchenko, and Petro Poroshenko, filed into the hall of the Ukrainian House, bringing wreaths and paying their last respects at Kravchuk's coffin, which was wrapped in a Ukrainian flag. Then, despite all the risks of attending a public event in wartime, Zelensky followed suit. Dressed in black rather than his usual green fatigues, he bowed for a moment and then, with his wife, comforted Kravchuk's family. The only missing president was Viktor Yanukovych, stuck in Russia since fleeing there in 2014. It was a remarkable display of the strength of Ukrainian state institutions, reminding me of the similar parade of one current and four former US presidents sharing a pew at George H. W. Bush's funeral in 2018.

A former Communist Party chief, Kravchuk had chosen to join the cause of Ukrainian independence as the Soviet Union started to fracture. In August 1991, he had disregarded Bush's infamous "Chicken Kyiv" speech to the Ukrainian parliament, in which the American president urged Ukrainians to abandon "suicidal nationalism" and remain under Moscow's rule.

Kravchuk was a controversial figure, blamed by many for maintaining

Ukraine in a post-Soviet limbo and preventing reforms. Yet at a time when Ukraine's statehood was fragile and perhaps seen as artificial and transitory by many in Russian-speaking cities like Kharkiv and Odesa, he had laid the foundation of the nation's long-term survival. He ensured that the new, multiethnic and multilingual Ukrainian state would be as inclusive as possible.

At independence in 1991, Ukraine—unlike Estonia or Latvia—granted citizenship to all its residents. It eliminated the Soviet-era ethnicity clause from identity documents. Under that Soviet concept of nationality, someone like Zelensky, because of his Jewish origin, was not considered a Ukrainian at all. Neither were the millions of other Ukrainians of Russian, Tatar, Bulgarian, or Hungarian blood.

"We decided that ethnicity should not become part of the creation of the state," Kravchuk recalled when I last met him in 2019. "What is important is how the person relates to Ukraine as a state, whether he builds it or destroys it."

CHAPTER 31

LOSING LUHANSK

Since the first days of the war, the White House's overriding priority had been not to overstep Russia's "red lines" and provoke a direct confrontation between Moscow and NATO—especially a nuclear one. In his speech on the day of the invasion, Putin threatened unimaginable consequences should the West try to intervene and help Kyiv. At first, those admonishments worked, and Washington scuttled a Polish proposal to transfer its MiG-29 fighter jets to Kyiv. "Two dozen NATO aircraft flying from a NATO country and into Ukraine and then to go to war? The intelligence community concluded that the Russians were likely to misperceive that as NATO entering the conflict," a senior Pentagon official told me. Only light Western weapons, such as portable anti-tank and antiaircraft missiles, were dispatched. Anything else, Biden administration officials fretted, would goad Putin to escalate.

When the US and US allies started shipping more heavy weapons, they carefully stuck to supplying only Soviet-standard equipment, such as T-72 tanks in Polish and Czech stocks and an S-300 air-defense system from Slovakia, that wouldn't provide Ukraine with a qualitative edge over Russian capabilities. Polish MiGs eventually made it to Ukraine, disassembled, overland. Ukrainian officials were exasperated with Washington tying itself in knots of self-imposed red lines, and dismissed the Biden administration's fears of Russian escalation as unwarranted. After all, as Zelensky kept telling his American interlocutors, Russia already used all its weapons except the nuclear bomb on Ukraine. What else could it do?

The US, however, took Russian nuclear threats seriously. "The Venn Diagram between our and Ukrainian interests overlaps about 85 percent, but that remaining 15 percent is pretty important," the senior Pentagon official explained. "The Ukrainians are already fighting for their existence. But the United States has a special obligation to avoid a nuclear war that would end all life on planet earth forever."

Russia's "red lines," however, proved very elastic. Every time the United States decided to step up its involvement, Moscow responded with only bluster and empty promises to destroy Western weapons convoys the moment they entered Ukraine. For a while, Russia fired barrages of cruise missiles at Ukrainian railway nodes, trying in vain to disrupt the country's logistics. With the Ukrainian air defenses denying Russian aircraft the ability to roam Ukrainian skies, these weapons continued to flow to the front lines largely unobstructed. Western howitzers that arrived in May helped improve the Ukrainians' odds, but they were far from sufficient to halt the Russian onslaught. Ukraine coveted a potent new weapon that Russia didn't have: Himars, or High Mobility Artillery Rocket System, a truck-mounted launcher carrying a pod of six high-precision missiles.

After months of denying Kyiv's requests for Himars, President Biden announced on May 31 that he was changing his mind. With Putin's sensibilities in mind, Washington still ruled out the more powerful ATACMS munitions for Himars, with their range of up to 190 miles and an ability to hit deep behind Russian lines. But Kyiv would receive the shorter-range GMLRS munitions that could strike some fifty miles away. Only four Himars trucks were to be shipped at first. As a condition, Kyiv had to pledge not to use any American-supplied weapons to hit targets on Russian sovereign soil. This limitation made it all but impossible to destroy the artillery and missile systems that kept battering Kharkiv from across the border.

"We do not seek war between NATO and Russia," Biden wrote in a *New York Times* essay that announced the decision. "So long as the United States or our allies are not attacked, we will not be directly engaged in this conflict ... We do not want to prolong this war just to inflict pain on Russia."

———

ON THE FRONT LINES, THE SITUATION TURNED GRIM FOR UKRAINE. THE failure of the Russian pontoon crossing attempts at Bilohorivka three weeks earlier had eased the threat of encirclement, but Russian troops led by Wagner continued to advance from the south, leaving only one tenuous and dangerous route to Lysychansk and Severodonetsk. Russian artillery had already destroyed the remaining bridges between the two cities, so Ukrainian troops had to ferry supplies and men to Severodonetsk using small boats and rafts that they pulled using cables strung across the fast-flowing Siversky Donets. There was no longer a way to move armor in or out of the city.

Four days before Biden's decision on Himars, Wagner troops operating from nearby woods managed to seize the Myr hotel complex on Severodonetsk's northern edge, a few hundred yards from the funeral parlor that I had visited on May 9. Having gained their first foothold in the city, the Russians started pushing Ukrainian forces into the industrial zone on the Siversky Donets riverbank, one neighborhood after another.

An overwhelming advantage in firepower helped the Russian advance. The bulk of Ukraine's artillery still relied on Soviet-standard 122mm and 152mm munitions, and hardly any of those shells remained in Ukrainian warehouses. On the front lines in Lysychansk, Ukrainian artillery was outgunned twenty to one. Casualties mounted fast, with 100 to 300 Ukrainian troops killed every day. The four Himars systems announced by Biden and the dozens of American howitzers shipped so far were a drop in the ocean as Ukraine fought Russia's giant military machine. Every day of Western hesitation, Ukrainian officials said, was measured in hundreds of Ukrainian lives.

"If Ukraine doesn't obtain enough weapons in time, it will bleed out," Anton Gerashchenko, an adviser to Ukraine's ministry of interior, told me at the time. Mykhailo Podolyak, Zelensky's adviser, published the Ukrainian wish list: 1,000 howitzers, 300 multiple-launch rocket systems, and 500 tanks. Western officials dismissed the request as outlandish. Five hundred tanks were more than what the United Kingdom and France had combined.

B y the beginning of June, Ukraine faced a critical decision: Should it keep clinging to its shrinking foothold in Severodonetsk and Lysychansk? In the early days of the war, Ukraine's military command, led by General Zaluzhny, often made the call to trade land for time, and lives, withdrawing to more advantageous defense lines. The priority was to preserve the army, and thus Ukraine's ability to defend itself. But as the government machinery in Kyiv returned to more normal rhythms, military concerns started to clash with broader political considerations.

Since May, Zelensky had consolidated decision-making at the Stavka, his supreme war council that met at least once a week. In addition to Ukraine's top military and intelligence officers, such as Zaluzhny and Budanov, the Stavka also included several civilians: Zelensky's powerful chief of staff, Andriy Yermak; the prime minister; the foreign minister; the national security adviser; and the speaker of parliament. Some moves, the president's aides argued, could be militarily sound but politically or diplomatically toxic. From Zelensky's perspective, a quick Ukrainian withdrawal from Severodonetsk would have been one of them.

More than four months after the invasion, Russia still didn't control the entirety of any Ukrainian region. Abandoning Severodonetsk and Lysychansk, and with them the remainder of Ukrainian-held Luhansk, would have finally given Putin a clear-cut political victory. It would also have strengthened the position of European politicians who, fearing the impact of the energy crisis on their economies, had already started pressing Zelensky to accept a cease-fire on Russian terms.

On June 5, Zelensky secretly traveled to the Lysychansk front line to see the situation firsthand. "You deserve victory," he told Ukrainian troops after his briefings. "But not at any price."

The heavy price that Ukraine was paying for holding on to its last sliver of Luhansk was revealed that very day by Masi Nayyem, one of the country's most famous lawyers and a younger brother of Mustafa Nayyem, the journalist whose Facebook post had triggered the Maidan revolution. Elected to parliament in 2014, Mustafa was now Zelensky's deputy minister of infrastructure. Masi, who had fought as a volunteer in the first war for Donbas, was under arms once again, serving in a reconnaissance unit.

On June 5, Masi's unit was scouting the Siversky Donets riverbank in Lysychansk, looking for the right spot to lay a pontoon crossing to Severodonetsk. As his car reversed, it hit a land mine. One soldier was killed and two others, including Masi, were badly injured. Shrapnel sheared off his eye and part of his skull. Photographs of the badly disfigured, bloodied celebrity lawyer quickly spread on social media. Masi survived, and regained his cognitive abilities, after multiple surgeries. The land mine that nearly killed him, he said in a TV interview months later, was likely placed by another Ukrainian unit. In the chaos of war, such mishaps weren't uncommon.

AFTER THE TRIP TO LYSYCHANSK, ZELENSKY CONVENED THE STAVKA AGAIN. As resupply over the river turned more and more tenuous, Zaluzhny became uncomfortable trying to hold on to Severodonetsk, and lower-level commanders on the ground pushed to withdraw from the city. But when pressed by the president, the generals told Zelensky that the military could continue resisting and avoid encirclement there, according to aides. The Stavka decided that the fight would go on. Ukraine poured more and more troops into the Luhansk battlefield. Some were special-operations forces, sent on regular infantry missions to plug holes in the defense. Some were fighters of the International Legion, who filmed high-adrenaline combat videos that showed an utter lack of tactical training. Many of these foreign fighters were dead days later. Ukrainian troops dispatched to the Luhansk front included reluctant members of the Territorial Defense, who had initially signed up to protect their hometowns and now found themselves, with little instruction and inadequate weapons, facing superior Russian firepower in faraway Donbas. Demoralized, many of these men started recording and posting videos, demanding to be withdrawn—or explaining why they had deserted their positions. "It's a clusterfuck," one Ukrainian soldier texted me.

The Russians, of course, also suffered tremendous casualties in the battle for the region—likely significantly higher than Ukrainian losses, though no reliable statistics exist for either side. The Russian dead on the Luhansk front included Major General Roman Kutuzov, commander of the 1st Army Corps—the military of the Donetsk "people's republic." According to Russian reports, he was cut down by Ukrainian artillery as he led troops into an attack southeast of Lysychansk on June 5.

As fighting continued, the Russians and the Ukrainians started carrying out small prisoner exchanges. On June 17, Zelensky announced that Ukraine managed to free Yulia Paevska, the medic taken in Mariupol. "We'll keep working to get all our people back," he promised. Russian *voenkors* were apoplectic at the exchange, which was apparently made for a prominent Chechen from Ramzan Kadyrov's circle.

❖

On the other side of Ukraine, Kyiv was winning in another battle. The arrival of Western artillery had finally put within range the strategic Snake Island, which the Ukrainians had failed to recapture in May.

Until then, imprecise Uragan rockets had been the only ordnance that could reach the island from the Ukrainian shore. Russian air-defense systems could intercept the few Uragan rockets that headed toward the island. They were helpless against the new hail of artillery shells that hurtled faster than the speed of sound.

In mid-June, Ukrainian forces ferried one of the new French Caesar self-propelled 155mm howitzers to the marshy Danube delta islands near the Romanian border. The terrain was muddy, and the gun got stuck repeatedly before it reached its position. The Ukrainian military also brought in a Ukrainian-developed 155mm howitzer, Bohdana, a prototype that was deployed to battle for the first time. Some twenty-four miles away, Snake Island was—barely—within range.

In late June, a sustained artillery barrage by the two howitzers started to hammer Russian positions and installations across the water. Buildings were leveled. There was nowhere to hide. As thick smoke rose into the sky on June 30, the Russians realized that holding the island was no longer possible, sending speedboats to evacuate survivors. Some twenty pieces of military hardware, including a slightly damaged Tor, had to be abandoned.

"The Russians made a huge mistake when they pulled in all these troops, cannons and rockets, thinking they could organize a garrison that would remain there," Zaluzhny noted later.

Refusing to admit defeat, the Russian ministry of defense announced that day that it had withdrawn from the island as a "goodwill gesture." A week later, after demining a path, Ukrainian soldiers returned to Snake Island, raising on the side facing Crimea a giant blue-and-yellow Ukrainian flag that they had picked up from the Odesa municipality. They found a treasure trove of abandoned documents, air-defense components, drone control terminals, weapons—and a hungry cat, which was evacuated to the mainland. At first, Moscow claimed, without proof, that it had destroyed that landing party. But Ukraine once again had sovereignty over the island, the war's most bitterly fought-over piece of real estate.

❖

Only a small part of Severodonetsk's industrial zone remained under Ukrainian control at the end of June. Lysychansk was on the verge of being surrounded, and the only remaining road, already under Russian artillery fire, was about to be cut off altogether. Zaluzhny concluded that the risk of encirclement was too high.

Ukrainian units in the Luhansk region were ordered to pull back to a new line of defense ten to fifteen miles to the west, established along the eastern approaches to the cites of Bakhmut, Soledar, and Siversk. The withdrawal was executed with considerable but not catastrophic losses of troops and equipment. "It was quick, and toward the end scary. We were nearly surrounded, the situation kept changing hour by hour, and we weren't certain until the last moment that we would be able to get out," recalled Captain Myron, commander of an artillery battery of the 80th Brigade. His battery, which at that time was armed with 120mm mortars, managed to drive out at dusk on the one dirt road left, at breakneck speed. Other units weren't as lucky, taking casualties along the way, he said.

In the following days, the Russians picked up enough destroyed, abandoned, or damaged Ukrainian howitzers, tanks, and fighting vehicles in Lysychansk to mount a small exhibition in Moscow.

Moscow's overwhelming superiority in artillery, ammunition, rocket systems, and aviation had made the withdrawal inevitable, the Ukrainian Armed Forces General Staff said on July 3. In an implicit rebuke of the West's hesitation to pump enough weapons into Ukraine, it added, "Unfortunately, a steel will and patriotism alone are insufficient for victory. We need materiel."

Zelensky, in a video address that night, promised that Ukraine would return to Lysychansk and other lost cities of the Luhansk region sooner or later. "We will rebuild the walls of homes, we will regain the land, but we must protect our people above all," he said. "Ukraine is not giving up anything."

KADYROV, THE RULER OF CHECHNYA, RESPONDED BY RELEASING TWO PRO-fessionally filmed videos of his own. In the first one, a Russian comic known as Maks Kamikaze—with an uncanny resemblance to Zelensky and clad in the same green fatigues—declares Ukraine's capitulation, his hand shaking, as Kadyrov towers above him. In the second one, the fake "Zelensky" is brought to the Chechen capital, Grozny, handcuffed, begging to join Kadyrov's militia and made to shout "Glory to Russia!"

The mood was just as giddy in Moscow. On the morning of July 4, Putin greeted Sergei Shoigu in his office in the Kremlin. The defense minister finally had good news to announce. The entire territory of the Luhansk "people's republic," he said, had been successfully liberated by the Russian military's Group Center, under the command of Colonel General Aleksandr Lapin, with the support of Group South, under the command of General Sergei Surovikin. There was no mention of Yevgeny Prigozhin, whose Wagner mercenaries played an indispensable role in this campaign.

"Good," Putin replied, announcing that Russia's highest military decoration, the Hero of Russia, would be awarded to Lapin. He also ordered a pause. "Units that took part in active military combat and that achieved success—a victory—on the Luhansk front must, absolutely, rest and regain their combat capabilities," Putin said, a tacit acknowledgment of the huge cost of this victory. Other Russian military groups, Group East and Group West, should continue pressing offensives, he ordered. "I hope that everything in their areas will be happening the same way as it has happened until present in Luhansk."

Putin's hope didn't come true. Lysychansk was the last Ukrainian city the Russians would capture in 2022. Holding on to the area for two bloody months paid off for Ukraine. Already short on manpower absent a mobilization, the Russian military had lost so many soldiers and so much equipment in the battles for Lysychansk and Severodonetsk that its offensive capacity was exhausted.

The war was about to enter a new stage, as Ukraine readied an American wonder weapon that would reshape the battlefield.

PART 7

ATTRITION

CHAPTER 32

HIMARS O'CLOCK

After driving the Russians out of Chernihiv in March, Lieutenant Valentyn Koval's Uragan rocket launcher unit was idling. There was no action in the liberated northeast. In any case, the Ukrainians were low on ammunition for their multiple-launch rocket systems—and there had been little success with restocking the Soviet-vintage rockets. In late May, Koval and his crew received orders to hand over their Uragans to another brigade, and to prepare their passports.

They were going to be the first Ukrainian crew to learn how to operate the Himars.

Days later, the Ukrainian soldiers were at an American base in Germany for a crash course on one of America's most sophisticated weapons systems. Himars missile launchers, also known as M142, are everything the Uragan isn't. The machine auto-loads pods of six missiles from a truck, meaning that it doesn't require a separate loader that can break down and sometimes needs to be replaced by eight men with belts. Its multiple-launch missiles are guided by GPS and can strike with the precision of a few yards from distances as far as fifty miles away. Russian air defenses have a much harder time shooting them down than Uragan rockets, too. Despite having an armored cabin to protect the crew, the Himars are also smaller—hard to distinguish from a regular truck on low-resolution Russian drone footage.

The American instructors lined up the Ukrainian trainees at the base, and then the fifteen Himars machines rolled onto the tarmac. "They were so pretty, like dolls," Koval recalled.

The Ukrainians soaked up the lessons. "In this unit, it normally takes a while to wake everyone up in the morning, but there, everyone was waiting for the bus to class ahead of time," Koval said. "We realized that we needed this to win."

Three weeks later, Koval and his men returned to Ukraine, relaxing in Lviv as they awaited further instructions. They expected weeks to pass before the first Himars would be delivered. But the next day, Koval's commander called with a question: "Are you ready for war?"

The first four Himars promised by Biden had just crossed the border. Koval's men were elated that these were exactly the same machines on which they had trained in Germany. "Every one of them has its own character, its own quirks, its own soul," he mused. Koval's men jumped into the cabins and, with military escorts to protect against Russian sabotage attempts, drove day and night toward Donbas.

They couldn't have driven fast enough. The Russians had established their network of ammunition and fuel depots, logistics nodes, command centers, and helicopter bases in what they considered to be the safe rear—at least twenty-five miles from the front line—beyond the reach of Ukrainian artillery. But with Himars, none of that network, indispensable for the Russian war machine, was safe anymore.

Ukrainian military intelligence had prepared a long target list, and Koval's four Himars trucks sprang into action, driving from town to town every day, sometimes for several hours, and unleashing their deadly payloads. "The entire front line was ours. There were so many targets everywhere—we kept firing without a stop for two weeks," he recalled.

A Russian ammunition and fuel depot in the town of Snizhne between Donetsk and Luhansk was among the first to be hit, giant fireballs of secondary explosions lighting up the sky. One facility after another went up in flames—not just warehouses and barracks, but also critical command centers. A Himars strike on July 8 in Shakhtarsk, east of Donetsk, killed much of the leadership of Russia's 106th Airborne Division, including two deputy commanders. Another the following day in the Kherson region devastated the forward headquarters of the 20th Motorized Rifle Division. According

to Russian government–controlled media reports that surfaced in the following weeks, that strike killed the division's commander, Colonel Aleksei
Gorobtsov; his two deputies; the division's chief of staff; and several other
officers.

Often, however, Russian propaganda denied the obvious. After a Himars attack on a major Russian ammunition depot in the city of Nova Kakhovka on July 12 caused a series of deafening, blinding explosions that
shattered windows in much of the city, Russian officials claimed that the
Ukrainians had hit a warehouse with humanitarian aid and saltpeter. The
Russian military kept making increasingly fantastical claims of destroying
Himars systems—with the count quickly exceeding the total number of Himars supplied to Ukraine. In reality, none had been hit. Every vehicle in
Koval's unit had a nickname. The lead one, with a toothy smile painted on
the cab that made it look like a dinosaur, was called *Trudyaga*—hard worker.
The battery's nighttime labors came to be known to the Ukrainians as "Himars o'clock."

Koval and his men occasionally had time to check the results of their
work on Telegram: footage of burning Russian facilities and maimed and
killed Russian troops. More important, he started receiving messages from
his friends and former military academy classmates serving along the front
lines. The intensity of Russian artillery fire was decreasing as Moscow found
it harder and harder to resupply frontline units, and as some of its biggest
ammunition depots turned into ash. "We started to realize, like the entire
country, that we were having quite an impact," Koval said. "This was a breakthrough."

On July 18, General Zaluzhny had good news to report on his regular
call with Joint Chiefs chair General Mark Milley, his American counterpart.
"We have managed to stabilize the situation. It is difficult, tense, but fully
under control," Zaluzhny said. "The timely arrival of M142 Himars was
an important factor that has allowed us to maintain defensive lines and
positions."

By then, Koval's unit was no longer the only one on the front lines. Several new batches of Himars systems arrived in Ukraine, as did their European tracked cousins, which carried pods of twelve instead of six missiles.

A day after Zaluzhny's conversation with Milley, Ukrainian Himars

struck an unusual kind of target. Four missiles punched holes in the Antonovsky Bridge over the Dnipro, one of only two lifelines that connected
the city of Kherson and the Russian forces on the right bank of the river
with the rest of Russian-occupied territory. Kirill Stremousov, the former
antivaccine blogger who now served as deputy head of the Russian occupation administration, visited the site to record the damage for Russia's TASS
news agency. "The bridge is intact for now. It's not really a problem, we will
fix it soon," he said, walking by the burning grass as panicked Russian soldiers ran behind him.

In fact, it was going to become a very big problem.

⬦

In previous months, Kostyantyn Ryzhenko, the journalist and activist in
Kherson, had established a network of Ukrainian insurgents to collect information on Russian air-defense systems, troops, and equipment locations. The data was sent to Kyiv via messaging apps, with Ryzhenko using
several e-sim cards from South Asia that he had purchased online as an
extra layer of protection.

"Our network was mostly people I trusted from before, and then friends
of friends started joining," Ryzhenko recalled. The new recruits were thoroughly investigated and vetted. Some were tasked to collect intelligence that
the partisans already possessed. Others were ordered to burn down a parked
Russian BTR while other members of the network secretly observed the area.

A public figure in Kherson who openly advocated resistance on his social media feed, Ryzhenko had to operate in disguise. He rarely ventured
out during daylight. He tinted his hair, grew a beard, changed the color of
his eyes with contact lenses, and put cotton balls inside his cheeks to alter
the shape of his face. A sharp dresser in normal times, he also started wearing disheveled clothes. Though the Russians announced a 200,000-ruble
($2,800) reward for Ryzhenko, he kept avoiding detention. "Someone not
from here, who has never met me before, would have had a great difficulty
spotting me," he said. "But people from Kherson who have known me for a
long time would recognize me. And it was a problem."

Targeting information for Koval's Himars battery came from insurgent cells like Ryzhenko's in occupied areas. Separated by the front line, the two men didn't know about each other's existence.

While the initial, July 19, Himars barrage on the Antonovsky Bridge didn't render it fully unusable for heavy military vehicles, strikes in the following days forced Russian authorities to shut down this vital connection to Kherson. Himars volleys also destroyed a separate railway bridge over the Dnipro, and damaged a bridge over the sluice of the Kakhovka hydropower station some thirty miles to the northeast. By the end of July, the entire Russian foothold on the right bank of the river in Kherson had essentially turned into an island. The tens of thousands of Russian troops in that part of the region could be supplied only by ferry or boat, dramatically constricting the flow of ammunition, fuel, and other vital provisions.

CHAPTER 33

"WE'RE NOT A BUNNY"

I went to see President Zelensky in his office in Kyiv on July 22. The entire government neighborhood had been cordoned off since February, the once-elegant city blocks devoid of traffic. Armored fighting vehicles stood at crossroads. Sandbags lined the sidewalks. I entered the presidential palace on Bankova via a back door past several layers of military security. The building was dank and deserted, with only essential personnel working from their offices.

The somber mood in that presidential enclave contrasted with the relaxed summer vibe in the rest of the Ukrainian capital. It had been months since Kyiv was struck by Russian missiles, and signs of the war were difficult to spot. The Kyiv Opera and Ballet Theater had reopened, though with only a skeleton troupe. The Pinchuk Art Centre hosted a new exhibition by Ukrainian artists, displaying their stark pieces about the war. A wall-sized installation by Oleksii Say contained dozens of frames with black twirls of ink that evoked rising smoke. It was called *News*. Kyiv's favored nightspots organized outdoor raves attended by thousands.

Oleksandr Melnychuk, the opera's lead baritone, who had joined the Territorial Defense in February, was back at his regular job, performing in *Nabucco*, *La Traviata*, and *Rigoletto*. "What are we fighting for if our art and our culture aren't there?" he asked me as we met for a coffee. "Our duty is not to surrender, and to return as much as possible to the way of life that we used to have. We must do it out of respect for all those who have given up their own lives to make it possible."

If all the men were to be needed under arms again, he added, he would rejoin his old unit, now deployed near Bakhmut in Donbas.

I HAD LAST MET ZELENSKY TWO AND A HALF YEARS EARLIER AT A BANQUET dinner in a Kyiv art space that once served as an ammunition warehouse. Then, he performed a short stand-up routine and deferred thorny questions about his relationship with then-president Donald Trump to the guest of honor at his table, whom he kept calling "the real president": actress Robin Wright, aka President Claire Underwood in the television show *House of Cards*.

That quick smile, the sparkle in the eyes, and the desire to please the crowd were gone. Zelensky was grim-faced, chronically tired, and visibly aged. He spoke fast, sipping espresso as he leaned forward from his dark-green leather chair, and sometimes lost the thread of the conversation. Months of life in the bunker were clearly taking a toll. "I used to come to work from my home like any other person, and after work I'd go home," Zelensky told me wistfully. "I'd wake up, have breakfast, exercise, and go to work. Now I live at work, I wake up at work." He picked up his phone to show the critical number he tracked every morning: Ukrainian battlefield casualties. It had declined to around 30 fatalities a day from some 200 a day at the height of the fighting for Severodonetsk weeks earlier, he said.

Again and again, Zelensky returned to the horrendous toll inflicted by Russia on the Ukrainian people. Only a fraction of the deaths went reported, he noted. "You have an explosion in a city center, and eleven people are missing. What does it mean? This means that nothing is left of these people, nothing at all." The Ukrainian president waved his hands. "Children without limbs, children without heads . . ."

By failing to seize Kyiv in March, Putin had already suffered a strategic military defeat in Ukraine, Zelensky believed. "He opened his mouth like a python and thought that we're just another bunny. But we're not a bunny and it turned out that he can't swallow us—and is actually at risk of getting torn apart himself." Yet despite a string of battlefield setbacks, Zelensky added, Russia's murderous intentions hadn't changed. "All they can do is kill all of us," he said. "And I fear that it may be their goal."

That was why Ukraine refused to consider a cease-fire on terms favorable to Russia. "It is a whale that has swallowed two regions and now says: freeze the conflict," Zelensky said impatiently. "Then it will rest, and in two or three years, it will seize two more regions and say again: freeze the conflict. And it will keep going further and further. One hundred percent."

For three years, Zelensky reminded me, Putin had refused to even take a phone call from him. "Now, nobody in Ukraine wants to talk to them. Talk about what? They're not even terrorists. Terrorists at least keep hostages alive for some benefit. But these people, they destroy cities, they murder people, and then they say: let's negotiate. With whom, with rocks?" Zelensky raised his voice. "They are covered in blood, and this blood is impossible to wash off. We will not let them wash it off. There are forty million of us. It's not one or two witnesses of murder, it's millions."

Zelensky was thankful for Western support but reiterated that the weapons supplied by the United States and its allies were too slow in coming and too limited, particularly when it came to sophisticated air defenses. Without those air defenses, he said, the millions of Ukrainians who had fled abroad at the outset of the war wouldn't come back. Zelensky was certain that the war would drag on and predicted that Putin would eventually be forced to start mobilizing Russian civilians.

The decision on when, where, and how to conduct counteroffensive operations was a complicated one, he replied, when I asked about Ukraine's plans to regain occupied land. But the overall goal of liberating all of the areas seized by Russia remained unchanged. "We would prefer to de-occupy in a way that is not by military means and to save lives. But we are dealing with who we are dealing with." Zelensky sighed. "Until they get smashed in the face they won't understand anything."

I DIDN'T KNOW IT, BUT THAT MONTH, UKRAINIAN, AMERICAN, AND BRITISH commanders were meeting at an American base in Wiesbaden, Germany, to figure out precisely where the Ukrainians should launch their attack. From Kyiv, Zelensky and Zaluzhny advocated for a push to the Azov Sea in the Zaporizhzhia region that, if successful, would sever Russia's "land bridge" to Crimea and deprive Moscow of its biggest prize in the war so far. After the losses in Severodonetsk and Lysychansk, the Russians were on their back foot, with as few as 100,000 combat-capable troops left in Ukraine. A better opportunity to strike a decisive blow might not present itself. What Ukraine needed to succeed, Zaluzhny calculated, were about ninety more howitzers and adequate ammunition, according to his aides.

It wasn't a huge ask, but the Americans weren't convinced. True, the Ukrainian Army had surprised everyone with its ability to defend territory and blunt Russian advances, a skill it had been honing since 2014. But the Ukrainian military had not yet demonstrated any capacity to carry out offensive operations, especially large ones involving complex coordination between multiple brigades, the Americans suggested. A Ukrainian attempt to push to Berdyansk, Melitopol, and the Azov Sea coast would leave flanks exposed to Russian counterattacks. Failure was likely, and its consequences potentially catastrophic. A Russian counteroffensive could capture the city of Zaporizhzhia and likely lead to the loss of the country's fourth-largest metropolis, Dnipro.

A much safer option was to focus on Kherson, US advisers suggested. Russian troops there were in no position to launch a sustained counteroffensive because of supply disruptions caused by the Himars strikes on river crossings. The consequences of a Ukrainian failure in Kherson would be unpleasant, but not strategic.

"The reason we recommended that they do Kherson was that they didn't have the trained personnel and the kit to go south," a senior Pentagon official involved in these discussions told me. "We thought that if they bit off more than they can chew in the South, they would get routed."

General Zaluzhny disagreed. "We must attack where we should, not where we can," he said, according to his aides. But without the requested package of American weapons and ammunition, the Zaporizhzhia offensive sought by Zaluzhny and Zelensky was impossible. For now, Kyiv had no choice but to focus on Kherson.

◆◆◆

Despite Zelensky's uncompromising language about Putin, Ukrainian and Russian representatives continued meeting for talks—not on ending the war, but on practical arrangements while the fighting went on. Turkey's President Erdoğan, who refused to join Western sanctions, remained the main intermediary.

There was a problem of global importance to resolve: Russia's invasion had prevented Ukraine—one of the world's largest exporters of wheat, corn, and sunflower oil—from shipping this food to its usual customers, most of whom live in the developing world. As Ukrainian grain remained stuck in Odesa warehouses, food prices climbed worldwide, pushing some of the world's poorest nations, particularly in Africa, to the brink of starvation. Many African governments that had remained neutral over Ukraine started pressuring Putin to find a solution. Erdoğan, who had long ago appointed himself as the spokesman for the developing world, couldn't miss this chance.

The recapture of Snake Island had already allowed the resumption of trade via Ukrainian ports in the mouth of the Danube, where ships could remain in the safety of Romanian waters until they docked. But these ports were too small for the large deepwater carriers that usually plied the route to Odesa, Ukraine's main export hub.

The breakthrough on the issue was made on July 22. That morning, Russian defense minister Sergei Shoigu and Ukraine's infrastructure minister, Oleksandr Kubrakov, flew to Istanbul for a ceremony attended by Erdoğan and the UN secretary-general, António Guterres. Shoigu and Kubrakov each signed separate agreements with Turkey and the UN that allowed Ukraine to resume food exports from Odesa, on the condition that these ships be jointly inspected off Istanbul.

The deal, as Kubrakov pointed out, was made possible thanks to Ukrainian military successes. The Russians made sure to bomb the Odesa port one last time, only a day after signing the Istanbul deal. But when I reached the city a few days later, a Ukrainian minesweeping patrol boat was already at sea, clearing up the grain corridor. On August 1, I watched from my seaside hotel as the first four ships laden with food gathered at the horizon, their horns blaring, and sailed toward Istanbul. By mid-November, eleven million tons of Ukrainian grain would be shipped this way.

In August, Odesa was packed with Ukrainian tourists. It was the only available seashore vacation for Ukrainian men barred from leaving the country. The seaside cafés and hotel swimming pools were crowded with families seeking a taste of normalcy. But the beaches in Odesa remained empty. Antiship mines had been laid, and it was forbidden to enter the water. Some brave youngsters defied the ban, jumping off my hotel pier for a quick dip, at risk of being detained by the police who patrolled the shoreline.

◈

Kyrylo Berkal, the Azov commander of Sector C in Mariupol, was in a high-security prison in Donetsk in late July. Initially, like most other detainees from Azovstal, except for senior members of Azov, he had been taken to the Olenivka detention camp run by the supposedly independent Donetsk "people's republic." The camp was overcrowded. The barrack where Berkal was jailed had been designed to house 150 inmates; there were 600 and counting.

Members of Azov and POWs from a variety of other Ukrainian units were imprisoned together, and Berkal waited days for his turn to be questioned. The Russian interrogator's eyes widened as he looked at the file. He instantly realized who was sitting in front of him: one of Azov's most famous commanders, featured in multiple videos. "Fuck me, this is Kirt." He jumped up, yelling at his colleagues to come to the room. Berkal was the biggest fish in the entire camp. "Why the fuck are you here with us?" the Russian asked, incredulous.

Conditions in Olenivka were rough. Prisoners were fed at best 700 calories a day: soup, bread, and some porridge. Beatings were frequent. But things were about to get worse for Berkal. At the end of June, he was spirited out of the camp and taken to a high-security jail for prisoners expected to face a death sentence in Donetsk. At the first interrogation, a bag was removed from his head, and he was offered water in a branded mug of the Azov military academy he used to head. A book about the fighting he oversaw in

2015 near Mariupol was on the table. "You are no longer a prisoner of war, you will be tried as a terrorist," he was told. He was tortured and beaten almost daily. As it turned out, he was lucky.

At the end of July, camp authorities in Olenivka built a new barrack specially for Azov, far away from the other POWs. As soon as the prisoners were resettled, on July 29, a huge explosion rocked the building. More than fifty Ukrainian prisoners died, and dozens of others were maimed. The Russians withheld medical assistance for hours and then announced that Ukraine had fired a Himars barrage at the camp, ostensibly to cover up Azov's alleged war crimes. According to the warped Russian narrative, it was Azov, not the Russian tanks and artillery, that had destroyed Mariupol.

There was no Himars barrage on Olenivka, of course. The deadly blast had come from within, likely from an explosive planted inside the building, according to survivors. The International Committee of the Red Cross sought an investigation but was denied access to the site of the massacre. "It was an outright execution," said Berkal.

Chapter 34

"TIME FOR SOME NONVERBAL COMMUNICATION"

By early August, Mykola Volokhov, the commander of the Terra drone unit, was in Mykolaiv. Bored after the Russian withdrawal from the Kyiv region, Terra's men had asked to come south and participate in combat. They were attached to a Ukrainian Marine brigade that held the front line on the way to Kherson.

The line hadn't moved since March, villages alongside it flattened by months of artillery fire and abandoned by civilians. Only stray goats, donkeys, and dogs wandered between the ruins of burned homesteads, coming out to greet Ukrainian reconnaissance squads and forward observation patrols that ventured into no-man's-land.

Much of the exiled Ukrainian administration for Kherson operated out of Mykolaiv. Cops with Kherson police chevrons on their shoulders and little to do with their time gathered for coffee and cake on Mykolaiv's main pedestrian street. "Kherson Resistance: The Partisans See Everything," proclaimed one billboard. "Kherson, we are near," promised another.

Kherson was known across Ukraine for its watermelons, yet none were available at the height of summer. Daily barrages of Smerch and Uragan rockets flew into Mykolaiv from Kherson, imprecise and sometimes laden with cluster munitions. They often missed their military targets and killed random civilians—at bus stops, outside grocery stores, inside their homes. It was no longer news, except when the victims were famous. On one of the days we stayed in Mykolaiv, a Russian rocket hit the bedroom of one of southern Ukraine's main entrepreneurs, the owner of the local grain port. He was killed, and Russian TV commentators exulted.

Aiming to render the city uninhabitable, the Russians also disabled the potable water filtration plant that used to serve Mykolaiv's half million residents. As an emergency alternative, the Mykolaiv municipality began to pump brackish water from the mouth of the Southern Buh River. It was good enough for washing dishes and floors but, after a few days of showering in it, I developed a rash and a newfound appreciation for the luxury of clean water.

Ukrainian officials had started openly talking about the upcoming Kherson offensive. Iryna Vereshchuk, the deputy prime minister in charge of occupied territories, urged Ukrainian civilians to leave the region so they would not become human shields for the Russians. I wanted to see the Kherson front line for myself, and to gauge just how likely the planned offensive was to succeed. Volokhov offered to take me for a ride.

In the late morning of August 4, I jumped into Terra's battered pickup, with its dirt-speckled British license plates, and we raced on dusty country roads to a small forest strip by an irrigation canal, exactly on the boundary between Mykolaiv and Kherson. We stopped some distance away from the position, so as not to give it away to any Russian drone that might be loitering above us. The driver sped off once we disembarked. We ran under the trees and into an area with two dugouts that would give us some shelter from artillery fire.

Volokhov and two of his men rigged up a mast and launched a DJI Mavic drone, a Chinese-made piece of equipment that had become a workhorse of the war. Sold for as little as $2,000 apiece, the Mavics were now used by soldiers on both sides—though much more by Ukrainians—to guide artillery fire onto the enemy with a precision that was previously unthinkable. All over the Ukrainian front lines, hundreds if not thousands of these commercial drones were in the air at any given time during daylight hours, augmented by fleets of more sophisticated DJI commercial quadcopters and winged drones manufactured specifically for the military.

With little ground movement on either side for over a month, the conflict had turned into a succession of drone-assisted artillery duels along most of the front line. Russia still enjoyed an advantage in firepower, but Ukraine increasingly offset it with greater precision. "It's a different kind of war now," Volokhov told me. "As people here say, if it comes down to exchanging small-arms fire, you have already made a mistake."

The Russians noticed Volokhov's drone and fired a few shells in our general direction, missing widely as we hunkered down in the dugout. Another, less careful drone team weeks earlier had parked their car next to their position down the road. Spotted from the air, it was hit, its members killed or maimed. The burned remains of the car were still there as we drove past.

After the Russian barrage ended, Volokhov and his men changed the drone's batteries and sent it out again, marking Russian positions on a tablet and then relaying coordinates to a Ukrainian howitzer. "It's time for some nonverbal communication with the Russians," Volokhov quipped. He didn't ask what kind of artillery was on the other end of the line, or where. All communication could be intercepted by the Russians and used to guide counterbattery fire. "Fire. Forty seconds to impact," he shouted. With a whistle, a Ukrainian shell flew over us and slammed into a field on the Russian side of the front line.

"Damn, too far," exclaimed one of his men, a project manager in civilian life who wore a patch reading "Avada Kedavra Bitch," a reference to the deadliest curse in the Harry Potter books. Russian positions south of us were covered by slabs of concrete, with only the noses of their armored vehicles visible through slim openings. Only a direct hit would have destroyed them. That day, several Ukrainian shells guided by Volokhov struck nearby, but none seemed to have scored a decisive hit.

"It's a cat-and-mouse game here," Volokhov told me. "They must be under stress every day. It's very important. If one day we have to launch an offensive, or they get the order to attack, they will be demoralized and fatigued." This, of course, was also the reason for Russia's incessant artillery barrages on Ukrainian lines.

The next day, Volokhov texted me that Terra had managed to guide Ukrainian artillery to a Russian ammunition dump. He sent me video footage of explosions rocking a Russian outpost.

·❖·

Under Ukrainian law, the Kherson region is composed of forty-nine *hromadas*, the main unit of local governance, established by decentralization reforms launched after the 2014 revolution. In early August, only one of them was fully under Ukrainian control: the town of Kochubeivka and surrounding villages at the very north of the region. The Russians briefly occupied it in February and March but had since been pushed back a dozen or so miles to the south. Russian troops were distant enough for the municipality to resume operations, and even for a grocery store on Kochubeivka's main square to reopen.

The mayor, Ludmyla Kostiuk, greeted me with a gift of a real Kherson watermelon. She gave me a tour of the municipal building, its windows blocked by sandbags. The US Agency for International Development had refurbished the building as part of its support for Ukrainian reforms, as the vandalized plaque on the wall attested. "All evil is from them" was scribbled next to the words "United States," a memento left by Russian soldiers who stayed in the building during the town's brief occupation.

Kostiuk told me she was praying every morning for the liberation of Kherson's forty-eight other *hromadas*—but not at any price. "We want it to happen as soon as possible, but we are also patient and realistic," she said. "It's important that as many of our defenders as possible remain alive. And so we wait—and we don't just wait, we help."

ONE OF THE FEW AREAS WHERE UKRAINIAN FORCES HAD MANAGED A RECENT advance was seventeen miles east of Kochubeivka. There, at the very end of June, Ukrainian troops captured the village of Potemkine, named after Kherson's founder, Count Grigoriy Potemkin. A lover of Russia's empress, Catherine the Great, Potemkin had governed that part of Ukraine after Russia detached it from Ottoman Turkey in 1774—and erected the famously fake "Potemkin villages" to impress the empress during her tour of the newly acquired parts of the realm.

The Potemkine operation allowed the Ukrainians to threaten supply routes to the nearby town of Vysokopillia, a major stronghold occupied by

Russian airborne forces. The ruins of Potemkine were now subjected to withering Russian shelling, and the Ukrainian military told me they wouldn't let us travel there. Instead, I met with the commander of a battalion responsible for the area, Lieutenant Colonel Serhiy Shatalov, at his base in a nearby town.

A career officer, Shatalov joked that he tried not to visit forward positions too often. "You know, to be honest, we don't have that many battalion commanders who are still alive," he said. Most of his men, including company commanders, were mobilized civilians rather than professional soldiers.

The battle for Potemkine, home to some 400 people before the war, lasted three days, and was won in part thanks to artillery support by American-provided M777 howitzers, he said. "The enemy outnumbered us in everything: men, ammunition, armor. And from our side, to be frank, it was more about heroism than about professional skills." On the Ukrainian side, there were also serious losses.

Most of the villagers had already escaped, mostly to government-controlled areas. But some of those who had stayed behind assisted the Russians during the assault on Potemkine, passing information on Ukrainian troop locations, he said. "They were the lovers of the Russian world who wanted to live in it." Overall, Shatalov was disgusted by how most Ukrainian officials in the Kherson region had abandoned their responsibilities, a contrast to other parts of the country where mayors and governors galvanized resistance. "It was a complete failure here," he said, "unlike in Mykolaiv, where simple people had come out to fight, with their own hunting rifles."

For the broader Ukrainian plan to retake Kherson to be successful, Shatalov told me, Kyiv needed to gather a much larger force made up of fresh, well-equipped, and well-trained brigades. "People must understand, what a fantastic reserve needs to be accumulated for a rapid move into the depth of the enemy lines, crossing a hundred kilometers in a few days," he said. "We need maximum preparation. This counteroffensive must happen at the least favorable time for the enemy. We should first weaken it on all fronts, make a deceptive maneuver, and then score the main thrust."

It didn't seem like such a thrust was imminent.

———

ONE OF SHATALOV'S COMPANY COMMANDERS, SENIOR LIEUTENANT VI-
taliy, was responsible for holding Potemkine. A civilian before the war, Vitaliy reminisced wistfully about how he had spent a month relaxing in a
military hospital after getting wounded. He complained theatrically that a
Russian shell had hit his position in the village a few days earlier and damaged his favorite fleece jacket.

On his stretch of the front, Vitaliy noted, Ukrainian Himars attacks on
Russian supply lines hadn't caused any decrease in the intensity of Russian
shelling. Just during the previous day, one of his platoon outposts was hit by
120mm mortars 138 times, and nearly 90 times by howitzer rounds, he said.
This was comparable to the amount of shelling that the entire contact line
in Donbas was getting in a monthlong period before the February invasion.

"Over there, it wasn't a real war compared to what we have here now,"
he said. "They were just basking in the sun."

As Vitaliy was checking his weapons, getting ready to drive to Potemkine, I asked him how much longer he thought the Russians would be able
to remain in Vysokopillia. "In a month, they will be gone," he said. "And if
they get kicked out of Vysokopillia, they will have to roll back very far.
There isn't much else left here. There are villages, but these villages don't
have any houses anymore."

⊰⊹⊱

Shatalov was right. Ukraine needed to create and train new brigades,
fresh formations with tens of thousands of new soldiers. The United
States and its allies still resisted supplying Ukraine with Western-made
tanks and infantry fighting vehicles but had already started to ship armored
personnel carriers such as the Vietnam War–era workhorse the M113, and
its Dutch modification, the YPR-765. Poland, the Czech Republic, Slovakia,
and Slovenia provided hundreds of Soviet-designed tanks, mostly T-72s,
from their reserves. Ukraine's most critical shortfall was in training the
men and women who would fight in these new units.

Conducting training inside Ukraine was dangerous business. Russia regularly fired devastating cruise missiles at known Ukrainian military training facilities. In a rare acknowledgment of such losses, Zelensky said that one of these strikes on the Desna training grounds in northeastern Ukraine had killed at least eighty-seven soldiers in May. When Prime Minister Johnson visited Kyiv the following month, he announced that Ukrainian troops would now be schooled in basic infantry skills on British Army training grounds. British military instructors had trained some 22,000 Ukrainian personnel in the country over seven years before leaving in February 2022. Now the British Army was going to train 10,000 Ukrainian troops every six months, the first such large-scale program by Kyiv's allies. Others would follow suit.

One of the first Ukrainian units to join this training in the UK was the new incarnation of the 36th Marine Brigade. Almost all of its existing service members had been killed or taken prisoner in Mariupol, and so the brigade was restarting from scratch. Buntov, a reconnaissance officer who had fought against Wagner mercenaries in Lysychansk and Popasna, was put in charge of one of the battalions. When I visited him at the battalion's base in a village outside Mykolaiv in early August, half of his recruits were in England. The other half, most of them lacking any military experience, remained to be trained locally.

BUNTOV HAD UNEXPECTED ASSISTANCE. A GROUP OF AMERICAN, BRITISH, Canadian, and Israeli military veterans had banded together in Mykolaiv to school Ukrainian recruits, setting up ten-day courses for the 36th Brigade, two platoons at a time. On the first day of these drills, I watched as Steven Tomberlin, a retired police officer from Colorado, towered over the battalion's recruits at a firing range. Many had never handled a Kalashnikov rifle before.

The men, in mismatched uniforms and some lacking helmets, were supposed to wait for a command to open fire. Something got lost in translation and, one by one, they started squeezing the trigger, in no order. "Cease fire!" Tomberlin screamed at the top of his lungs. "Until I give the command. You. Do. Not. Do. Anything." Once he ordered firing to resume, most bullets hit the berm, missing the targets.

Motivation among these brand-new Marines varied wildly. Two men from the Khmelnytski region in central Ukraine seemed more interested in scrutinizing the ripe sunflower pods in the fields. "It's going to be a great harvest this year," the older of them said. They were both called Vova—shorthand for Volodymyr. "Like Zelensky?" I asked. "Like Zelensky and Putin, the two Vovas that got us into this crazy war," the older Vova replied.

"We're farmers, we're not really warriors," said the younger one, smiling. So far, he had survived a Russian missile strike on his barracks near Lviv and another in Mykolaiv, without seeing any other action. Both men had been rounded up in their village and sent to the military as part of the emergency mobilization. "Only the farm boys get drafted," the younger Vova complained. "Have you seen anyone from the big cities here?"

Others were far more eager to fight. Another Marine in the same platoon told me he had risked his life, crossing the front line from a Russian-occupied part of Kherson, so that he could join the Ukrainian military and liberate his hometown. His family was still there. Another man said he had been working, along with several other Ukrainian men, for a construction company in Croatia before the invasion. Like many of them, he volunteered to come back to Ukraine and join the military. Several of his friends from the Croatian construction site were already dead.

Buntov, the battalion commander, was a native of Kherson. Only recently had he managed to smuggle his own family from the city to government-controlled territory. "My motivation is ironclad," he said. "To liberate my home."

I noticed that one of his deputies, a Navy special forces diver who had been assigned to the reconstituted brigade, was wearing an unusual patch on his body armor. "I kill for Zelensky," it said. This was the first time I had spotted any reference to the Ukrainian president on the front lines, and the patch was clearly meant ironically. Zelensky may have become a symbol of the Ukrainian struggle around the world, but the men and women of the Ukrainian military were fighting for their homeland. If anyone was publicly admired on the front, it was Ukraine's top general, Zaluzhny, who hadn't appeared on TV since the war started. Stenciled portraits of him flashing a victory sign became increasingly frequent on the pockmarked walls of buildings on the battlefield.

———

THE WESTERN INSTRUCTORS WHO TRAINED THESE MARINES WERE PRIME targets for the Russians. After I first met some of them in Mykolaiv, a Russian Smerch missile struck near the home of the group's commander, retired US Army sergeant first class Bradley Crawford. He got away with light burns and some wood splinters in his rear. "The Russians, they sure don't like us being here," Crawford told me on the range, US and Ukrainian flags on his uniform.

Crawford had served in Iraq, while Tomberlin had trained Afghan special-operations forces. At the height of the battle for Severodonetsk and Lysychansk, Ukraine, a country with one-eighth of America's population, had more military fatalities every week than the US military had sustained in an entire year at the peak of either the Afghanistan or the Iraq war. Ukrainian Marines in the field around us were about to experience the kind of bloody, merciless combat that American troops hadn't seen in decades.

"In Afghanistan and Iraq, we did have dangers, but here we are sending these guys to full kinetic warfare, not some kind of counterinsurgency," Tomberlin said. Like many other American trainers, he had come to Ukraine because he was moved by images of destruction wrought by Russia and wanted to help. At sixty-two, he had cashed out his retirement fund to remain in Ukraine, hoping to increase his students' chances of staying alive.

I checked back on the training twice more, tagging along for a twenty-four-hour exercise in a forest where the two platoons practiced attacking and ambushing each other. Compared with the first day, the difference in how the men handled themselves and their weapons was obvious. So was the difference between the two units. Men in the first platoon, led by a Merchant Marine engineer from Odesa named Ihor who spoke fluent English, were energetic, thinking up unusual plans of attack. The second platoon, led by a mobilized reserve lieutenant who used to be an accountant in Donbas, was a mess, with some of the men openly challenging their commander. Unsurprisingly, the second platoon was routed in the exercise. "You're dead, you're dead, you're dead," Tomberlin told one Ukrainian Marine after another.

"If we have to go with these guys to Kherson, I want to embed with Ihor," I said, turning to Manu.

"For sure," he said. "If we embed with the other platoon, we'll be slaughtered."

⊰⊹⊱

On August 9, Russian tourists in the Crimean beachfront town of Saky were jolted by giant explosions. One after another, fireballs burst into the sky over the main Black Sea Fleet naval aviation base just behind the beach. Abandoning their seafront cabins, the tourists started to run in a panic. "Mama, Mama, we need to get the hell out of here!" one Russian woman yelled. The commotion was recorded in a video that Ukrainians would savor for weeks.

"No, this wooden cabin won't protect you. Let's go, before it's too late, Mama!" she screamed as a black mushroom cloud rose behind her, and then another. Nobody was hurt on the beach, but the air base was gone.

Ukraine had carried out daring attacks before—in Crimea and in adjoining parts of Russia, using drones to hit refineries and weapons depots—but this was something else. In one strike, Ukraine had wiped out a significant part of Russian naval airpower, its home airfield that was supposed to be well outside Kyiv's reach. Once the fire at the base was extinguished and commercial satellites circled above, imaging showed that at least eight aircraft, Su-24 tactical bombers and Su-30 multirole fighters, had been destroyed, and a few others damaged. The exact method of Ukraine's attack remained a mystery until Zaluzhny, a month later, acknowledged in passing that Kyiv had hit the Saky airfield with missiles.

No missiles with this kind of range had been known to be in Ukraine's possession. In underestimating the capacity of Ukraine's military industries, Russia had once again made the same mistake it had made with the cruiser *Moskva*, which now lay on the bottom of the Black Sea.

CHAPTER 35

MORE SHELLS
THAN STALINGRAD

The transfer of Russian forces to Kherson in July and August meant that the intensity of combat declined in most of Donbas. There was, however, one major exception: the city of Bakhmut. As Russian offensives petered out elsewhere, Putin's former chef Yevgeny Prigozhin and his Wagner private military company pursued a relentless attack on Bakhmut's defenses, sending in small groups of storm troops despite a level of casualties that would have made conventional military units disintegrate.

Prigozhin had grandiose plans to turn this private army into Russia's most important fighting force. A Wagner victory in Bakhmut could make him a key player in Russia's domestic politics, a national savior, perhaps even Putin's successor.

Between May and early July, Wagner had proven its mettle in the Luhansk region with the "Flower of Popasna" offensive that relied on its highly experienced cadre of mercenaries. High losses, however, meant that Prigozhin had to switch to a different business model. He spotted an exceptional opportunity in Russia's vast penitentiary system, with which he was intimately familiar. Hundreds of thousands of murderers, robbers, rapists, and other violent criminals languished in Russian prison camps, many of them facing decades-long sentences or life behind bars. Imprisoned in Soviet times for robbery and theft, Prigozhin was uniquely qualified to tap this manpower reservoir. Under a deal he worked out with Putin in the summer of 2022, prisoners willing to join Wagner in Ukraine would be pardoned and allowed to return to their homes if they survived for six months. A big if.

This arrangement became public in early August, after Nikita Mikhalkov, a film director and actor who had once won an Academy Award and the Grand Prix in Cannes, shared the story of the country's newest hero. Surrounded by Orthodox icons on his TV show, Mikhalkov, now one of Russia's most virulent war propagandists, recounted how Konstantin Tulinov, a twenty-six-year-old recidivist imprisoned on drug and robbery charges, had volunteered to redeem his sins by fighting in Ukraine. "He had many reasons to dislike the authorities, the country. It wasn't very affectionate between him and the state," Mikhalkov said in a soothing voice as melancholic music played in the background. "But he knew what to die for. He felt that he was needed over there." One of the first prisoners recruited by Wagner, Tulinov was killed in Donbas on July 14, just a few days after arriving in the war zone. Life expectancy for people like him was measured in days. That didn't matter. Tens of thousands more Russian convicts were about to pour toward the front line.

In mid-August, traveling to Bakhmut to report on Wagner's campaign to capture the city, I sent questions to Prigozhin. He was still coy about acknowledging his ownership of Wagner, claiming ignorance. Instead of providing answers on his private army, he wrote back mockingly, "If you have any information about it and are ready to share it, I would be very grateful, as other news organizations keep asking the same question." As for my question about whether he was visiting Russian prisons to recruit inmates, Prigozhin replied that he didn't just visit Russian prisons but had served a ten-year sentence in many of them. "Sadly, I do not recall the addresses of all the penal colonies where I have been," he added.

Less than a month later, Wagner leaked a video of one of Prigozhin's recruitment speeches to inmates, likely in the Mari El republic on the Volga. "The only two who can get you out of here are Allah and God, and even then, only in a wooden box," he told the assembled convicts. "I can take you out of here alive, though I can't always return you alive."

Those who attempted to desert or surrender would be executed on the spot, Prigozhin said—a remarkable promise given that Russia doesn't even have the death penalty. Other sins for which summary justice would be dispensed, he added, were the use of alcohol or drugs, looting, and "sexual contact with local women, flora, fauna, men, or anything else."

The first group of convict recruits, forty men plucked from a penal colony in Saint Petersburg, joined Wagner in June. Three of them were killed and seven wounded in their first skirmish, but the unit succeeded in taking a Ukrainian position and slaughtering its defenders. Now, Prigozhin added, Wagner possessed its own warplanes, rocket systems, tanks, and "everything else necessary to advance." Potential recruits had five minutes to decide whether they wanted to enlist.

"This war is trying, nothing like the Chechen war," he said. "My ammunition expenditure is roughly two and a half times higher than in Stalingrad."

❖

I watched the impact of Prigozhin's ammunition expenditure as we drove into Bakhmut on August 8. Rows of black smoke rose from the town of Soledar north of us, and from the eastern approaches to Bakhmut itself. Cluster munitions flew into a built-up area in the city center. The remains of Russian rockets and shells that had hit the neighborhood in previous days were piled up on the edge of a lawn outside the municipality. The city, home to 72,000 people before the war, was being wiped off the face of the earth, as had happened already to other cities of Donbas: Popasna, Mariupol, Volnovakha, Severodonetsk.

Known as Artemivsk in Soviet times, Bakhmut used to be one of the more pleasant towns of Donbas. In January, before the war started, Stevo and I had visited the giant underground winery where local sparkling wines were maturing in a network of former gypsum mines, using the *méthode champenoise*—Bakhmut's main claim to fame. We drank an excellent bottle of brut in one of Bakhmut's nicer restaurants.

By May, the winery and the restaurants had closed, but the city still had functioning hotels, a busy market, and a few fast-food and coffee outlets. In mid-August, the front line ran right across the winery compound. The hotel where we had stayed had been destroyed by a Russian airstrike. The city no longer had running water or electricity. Apart from a few dark grocery stores with erratic supplies, all the shops and offices had been boarded up.

We stayed at Bakhmut's central hospital, which had been turned into the Ukrainian military's field clinic. With all the civilian doctors and most nurses gone, it was operated by personnel from the three Ukrainian brigades defending the city and by the Hospitallers, a volunteer organization of medics that worked with the military, often in some of the most dangerous stretches of the front line.

The wounded—and sometimes the dead—were ferried to the hospital in military pickup trucks, regular civilian cars, ambulances, and, in one instance, special forces buggies. The medics usually had only a few minutes to prepare the operating table, immediately triaging the patients most in need of stabilization surgeries. Some had grotesque wounds—pieces of flesh ripped off their sides, bones sticking out. Others with just a concussion and a few cuts were told to sit and wait in a corner room. Nurses collected everyone's weapons and ammunition. None of these patients lingered long in Bakhmut because the facility could be shelled anytime. Once stabilized, the wounded soldiers and civilians were rushed to hospitals outside Russian artillery range.

I talked to a soldier in a striped T-shirt who had just arrived at the front line three days earlier. He had once served in the military, but most of his comrades had no experience and sought to flee the position within hours. "They are fucking us up real hard there," he said. "Real hard." A Russian munition that hit his trench in the morning, he said, sprayed his back with shrapnel. Luckily, most of the fragments were stopped by his body armor, with only a few causing non-life-threatening injuries. He was agitated, adrenaline still pumping through his veins, and licked his dry lips as he smoked. I asked him if he was thirsty or hungry. He nodded vigorously, and downed two cans of Coke, followed by two Mars bars, seconds after I handed them over.

Taken to the hospital minutes later, Yuri Vyshchepanko, a civilian patient, had been sheltering in his basement most of the day as his neighborhood of Bakhmut came under Russian fire. During a lull, he went up to his kitchen to get some water and to call his daughter to say that he was fine. That was when a Russian rocket punched through the ceiling and hit his kitchen. "Smoke everywhere, stink, darkness—we thought we're on fire," Vyshchepanko told me as he was treated for moderate burns and cuts. The rocket was faulty and didn't detonate. If it had, there wouldn't have been much left of him and his wife.

Another patient had been hit in the knee by a Russian cluster munition in what had seemed one of the safest areas—his vegetable patch, far from the front line. The man crawled through the field for an hour that morning until he was spotted by neighbors. Afraid of stepping on an explosive, they threw him a rope and pulled him out to hard ground. He got to the Bakhmut hospital just in time. One of the neighbors who called the ambulance, Valeriy, told me that he used to be a Putin fan before the war. "In January, I would have voted for Putin with both of my hands," Valeriy said. "Now, I just want to cut off every one of his fingers, one by one, slowly. So many people here have died because of what he has done."

Such loathing wasn't universal. An elderly woman who stood in a Bakhmut grocery line whispered that I should be careful. Some of the locals were gathering intelligence for the Russians, she said. "Those are the real scoundrels. In the morning, they come and get welfare payments from the Ukrainian state, and in the evening they guide Russian fire onto the city."

Bakhmut was a city of heartbreak. Some of those fleeing it now were escaping the Russians for the third time. One family had already fled their home in Horlivka in 2014, in what had become part of the Donetsk "people's republic," to a suburb of Lysychansk. They had moved to Bakhmut after Lysychansk's fall in July. The parents were staying behind, for now, while their daughter and her small child were departing on a bus to Dnipro. "Tanya, please make sure to call!" her mother called out as the bus began to pull away from Bakhmut's main square. "Mama, Mama, don't cry!" the daughter shouted back. Her father hugged his wife, wiping off his own tears as he led her away. Minutes later, Russian shells landed with a thump near the square, and everyone scurried away. Doctors would be busy again soon.

PART 8

LIBERATION

CHAPTER 36

INTO THE STEPPES
OF KHERSON

Offensive operations are more difficult than defense in any terrain. The flat, boundless steppes of southern Ukraine are particularly challenging, especially when attacking an adversary that possesses superior firepower and can operate tactical aircraft. Unlike in northern Ukraine, where forests, hills, and ravines can provide cover and concealment, movement can be spotted from long distances in the Kherson countryside. Any wooded strips between fields are sparse and narrow. Soldiers trying to move ahead have nowhere to hide from artillery, fighter-bombers, and helicopter gunships before crossing the steppe and battling their way into the next village. In these villages, troops can weather bombardments in basements and vehicles can be hidden in courtyards, shielded from drones by tree foliage, at least for a while. Weeks of artillery barrages would destroy much of that shelter, too.

In the first weeks of the war, the Russian Air Force had enjoyed air superiority in this part of the country, an advantage that allowed Russian ground troops to swiftly move forward. At the end of August, as Kyiv began its long-anticipated offensive to retake Kherson, neither side had control of the skies and Ukrainian troops couldn't rely on air cover. In the villages of Kherson, some of Russia's best-trained forces, redeployed from Donbas, were ready and waiting behind concrete fortifications erected during the summer. Adding to the complexity of Ukraine's effort was the Inhulets River, which presented a natural obstacle to any advance in many parts of the region.

As the Ukrainian military prepared for the push, Kherson partisans continued providing intelligence to Himars teams striking the region. They also kept assassinating senior collaborators. On August 28, Oleksiy Kovalyov, a Ukrainian parliament member from Zelensky's party who had joined the Russian administration and survived a car bombing in June, was gunned down by assailants in his home near Kherson. Later that night, Ukrainian units comprising infantry, tanks, and armored vehicles began a major offensive from four different directions, pushing south all along the Kherson front line. Military engineers established pontoons over the Inhulets, allowing these forces to cross the river. The Ukrainian push failed to make much headway in most areas, as Russian artillery annihilated the advancing columns. But the Ukrainian military punched through Russian defenses in the central part of the front, taking the village of Sukhyi Stavok across the Inhulets. Ukraine also gained more terrain between Potemkine and Vysokopillia in the northeast of the front. Ukrainian casualties were high, and it wasn't the kind of rapid breakthrough that Ukrainian commanders desired. The operation, however, started to put pressure on Russian forces.

The night of August 29, after the first full day of the Kherson offensive, Zelensky steered clear of specifics in his public address. "Some people want to know what our plans are. You won't hear any concrete details," he said. "Ukraine is reclaiming what belongs to it, and will keep doing that . . . If the Russian soldiers want to survive, it's time for them to flee."

The next day, the Russian ministry of defense reported triumphantly that the attempted Ukrainian offensive had failed completely, and that the remaining Ukrainian troops in Sukhyi Stavok were being eliminated. The deputy head of the occupation administration, Kirill Stremousov, went on TV to crow about Ukrainian losses and forecast that the "utopian" Ukrainian attempt to advance would turn into a lightning-fast Russian counterstrike. "Maybe it was all a trap for the Nazis?" he mused on August 30. "I think we will see a liberated Mykolaiv soon . . . Russia is in the liberated territories forever."

The Ukrainian military, for the first time since the war began, imposed a tight information blackout on its Kherson operations, barring media access to the front lines. The only news came from military hospitals, which overflowed with maimed soldiers. "When they started to bring in such a large number of wounded, then, honestly, I felt sorry for them and started wondering if this was worth doing at such a cost," the head of an intensive care unit in a Mykolaiv hospital told one of my colleagues. "I don't know. There is no right answer here."

❖

With the Kherson offensive under way, Zaluzhny and another Ukrainian general, Mykhailo Zabrodsky, who also served as a lawmaker, published a lengthy article outlining Ukraine's long-term military strategy. Even a sweeping Ukrainian military victory on the ground in the coming months, including the liberation of Crimea, wouldn't end the war, they warned, because of the fundamental disparity in long-range firepower. Russia had the ability to strike anywhere in Ukraine with cruise missiles while Ukraine lacked long-range weapons to hit back.

The real center of gravity in the conflict lies in the fact that most Russians perceive the war as remote, Zaluzhny and Lieutenant General Zabrodsky wrote. "Because of that remoteness, Russian Federation citizens don't feel so much pain about the losses, the failures and most importantly the cost of this war . . . In simple words, the issue is the impunity that is ensured by physical distance." To win the war, the two generals added, Ukraine needed to affect the lives of everyday Russians.

That would take only three more weeks.

CHAPTER 37

THE KHARKIV BREAKTHROUGH

With attention focused on the Kherson front line during the first week of September, Ukrainian units started to gather near the town of Balakliya, south of Kharkiv. The front line in the area had remained stable for months, except for artillery exchanges that had gradually—but, so far, invisibly—eroded Russian combat power. The Russians had seized this town of 30,000 people in the initial days of the war because of its vast, fortified Soviet-era ammunition depots. In 2017, a large part of that storage facility holding 122mm and 152mm artillery shells had caught fire and exploded, in what Ukrainian authorities said was a Russian sabotage operation. Hundreds of buildings in Balakliya had been damaged in the blast, and Ukraine had lost a large part of the ammunition reserves it would desperately need five years later.

In late August, most professional Russian units from that stretch of the front line had been sent to Kherson. Only mobilized reservists from the Luhansk and Donetsk "people's republics" and volunteer Russian units, known as BARS, manned the forward positions. Chronic corruption in the Russian military meant that Russian generals overseeing that part of Ukraine had been deceived about the strength of their forces, some Russian officers acknowledged later.

Oleksandr Syrsky, the head of Ukrainian Ground Forces who oversaw the planned Kharkiv offensive, and other Ukrainian commanders carefully examined the Kharkiv front line and concluded that this was the most vulnerable spot—between large Russian troop concentrations in Izyum to the south and along the Russian border and Kharkiv city to the north.

Despite the media blackout, the gradual arrival of Ukrainian reinforcements in Balakliya wasn't a complete secret. Russian military bloggers and analysts wrote about the units that poured into the Kharkiv front line during the first week of September. But the Russian high command, preoccupied with defending Kherson, didn't seem to be paying attention.

In the occupied Kharkiv region, just as in Kherson and Zaporizhzhia months earlier, Russian authorities had adopted a policy of fully absorbing the conquered areas into Russia. They appointed as governor Vitaliy Ganchev, a former Ukrainian police officer who had fled to the Russian-occupied Donbas in 2014. In a meeting with hospital staff in the occupied town of Shevchenkove on August 23, Ganchev exuded confidence in the permanence of Russian rule as he demanded that the doctors and nurses sign up for the Russian health system. "You still hope that the Ukrainians will come back? No, they will never come back," Ganchev said, according to those present. "In a month, we will all be in Kharkiv city."

Indeed, a new Russian military formation, the 3rd Army Corps, had started preparing for another offensive on Kharkiv. On September 1, the beginning of the Russian school year, a handful of schools reopened under the Russian flag in the occupied parts of the region, though most teachers and parents stayed away. The headquarters of the occupation authorities in Kupyansk, the de facto capital of the Russian-held part of the region, was packed with freshly imported Russian schoolbooks and teaching materials.

As six elementary school students gathered for the cameras under Russian flags in Kupyansk, Russian poet Anna Dolgareva delivered the back-to-school address. A Kharkiv native and the former wife of a pro-Russian sniper in Donbas, Dolgareva had become a star with Russian nationalists. By her own admission, she also no longer talked to her brother, who had sided with Ukraine. She recited a poem by Anna Akhmatova, the canonical Odesa-born twentieth-century Russian author, about how it was worth getting killed by a bullet to maintain the great Russian language. "You, kids, will be the ones who will carry forward the Russian word," she told the six children, who blinked, uncomprehending. The remaining part of the Kharkiv region would hopefully be "freed" soon, she added.

The first of a series of Ukrainian Himars strikes hit Kupyansk that day, leveling the compound that housed Russia's FSB intelligence service.

✣

Before dawn on September 6, Ukrainian troops started to probe Russian defenses northwest of Balakliya. There wasn't much resistance. Undertrained and underequipped conscripts from Donetsk and Luhansk had been on the front lines since February, many of them suffering from chronic diseases. Their sky-high casualty rates had sapped morale, and many of the draftees were posting videos complaining about the conditions and demanding to be sent home. With so many dead or missing in action, their mothers, sisters, and wives were posting separate group videos of their own, asking commanders about their loved ones. These soldiers were not in a mood to fight.

Unlike the much-advertised Kherson offensive, the attack on Balakliya had been shrouded in secrecy. The Ukrainian military banned journalists from the area and made no statements of its own.

Late in the afternoon of September 6, the first reports that something had gone terribly wrong for the Russians came from Russian military bloggers and *voenkors* on Telegram. Photos taken by locals and posted on social media showed a Ukrainian BTR in the suburb of Verbivka northwest of Balakliya. Russia's ministry of defense maintained strict silence, but Ganchev, the Russian-appointed governor, issued reassurances that Balakliya remained, and would forever remain, in Russian hands. "Don't succumb to panic. Don't read lying posts. Don't pollute your brain," he urged.

Balakliya was still in Russian hands that night, but only because Ukrainian commanders had far more ambitious goals. Instead of getting bogged down in battles over every village and every town, they were about to execute the kind of rapid maneuver warfare that Russia had botched at the start of the war.

On the evening of September 6, in the town of Shevchenkove, more than twenty miles northeast of Balakliya, some seventy battered Russian troops took over the local civilian hospital, bringing in their wounded. For the hospital's acting director, Natalia Nesvoyeva, this was the first sign that something unusual was happening. The Russians, who had fled from the Balakliya area, seemed intent on staying awhile, asking Nesvoyeva to show them the basement shelters. A Russian woman showed up in the hospital that night. She had come to the area to visit her husband, a soldier with that unit, and was frantically asking about his whereabouts. The troops had bad news. "He's not here, which means that he's been left behind over there," one of the soldiers told the woman. "He's gone."

When Nesvoyeva woke up the next morning, the Russians had already abandoned the hospital. A few hours later, she spotted a Ukrainian patrol carefully moving just outside the fence. "You can't imagine the joy, the euphoria we all felt when we walked out and suddenly saw that our boys are back here, with our own flags," she recalled.

Ukrainian troops that bypassed Balakliya were fanning out rapidly through the Kharkiv countryside, moving through forests and popping up on key routes that the Russians had still considered safe. The 80th Brigade under Ihor Skybiuk managed to stealthily move into the Russian rear near Izyum. "We were their fata morgana," he recalled. "The enemy just didn't understand what was happening."

One after another, Russian convoys that believed themselves to be in safe areas were ambushed. One video posted on September 7 showed a captured Russian lieutenant colonel kneeling on the roadside as Ukrainian troops with blue armbands stood around, enjoying the spectacle.

The entire Russian front line was crumbling. Panicked Russian units retreated chaotically, often leaving their tanks and artillery pieces behind. Professional Russian troops were frequently the first to escape, leaving the draftees from Donetsk and Luhansk to fend for themselves.

Asked about the developments on September 7, Putin denied that anything untoward was afoot. "We haven't lost anything and we won't lose anything," he said. "As for gains, I can say that the main gain is the strengthening of our sovereignty."

The Russian military still maintained a sizable force in the Kharkiv region. At least a dozen battalion tactical groups had been stationed in Izyum, the headquarters of the 1st Tank Army, with more than adequate stocks of ammunition and heavy weapons. But a Ukrainian Himars strike on Russian headquarters in the first hours of the offensive had wiped out a large part of their command, disrupting the Russians' ability to coordinate their forces and magnifying the chaos on the battlefield.

On September 8, Ukraine finally acknowledged the Kharkiv operation. By then, Ukrainian forces had advanced nearly thirty miles into Russian-held areas, liberating more than twenty towns and villages, the Ukrainian General Staff reported. At 4 p.m. that day, Lieutenant Colonel Vito, the deputy commander of the Kraken unit from Kharkiv, raised the Ukrainian banner above the municipality of Balakliya. "The order has been executed," he said in a recording addressed to Zelensky, a Russian flag under his boots. In the city itself, Ukrainian forces started peeling off giant billboard signs that proclaimed, "Together with Russia—Forever."

Ganchev recorded a statement that day, standing by the roadside next to a car with a running engine, anxiety in his eyes. Civilians, he said, should be evacuating Kupyansk: "Today, I don't see any other solution, if only to save our children." He and other senior collaborators were already on the way to Russia, fearing retribution. A few who hadn't managed to escape were already being rounded up by advancing Ukrainian forces.

⋯

The following morning, on September 9, Ukrainian soldiers reached the entrance to Kupyansk. Their initial plan was to push as far as the city, not to storm it. But with the Russian defenses collapsing, the way into the capital of the occupied part of Kharkiv was open. Realizing the huge opportunity provided by the Balakliya breakthrough, Zaluzhny and Syrsky started to send additional forces to the Kharkiv region. While the Russians needed circuitous routes around Ukraine to move troops from Kherson to Kharkiv, Ukraine's road and rail infrastructure allowed reinforcements to arrive in a matter of hours.

By the morning of September 10, the predicament for Russian forces had become catastrophic. Overnight, Ukrainian troops seized the western side of Kupyansk, with Russian troops retreating to the eastern bank of the

Oskil River and blowing up the only bridge connecting the two shores. Russia's ministry of defense that day released videos of what it said were Russian reinforcement columns rushing to Kupyansk, tanks and trucks that were painted with a circle inside a triangle—the logo of the vaunted 3rd Corps. Another recording showed military vehicles driving across a field and being loaded into helicopters, ostensibly also on the way to Kupyansk. Open-source intelligence analysts quickly discovered that the footage showed the same vehicles being unloaded from the choppers. It was all for show.

One viral video shot by Russian troops on September 10 illustrated what had really happened to the promised 3rd Corps reinforcements. Sitting in an infantry fighting vehicle as it sped away from the eastern entrance to Kupyansk, a soldier cursed that "we've barely had time to fuck off" as Ukrainian shells exploded behind him. The remainder of his column had been destroyed.

Pushing south, Ukrainian soldiers from the 80th Brigade reached the northern edge of Izyum. The huge Russian grouping in the city had only one supply—and escape—route left, to the east via a pontoon crossing over the Oskil, which was vulnerable to Ukrainian Himars and artillery attacks. Anticipating a Russian rout, Ukrainian social media bloomed with memes depicting Zaluzhny cooking raisins—the meaning of Izyum in Ukrainian—in a giant cauldron.

Russia's ministry of defense ordered Izyum to be abandoned. "In order to achieve the declared goals of the special military operation to liberate Donbas, it has been decided to regroup Russian forces in the Balakliya and Izyum areas to strengthen efforts in the Donbas direction," the ministry said, claiming that Russian forces had killed 2,000 Ukrainian and mercenary troops in the previous three days. "Regroup" was a euphemism for withdraw.

Igor Girkin, the former Donetsk "people's republic" minister of defense, was apoplectic. "If you have to characterize the situation with an analogy to the Russian-Japanese war, only one word comes to mind—MUKDEN," he wrote, referring to the 1905 battle in the Chinese city of Shenyang, formerly known as Mukden, in which Japan routed Russia's land forces, a prelude to Russia's overall defeat. Russia had considered Japan an inferior opponent.

As the Russian Empire's hawkish interior minister Vyacheslav von Plehve had put it at the time, Russia needed "a little victorious war" with Japan to distract from political tensions at home. Plehve himself didn't witness the consequences of his warmongering: he was killed by a leftist assassin in 1904. That "little victorious war" had led to the collapse of the Russian Empire—and the proclamation of an independent Ukraine thirteen years later.

BY THE AFTERNOON OF SEPTEMBER 10, UKRAINIAN UNITS THAT HAD BEEN fighting on the Izyum front line since the spring broke through Russian lines and attacked the city from the south, ascending the Kremyanets mountain with its giant ancestral stone *babas*. The Carpathian Sich battalion had finally left the flattened ruins of the village of Virnipollia. As most of the battalion headed to Izyum, some of the troops were left behind to control a road in the village of Topolske some four miles to the southwest.

It was already dark when a Carpathian Sich soldier going by the call sign Simpson heard the roar of an approaching infantry fighting vehicle, which he assumed to be Ukrainian.

The BMP-2 stopped at his improvised checkpoint. One of the soldiers in it shouted over the din of the running engine, asking, "Where is everyone else?" He spoke Russian, but so did many Ukrainian soldiers.

"In Izyum," Simpson said, shrugging.

"Where are we exactly?" the soldier inquired.

"Topolske," Simpson said. That was when he noticed that the soldiers' helmet covers looked different.

"Which brigade are you from, guys?" he asked them.

"The 423rd."

There was no such brigade in the Ukrainian Army. The 423rd Motor Rifle Regiment was part of the Russian Army's 4th Kantemirov Tank Division that Carpathian Sich had been battling for months.

Simpson shot his Kalashnikov in the air as fellow Ukrainian soldiers rushed toward the checkpoint. "Get the fuck down on the ground!" he screamed at the Russian troops in the BMP. He recalled the words of Vitaliy Kim, the governor of Mykolaiv. "All summer," he said, "I had been dreaming to have such an occasion to say it."

"Good evening, we are from Ukraine!" he roared at the Russians.

Their eyes widening, the men surrendered and asked if they could smoke. Only if you have your own cigarettes, Simpson told them. The battered pack of cigarettes in his pocket had come from Ukrainian volunteers who risked their lives under Russian artillery fire to deliver supplies to the front line. It would have been disrespectful to share these smokes with the Russians.

Many other Russian troops fleeing Izyum didn't make it out alive. Ukrainian Himars strikes hit retreating Russian columns east of the Oskil River, destroying dozens of tanks, trucks, and artillery pieces. One tank crew with Russia's newest T-90 was so desperate to escape the kill zone that it missed the pontoon, toppling into the fast-flowing river, only its gun sticking up above the water.

Inside Izyum, Ukrainian forces found abundant weapons and ammunition depots. Some of the equipment had been damaged, but there were also brand-new tanks and BMPs, their gas tanks full and their guns loaded. In the pine forests on the edge of the city, the advancing Ukrainian forces also discovered hundreds of mass graves. Some of the bodies had their hands tied behind their backs, executed in cold blood. Bucha hadn't been an exception.

❖

The collapse of the Russian military wasn't limited to the Kupyansk and Izyum areas. On September 10, Russian troops also began fleeing from the northern part of the Kharkiv region, the strategic terrain between the city and the Russian border, an area that wasn't under any threat of encirclement by Ukraine. On September 11, Vsevolod Kozhemiako and his Khartiya soldiers reached the frontier. The entrepreneur turned commander stepped a few yards onto enemy land, recording a message from Russian soil.

"This is the land of the *katsaps*, and this is the crossing point of the international border, and that, on the other side, is the Ukrainian flag that Khartiya has restored," he said. The Russian tricolor was already in the mud, by the concrete roadblock. "This is where that flag is supposed to be,"

Kozhemiako added. "Shut it down," he shouted at one of his men, who ran to lower the boom barrier. "And turn the stop sign their way, so they can see it!" Kozhemiako later told me he had been mildly reprimanded for his unauthorized invasion of Russia.

By September 14, Izyum was so far in the rear that Zelensky, accompanied by Syrsky, was able to visit the city. "You can occupy the territories of our state, but you can't occupy our people," he said in a speech on the city's main square, with not a single building left undamaged. Soldiers then raised a large Ukrainian flag on the mast in front of the bombed-out municipality. Zelensky and the soldiers mouthed the words of the national anthem.

> *Our enemies will vanish,*
> *Like dew at sunrise,*
> *And we, oh brothers, will become the masters once again*
> *Of our own land.*

Ukraine wasn't advancing just in the Kharkiv region. Ukrainian forces in mid-September also managed to inch ahead in Kherson, finally taking the town of Vysokopillia near Potemkine. They also began to attack Russian positions in the Donetsk region, north of Slovyansk.

Impotent on the battlefield, Russia lashed out against Ukrainian infrastructure. On September 11, Russia fired missiles at power stations in Kharkiv and Dnipro, disrupting electrical supplies in large parts of eastern Ukraine. These were the first of many such strikes against the country's electricity generation and distribution network. The Russians also fired cruise missiles to destroy a dam in Kryvyi Rih, flooding parts of the city to raise the water level of the Inhulets River and wash away Ukrainian pontoon crossings downstream in Kherson.

While Russian propagandists gloated, anticipating how Ukraine would be plunged into nationwide blackouts, Zelensky addressed the Russian enemy with defiance. "Read my lips. Without gas or without you? Without you. Without electricity or without you? Without you. Without water or without you? Without you. Without food or without you? Without you. Cold, hunger, darkness, thirst—none of that is as scary and lethal to us as your 'friendship and brotherhood,'" he told Russians in his September 11 address. "History will put everything in its place. And we will end up with gas, electricity, water, and food—and without you."

The Russian plan that week was to regroup and stabilize the front line along the defensible natural barriers, the Oskil and Siversky Donets rivers. But Ukraine had different aims. The Kharkiv offensive was going to continue—beyond Kharkiv.

CHAPTER 38

MOBILIZATION
AND ANNEXATION

The footage of Zelensky's triumphant visit to Izyum caused uproar and recriminations in Russia, denting Putin's carefully cultivated image of strength. Moscow's late March withdrawals from Kyiv and northern Ukraine had been spun as a goodwill gesture to further peace negotiations. But what had happened in Balakliya, Kupyansk, and Izyum exceeded even Russian TV's unmatched ability to manipulate public opinion. Putin's decision to participate in extravagant Moscow Day celebrations on September 10, opening a new Ferris wheel just as the Russian Army was collapsing, stirred so much criticism from the nationalist right that one Russian city after another canceled their own public festivities in the following days. Something had to be done, and Russian hawks were clamoring for a fierce response.

> "The darkest night comes before dawn,
>   The darkest night is already here,"

wrote Dolgareva, the poet who just two weeks earlier had opened the Russian school in Kupyansk.

THROUGHOUT THE SUMMER, RUSSIAN AUTHORITIES HAD BEEN MULLING plans to formally annex the two "people's republics" of Donbas, as well as other captured regions. Occupation officials there were slowly laying the groundwork for sham referendums on joining Russia, similar to the vote that Moscow had organized in occupied Crimea in 2014. These plans, however, kept being postponed because of one important problem: none of these Ukrainian regions except for Luhansk were under full Russian control. There are few examples in history of a nation formally annexing a land that it doesn't occupy.

As recently as on September 5, Kherson's Russian-appointed deputy governor Stremousov, who by now wore uniforms with his chosen call sign, Stalin, declared that referendum preparations had been put on hold because of the Ukrainian offensive.

On September 20, the Kremlin suddenly changed course. The Russian-appointed leaders of the occupied parts of the Donetsk, Luhansk, Zaporizhzhia, and Kherson regions (there wasn't much of Russian-occupied Kharkiv left anymore) announced that they would hold referendums on joining Russia. "The biggest desire of the people of Donbas is to become part of the Russian Federation. That is why we are absolutely certain about the referendum's outcome," said the head of the Donetsk "people's republic," Denis Pushilin. He certainly had no reason to doubt the result. The snap vote in all four regions was to be held only three days later, obviously without any right to campaign against the annexation or any ability to independently verify the results. Boycotting also wouldn't be an option: election officials, accompanied by Russian soldiers, were ordered to go with the ballot boxes from apartment to apartment. These referendums were to be held, literally, at gunpoint.

The next day, a stern-faced Putin delivered his speech to the nation. Russia had an obligation to the five million people living under its rule in what used to be Ukraine, and would accept them into the motherland's fold, he pledged: "We don't have the moral right to let butchers tear to pieces the people who are close to us, we cannot fail to respond to their sincere desire to determine their own fate."

Once these new territories formally became part of Russia, the rules of the game would change, Putin cautioned—a reminder of Moscow's nuclear weapons. "In case of a threat to the territorial integrity of our nation, to defend Russia and our people, we will, without a question, use all the means available to us," he warned. "This is not a bluff."

Then came the most important announcement. The war, he said, was no longer just against the regime of Ukraine but against "the entire military machine of the collective West." To win, Russia needed more troops. At least three hundred thousand more.

On that same day, September 21, Russian recruitment offices throughout the country started rounding up men and shipping them to military camps. Despite promises of thorough training, some of these recruits ended up on the front lines just days later. Soon, body bags started traveling in the other direction, toward their hometowns. Hundreds of thousands of Russian men stampeded to flee the country through the few available exit routes. Daylong lines formed overnight on the mountainous border crossing into Georgia, so Russian authorities eventually established a mobile recruitment office to press-gang fugitives on the spot. Flights to the few international destinations still linked with Russia sold out in a matter of hours. On September 22, the cheapest one-way economy ticket from Moscow to Dubai cost nearly $8,000.

The average Russian was feeling the consequences of the war.

❖

American fears of a Russian nuclear escalation reached their highest point that week. According to US intelligence estimates, Putin was likely to consider a nuclear strike under three scenarios. One was a major attack on Russia proper, especially with NATO involvement. Another was the possibility of losing physical control over Crimea. And the third, according to a senior Pentagon official, was a Ukrainian battlefield victory "that would completely and totally shatter the Russian military, such that the Russian state would sense an existential threat."

Crumbling in Kharkiv and Kherson, the Russian military now seemed on the verge of such a collapse—a consideration that tempered American assistance to Kyiv.

On September 25, Biden's national security adviser, Jake Sullivan, went on American TV networks to make public the warnings that Washington had already relayed to Moscow. "We have communicated directly, privately, to the Russians at very high levels that there will be catastrophic consequences for Russia if they use nuclear weapons in Ukraine," Sullivan said. "We have been clear with them, and emphatic with them, that the United States will respond decisively alongside our allies and partners. They well understand what they would face if they went down that dark road."

❖

Kyrylo Berkal and other Ukrainian prisoners on death row in Donetsk had only one source of news: Russian state TV that blared into their cells. The power of the Russian propaganda stunned him. "If I had been a slightly simpler man, I would have started to hate myself, too. All the Ukrainians are Nazis, every Ukrainian rocket and bullet kills an old lady and a child, and every Russian missile destroys a thousand Ukrainian war criminals," he said. "And the worst thing was that the prison staff genuinely believed all that."

Authorities in Donetsk had already built special cages in which they planned to display Azov prisoners for a much-anticipated trial. The verdicts were a foregone conclusion after the three foreign-born Ukrainian Marines— two Brits and one Moroccan—were sentenced to death in July. They were held in the same Donetsk facility.

When the Kharkiv offensive began on September 6, Russian TV propagandists suddenly turned on each other in a bout of recriminations. The news channel was abruptly disabled. From then on, the TV set just blared Russian pop music. "That's how we understood that our troops had achieved success," Berkal recalled.

Almost two weeks later, he was pulled out of his cell and taken to a holding room with some thirty other senior Azov commanders and fighters. They were blindfolded, tied to each other, and packed into trucks that bounced on roads for a day and a half, destination unknown. The men, many of whom were seriously injured, weren't allowed to leave the vehicles. Berkal almost suffocated. His hands remained numb for months afterward because of how tightly his wrists had been tied. On day two, the Ukrainian POWs were transferred onto a Russian military plane. Once they landed a few hours later, they heard a different accent. They were in Belarus, and soon would be headed down the highway to the Ukrainian border.

It was only after a Ukrainian intelligence officer stepped onto their bus, greeting the men with a loud "Glory to Ukraine," that Berkal allowed himself to believe that he was indeed returning to freedom. "This was," he told me over cappuccino in a Kyiv café, "the biggest euphoria of my life."

THE SEPTEMBER 21 PRISONER EXCHANGE WAS ONE OF THE LARGEST IN THE entire war so far, a complex swap mediated by Turkey, Saudi Arabia, and the United Arab Emirates. Under the deal, Viktor Medvedchuk, the pro-Russian politician, and fifty-five Russian POWs, including senior Russian officers just captured in the Kharkiv offensive, were handed over to Moscow. Ukraine secured the release of 215 POWs, most of them from Azovstal and half of them members of the Azov Regiment. Ten foreigners who had fought for Ukraine, including the three already sentenced to death, were included in the swap. Russia also released the legendary commanders of the resistance at Azovstal—Denys Prokopenko and Svyatoslav Palamar from Azov, and Serhiy Volynski from the 36th Brigade. Moscow's condition was that they would have to spend the rest of the war in Turkey, but Ankara sent them home nine months later.

"We thank you and your entire team for what you have done," Prokopenko told Zelensky over video link from Turkey after GUR chief Budanov reported on the release. The Ukrainian president audibly gasped as he saw how gaunt and tired the men were after months in Russian captivity. Volynski, he remarked, had become impossible to recognize.

"I thank *you* for what you have done, and for what you will do for Ukraine in the future. We will celebrate victory together," Zelensky said.

A new wave of outrage poured from Moscow, both over the liberation of Azov's commanders and the fact that they had been swapped on the very day when Putin announced the unpopular mobilization decree. "You know how it looks? Like this: you come out to the Russian people, ask them to defend Russian land, and then . . . shit on the head of those who have responded to the call," fumed Igor Girkin. "Openly, mockingly, with laughter and jokes."

CHAPTER 39

EAST OF OSKIL

The big square in front of the Kupyansk municipality was empty when I arrived on September 22, except for two Ukrainian troopers who ran from building to building to evade any Russian snipers, making sure there were no infiltrators in the neighborhood. Several Russian flags and the red, blue, and pink banners of the Russian occupation administration for Kharkiv were scattered in the dirt, some half-burned.

A billboard with the words "We are a single people with Russia!" in the colors of the Russian flag was still hanging on the building's facade, on a plaza overlooking the Oskil River. The Russians had hoped to stabilize the front line on the river's opposite bank, but the Ukrainians had already established a pontoon crossing and started pouring tanks and armored personnel carriers across the river. They clearly weren't deterred by Putin's nuclear threats. The offensive continued.

For the first time, I saw Ukraine's International Legion, which was fighting on this stretch of the front. They rolled up in several pickup trucks to the only bridge over the Oskil in the city, a structure that the Russians had repainted in their country's colors before trying to destroy it. One of the road's sections was missing, but the bridge remained passable on foot. As the Legionnaires pushed into eastern Kupyansk, Manu and I ran behind them.

We advanced around the remains of burned-out Russian tanks and armored vehicles, past the anti-Russian graffiti that testified to local Ukrainian resistance, and past the bloated remains of a Russian soldier. He was lying in a pool of dirty water under a billboard advertising a Ukrainian fish processing company that proclaimed, "We value everyone, we work with the best!"

The previous day, the Legionnaires told me, they had captured one of the tallest buildings in eastern Kupyansk, a grain elevator that provided valuable firing positions for the Russians. The soldiers, commanded by a Ukrainian officer, said they had expected a fierce firefight, but the enemy was gone by the time they arrived. "They just ran away," said one of the team leaders, a Latvian soldier with the call sign Ulvis. "They know they are finished here."

I asked one of the Legionnaires, a Tennessean medic who went by the call sign Doc, why he had decided to come fight for Ukraine. He told me it was the images of destruction wrought by Russia that he had seen in the media. "Everybody saw these pictures. For me, it wasn't a choice, really. If I didn't do this, I would have hated myself," he replied. "I just don't like fascists and I don't like people raping and murdering."

Past the intersection farther ahead, there were abundant signs of a Russian rout. A white truck with Russian "Z" markings spray-painted on the sides in orange sat in the middle of the road, its windows shot out and two corpses spilling out from the cabin. A tank with a lollipopped turret smoldered nearby alongside a stack of carbonized cadavers. The Russians were fleeing in chaos, without realizing how close the enemy was. I took a photo with the squad of Legionnaires. Within a few weeks, some of these men were killed.

AS THE LEGION'S SOLDIERS PREPARED FOR ANOTHER ATTACK, I WALKED BACK through a side street, trying to speak to some locals. Kostyantyn Zdorikov, a former Ukrainian border force officer, was eager for some news. For weeks, there had been neither phone service nor electricity in Kupyansk. When he first saw the Russian columns enter the city in February, he admitted, he had lost all hope. "For three days, they were rolling through without a stop.

Thousands of tanks, all these new vehicles I had never seen before. At the time, the Russians seemed invincible," he said. "I'm not going to lie, I couldn't believe that Ukraine would ever be able to overcome all that. That is why so many people here collaborated, so many kowtowed and bowed to the Russians."

The Russian rule wasn't as harsh in Kupyansk as it was in, for example, Bucha, he said. The retirees and the employees of the local hospital and other public services working under the Russians had received one-off payments of 10,000 Russian rubles (roughly $150). Zdorikov went unpaid through the seven months of occupation. But, he added, he hadn't been mistreated.

The real trouble began once the Ukrainian forces entered Kupyansk and Russian artillery began indiscriminately shelling the city from the east. "That's when the Russians have shown us their true face, firing at random, without any regard," Zdorikov said. One Russian shell had fallen the previous night on the street just outside Zdorikov's home. Another, two days earlier, killed his twenty-four-year-old neighbor, Bohdan Kostenko.

"The lower part of his body was intact—but the head, there was nothing left anymore," Kostenko's father, Oleh, explained to me matter-of-factly, still processing his grief. Bohdan used to be a soldier, and in 2019 his father had traveled to Kyiv for the ceremony of his son taking the oath. Petro Poroshenko, then still president, attended the event and read out Bohdan's name to the assembled crowd. It was the third on the list, Oleh recalled with pride.

"My son had taken an oath to serve in the Armed Forces and to defend Ukraine, but when the Russians came here, there was nothing to stop them. Everyone had run away." Tears appeared in Oleh's eyes. "Just a horde of tanks showed. We were abandoned to ourselves. No weapons, no help. We tried. But how were we supposed to fight? With pitchforks?"

I asked Oleh if he, too, had lost faith in Ukraine's return to Kupyansk.

"No." He straightened up. "Those who didn't have faith are by and large gone now. They have escaped to Russia. Those who are still here are those who have kept the faith."

As I was leaving, Zdorikov asked me for a favor. His father was living in Kharkiv, and they hadn't been able to communicate for weeks. Could I give him a call once out of Kupyansk, and tell him that his son and grandchildren were fine? Of course, I replied as I scribbled down the number. The father was suspicious at first, then relieved.

Another neighbor, Natalia Somova, warned me that Russian soldiers might still be hiding in the area. "The truth is that some people are giving the Russians shelter. There were many people here for Russia, and they still are, hoping that Russia returns." Somova told me she had informed a Ukrainian patrol about a Russian hideout nearby. Forty minutes later, her house was shelled. Luckily, the projectiles only broke the glass and lightly damaged the roof.

Artillery fire picked up and we decided to retreat to the western side of the Oskil River. As we sprinted toward the bridge, a pickup truck sped past us. In the back, a Ukrainian soldier winked and raised a thumb. There was a black bundle at his feet, and it took us a minute to realize that it was a person. Two medics at the bridge unloaded the passenger, helping him walk, slowly, with a limp. From the back, it seemed like a hunched old woman. It was only once we approached that we realized it was a wounded Russian soldier, just detained somewhere in eastern Kupyansk. He had been hiding.

The Ukrainian escorts asked the blindfolded prisoner where he was from as they crossed the bridge.

"Belgorod," he said, from Russia's 200th Motor Rifle Brigade.

"Ah, neighbors! Have you been to Kharkiv before the war?" a Ukrainian soldier asked him, puzzled.

"Of course," the Russian replied. It used to be common for the people of Belgorod to visit the much bigger Kharkiv on weekends. The two cities were only an hour-and-a-half drive apart, back when there was no war and when the border was easy.

"Did you see any Nazis there?" the Ukrainian asked, squinting.

"No," the Russian mumbled.

"Then why the fuck did you come here to fight?"

There was no reply.

On the other side of the bridge, another team of Ukrainian medics patched up the prisoner's flesh wound and took him to safety in the rear. Ukraine needed as many prisoners as it could get to trade for the Ukrainian captives in Russia.

❖❖❖

Back in the center of Kupyansk, I walked through the broken glass door of the municipality building, carefully looking under my feet so as not to step on a mine or trigger a tripwire. Abandoned in haste, the building had been the inner sanctum of the Russian occupation administration.

At the very entrance, the occupiers left behind hundreds of copies of IDs of Kupyansk citizens who had come to collect subsidies or apply for Russian passports. On the top floor, inside the offices of senior officials, rotting fruit and half-drunk cups of coffee remained on the desks next to dust-covered portraits of Putin and innocuous trinkets, such as a carving of the Burj Khalifa skyscraper in Dubai. Some of the rooms were full of brand-new textbooks and teaching aids in Russian, still wrapped in cellophane, meant for the new schools that were supposed to supplant Ukrainian education. There hadn't been enough time to distribute them. I was surprised by the sheer quantity of paperwork left behind. Minutes of meetings, agendas, guidelines, allocations were spilling from cupboards. The Russian bureaucratic machine in Kupyansk had been preparing for permanence.

While the municipality building was relatively intact—minus its windows—the former headquarters of the Russian FSB intelligence service had been destroyed by a Ukrainian Himars strike at the very beginning of the offensive. Its courtyard had served as a Russian military camp, with burned armored vehicles and assorted detritus of Russian military presence still left behind. As I examined a collection of cassette tapes of Russian and Soviet patriotic songs—something I hadn't seen for a while—a family from the neighborhood walked in: a man, a woman, and a young girl. With determination, they scavenged a large piece of camouflage tarpaulin.

Unlike the people I had met across the river, they weren't happy that the city had returned to Ukrainian rule. In a way, I could understand. The Russian takeover had been quick and painless, with uninterrupted electricity, heating, and water. And for seven months, there was no shelling. Now the power outlets had gone dead, the water taps were dry, shops and bakeries were closed, and one building after another was being destroyed by Russian artillery. "To tell you the truth, life was better under the Russians," said the woman, Marina. During the occupation, she had been working as a nurse in the local hospital, making $700 a month (more than three times her Ukrainian salary, she said) in addition to more generous Russian child benefits. She had heard about Putin's nuclear threats, and I sensed hope in her voice—hope that Ukraine would give up and make peace on Russian terms.

Experience shapes perceptions. For the citizens of Kharkiv, which had resisted the Russians and suffered death and destruction from the first days of the war, the enemy was clear. But in Kupyansk, the worst for people like Marina had begun only with the return of Ukrainian forces.

⊶

Citizens of Kupyansk and other de-occupied areas who moved toward Kharkiv and the rest of government-controlled Ukraine had to undergo filtration in Shevchenkove, a town half an hour's drive to the northwest and outside Russian artillery range. They were questioned about whether they had collaborated with the Russians, and in almost all cases were released. Ukraine's interior ministry had already sent a mobile office to Shevchenkove, issuing passports and ID cards from a van linked to the database by Starlink.

Russian state media was brimming with horror stories about alleged Ukrainian retribution against suspected collaborators. To believe Russian TV, everyone who had ever greeted a Russian soldier was being executed on the spot by Nazi death squads. The Kremlin's propaganda aside, revenge is common in such circumstances. In liberated France in 1945, scenes of summary justice—local partisans shaving, tarring, and parading women who had consorted with the enemy—were commonplace. I was half-expecting to see something similar in liberated parts of Kharkiv.

What I found on Shevchenkove's main square instead was a gaggle of schoolteachers who had refused to collaborate with the Russians, and who were outraged that their colleagues who did collaborate hadn't been fired, let alone detained. "Why are our boys dying out there? Why has my grandson not seen his father for seven months? So that we forgive all these people as if nothing had happened?" wondered Olha Usyk, whose son-in-law was fighting in the military.

While Shevchenkove's mayor had fled to Kharkiv in April, unwilling to submit to the Russians, his second-in-command, the municipality's executive secretary, Nadiya Sheluh, had stayed on. She had urged teachers to re-open schools under the Russian curriculum. Sheluh had been interrogated by Ukraine's security services but let go. When I found her in her home, she said that all she had tried to do was provide humanitarian assistance to Shevchenkove's residents. She had gotten the Russians to demine the local garbage dump, which had become a health hazard, and had arranged for a gravel road to be built to the local cemetery, she said proudly.

"I was defending the interests of our local citizens, making sure they get the medication and the humanitarian aid," Sheluh told me. "Mostly old people and children stayed here, and they needed the baby formula, the diapers."

I ran into an SBU investigator on the town's main square later that day. The Ukrainian government, he said, had no choice but to be lenient to everyone except the most egregious collaborators: security personnel who had joined the Russians with arms, senior local government officials, businesspeople who had enabled the logistics of the Russian military. Rounding up everyone tainted by collaboration, he said, would be impossible. "There are just too many. We can't behave like Stalin, pack trains with everyone who worked with the enemy, and send them away. Where would we send them, anyway?" he wondered. "In every village here, they tell us that everyone in their own village resisted, but that the next village over is full of collaborators."

In the Shevchenkove hospital, doctors and nurses had just returned from a visit to the regional health directorate in Kharkiv. Some of the nurses had dated the Russians and were now shunned by their colleagues. "They wanted to fix their personal lives but chose the wrong men. Now they are despised by the entire staff," said Natalia Nesvoyeva, the hospital's acting director. The retribution didn't go beyond social ostracism. "They are good workers and I cannot fire them. But they are crying all day that other people have a bad attitude to them. What else did they expect?"

✥

A few days later, Vsevolod Kozhemiako, the commander of Khartiya, picked me up at the Scandinavian fusion restaurant that had reopened in Kharkiv. His friends Volodymyr and Gelya Radchenko had just returned from Germany after a seven-month absence. Access to their home in Velyki Prokhody on the Russian border remained restricted for civilians so he offered to escort them there. Gelya's mother, Tetyana, unlike many neighbors, had survived the occupation unharmed.

On the way, Kozhemiako explained to me that in previous months, as he was checking up on Tetyana via a neighbor who had somehow established a mobile phone connection, he also gathered intelligence. The neighbor passed him information about Russian positions and about which houses were still inhabited by locals, so that Ukrainian artillery would spare them.

We drove past the ruins of Ruska Lozova, on what used to be a broad highway but had been turned into a track covered with debris, broken trees, and remains of Russian fortifications. Gelya was tense as we approached her house. It was intact. She knocked on the gate and her dog was the first to run out, beside itself with excitement, squealing and wagging its tail. "I've missed you so much," Gelya exclaimed as she knelt to pat it.

Her mother emerged a minute later. "It's been so long." Tetyana exhaled. She welcomed us in, making coffee with an espresso machine. The Russians had tried to steal the generator, but she said her ferociousness had scared them away. She showed us the basement, which still contained an impressive collection of pickled preserves. In the absence of news, she had learned to recognize changes in the tide of war by the music the Russians played via loudspeakers at a nearby outpost. When the Russians had losses and setbacks, they broadcast a sad 1960s song, "Do the Russians Want War?," that mourns heavy casualties in Russia's past conflicts. When they had victories, they put triumphant Soviet marches on repeat.

Kozhemiako, clad in his body armor and uniform, was standing by the entrance, observing how his friends' family reunited. "It's kinda nice," he told me quietly before slipping away. "I guess that's what we've been fighting for."

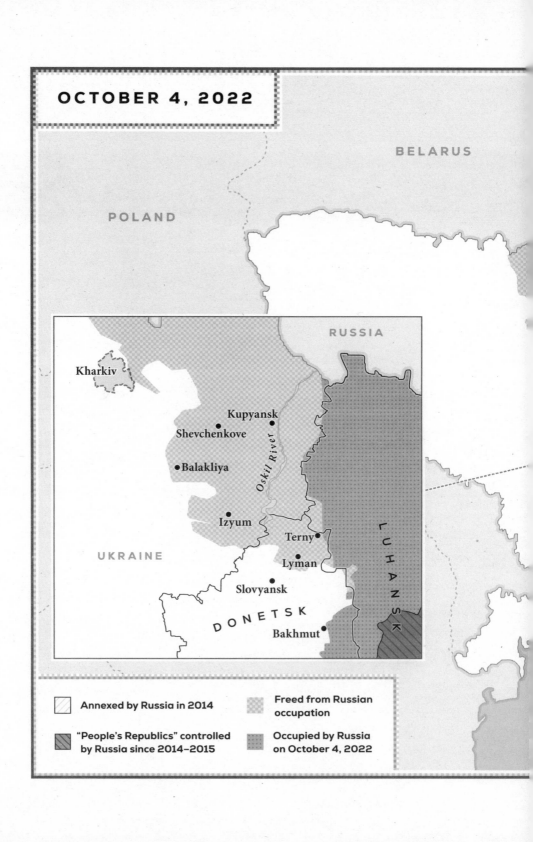

OCTOBER 4, 2022

BELARUS

POLAND

RUSSIA

Kharkiv

Kupyansk

Shevchenkove

Balakliya

Oskil River

Izyum

UKRAINE

Terny

Lyman

Slovyansk

L U H A N S K

DONETSK

Bakhmut

Annexed by Russia in 2014

Freed from Russian
occupation

"People's Republics" controlled
by Russia since 2014–2015

Occupied by Russia
on October 4, 2022

KILOMETERS

0   50   100   150

0   50   100   150

MILES

N

RUSSIA

Sumy

Kyiv

Dnipro River

UKRAINE

Kharkiv

AREA OF DETAIL

Donbas

Luhansk

Dnipro

Donetsk

Zaporizhzhia

Mariupol

Kherson

Odesa

Azov Sea

Crimean
Peninsula

*Snake
Island*

KERCH BRIDGE

Sevastopol

Black Sea

PART 9

✧◻✧

PURSUIT

CHAPTER 40

BACK TO DONBAS

Russia's referendums did not surprise: support for annexation ranged from 99 percent in the Donetsk region to 87 percent in Kherson, the Russian election commission announced on September 27. Three days later, Putin greeted the Moscow-appointed leaders of the four regions and presided over the formal annexation ceremony in the gilded St. George's Hall of the Kremlin. Russia, he said in his speech to mark the biggest land grab of the century, now led the world's anticolonial struggle, inspiring mankind in its struggle against decadent values imposed by the West.

The zeitgeist of the day, however, was most eloquently conveyed not by Putin but by one of his guests of honor at the ceremony, Maksim Fomin, a former bank robber who was a gunman for the Donetsk "people's republic" in 2014 and had become one of Russia's main *voenkor* propagandists while also continuing to fight in the military under the call sign Hot Dog. Trading his oversize fatigues for a suit, Fomin, aka Vladlen Tatarsky, posted a short video from St. George's Hall that day. "For two hundred years, we have been capturing all of Europe and fucking it doggy-style," he said as he pointed to marble plaques commemorating Russia's past feats of arms. "We will do the same now . . . We will kill everyone, we will rob everyone that we must, everything will be the way we love it."

It didn't turn out to be that way. In April 2023, Fomin was hosting a talk at a venue in Saint Petersburg owned by Yevgeny Prigozhin when a young woman handed him a gift—a gilded statue of himself. Smiling, Fomin put it on a table by his side. A minute later, the bomb hidden inside exploded, killing him and injuring several attendees.

◆◈◆

The problem for Russia was that the Ukrainian forces had already moved beyond the Kharkiv region and started reclaiming the northern parts of the Donetsk region—which Moscow considered its sovereign soil. On September 26, crossing the Oskil River on a pontoon bridge east of Izyum, Manu and I entered the first liberated villages of Donetsk. Bloated bodies of Russian soldiers who had tried to flee from Izyum were still sprawled on roadsides. The pine forest along the road was filled with the burned remains of Russian tanks, artillery pieces, and missile launchers—the result of Ukrainian Himars strikes two weeks earlier.

The village of Yatskivka, just past the huge concrete Soviet-era sign marking the boundary of the Donetsk region, was a scene of destruction of a scale I had rarely witnessed in this war or any other. Twisted metal, concrete, bricks, melted parts of weapons, human remains—it was all threshed and churned together as if by a supernatural force, and then scattered over muddy craters. This is what a nuclear explosion site must look like, I thought. On the left side of the road there were hardly any buildings still standing. On the right, we noticed smoke from one shattered house, and an old woman with a soot-covered face holding a small plastic bucket. The house wasn't hers, she told us, but she was afraid that with the wind fanning the flames, the fire could jump over a meadow and spread to her own home.

She asked whether we could help her extinguish the flames using water from a swimming pool in what looked like an abandoned resort nearby. A scribbled sign warned "Mines" at the entrance. It had been used as a Russian military outpost, judging by tattered uniforms and several molten walkie-talkies amid the ruins. Gingerly, our new security adviser, Hutch, stepped in, saying that the path to the pool was probably safe. As we carried the water and Hutch threw it onto the smoldering roof, the woman kept talking, happy for her first human conversation in days. Nobody else appeared to have remained in Yatskivka.

"I have lived here all my life, happy with everything Ukrainian, and Putin just came here and brought his Russian world." She cursed furiously. "Look at this Russian world! Everything is burned down, nothing is left here!"

I asked her name. She shied away from me. "I am too scared to tell you," she said. "If the Russians come back, they could execute me for talking to you."

In the next village down the road, Rubtsy, destruction was limited, and many civilians remained. The Ukrainian military had just established an outpost and a small field clinic on the main square.

I watched as several villagers spilled out of a battered car, asking soldiers for the password to the Starlink Wi-Fi—their only way of communicating with the outside world. One of them, a retired woman named Maria Savchenko, had a message for the officer who greeted them. "Please, don't hand us over again" to the Russians, she said. "We've had enough of all this shooting. I can't take it anymore."

✛

On the evening of September 30, Putin attended a concert on Moscow's Red Square to celebrate Russia's new territorial acquisitions. Onstage, he was flanked by the collaborationist governors of the four annexed Ukrainian regions. "Russia had created contemporary Ukraine, giving it significant territories, historical Russian territories, together with the population that was never asked where and how they want to live," he said, urging the crowd to honor Russian forces that had restored these lands to their rightful owner with a triple "Hurrah."

One of the speakers who shared the stage with Putin was the nationalist actor Ivan Okhlobystin. "This is a holy war!" he screamed, wearing black gloves and dressed in a black leather overcoat. "*Goyda*, brothers and sisters! *Goyda!*" he shouted into the microphone. "Be afraid, the old world, lacking true beauty, lacking true faith, lacking true wisdom, ruled by madmen, by perverts and satanists! Be afraid! We are coming. *Goyda, goyda, goyda!*"

Goyda was the battle cry of the *oprichniks*, the murderous private army of the deranged Muscovite czar Ivan the Terrible. Okhlobystin once

performed in a movie about the *oprichnina*, one of the most terrifying epi-
sodes in human history, which began in 1565. Riding on horses with dogs'
heads attached (to symbolize ferociousness) and carrying brooms (to
symbolize their intent to sweep away dissenters and traitors) the black-clad
oprichniks devised ever more gruesome methods of torture and killing as
they slaughtered anyone suspected of disloyalty, along with their servants
and families. The head of the Russian Orthodox Church was one of their
myriad victims.

Russia indeed seemed to be headed into dark times.

❖

For Ukraine, the biggest prize in the northern part of the Donetsk region
was the railway junction of Lyman, a city of 20,000 people before the
war. The Russians had conquered it in late May, at the peak of their big Donbas offensive. Ukrainian forces were now pressing into Lyman from the
north, the south, and the west. But instead of fleeing like they had done in
Izyum three weeks earlier, the Russians had regrouped and were putting up
fierce resistance. The status of Izyum or Kupyansk had been uncertain. But
Lyman was now a full-fledged part of the Russian Federation, at least as far
as Russian law was concerned.

The Carpathian Sich battalion, whose men we had followed through
the no-man's-land of Virnopillia in May, was engaged in heavy combat on
the Lyman front.

Early on the morning of October 1, I drove with Manu and Hutch to link
up with Carpathian Sich and its deputy commander, Rusyn. Izyum—the
town where I had suggested we should meet next—was already more than
twenty miles behind our backs. The battalion's new rear base occupied a
former village school that until days earlier had served as a Russian Army
outpost. The brick building had a car-sized hole in its side from a direct artillery hit, just above graffiti that proclaimed, "For Putin, for Empire." A
shrapnel-pierced water cistern was painted over with Russian words: "Don't
touch. Only for the injured." Russian garbage was scattered around.

The compound was busy. In these five months, Carpathian Sich had expanded, absorbing many foreign volunteers. A new rotation of troops had

just arrived, most of them Spanish-speakers—Argentineans, Colombians, Venezuelans, and three Spaniards in Spanish Legion fatigues. Manu chatted with his compatriots, who preened in their *chapiri* caps with red tassels as they unloaded the truck. The Spanish soldiers were elated to be at the front. "We've finally got to see some action, after so many years of boredom," one of them said, laughing.

One of the few Ukrainian soldiers, Kay, originally from Kharkiv, told me he was also raring for battle. The Russians had killed four of his friends, and he didn't have any confirmed hits of his own just yet, though he said he had repeatedly fired in the Russians' general direction. "I need to at least even the score, to minus four." He smiled sheepishly.

A handful of other volunteers, mostly English-speakers, were getting ready to leave for a break, some to go home to England and the United States and never return. They were dazed, speaking of the comrades they had lost while storming a village just to the south earlier in the week. "It's tough here, very tough," one of them said.

WE DIDN'T KNOW IT YET, BUT THAT MORNING CARPATHIAN SICH WAS CARrying out one of its most daring operations in the whole war: the assault on the village of Terny northeast of Lyman. Located east of the Zherebets River, Terny sits on the edge of the Donetsk and Luhansk regions, separated by a thick forest from the strategic Russian-held city of Kreminna, the gateway to the rest of Luhansk.

We needed an escort to show us the way around minefields to the battalion's command point farther east. A stocky Ukrainian soldier in his fifties jumped into our armored Land Cruiser. He seemed content at first, and his radio crackled with news of the battalion's advances.

As we stopped so he could show us the bodies of Russian soldiers and the destroyed Russian tanks and BMPs on the roadside, bad news began to pour in. Carpathian Sich's assault squads had sustained casualties. Two wounded, one badly. "Do you know who?" the soldier asked on the radio. "Negative," came the reply.

Agitated, he raised his Kalashnikov rifle and fired a volley into one of the dead Russians whose body lay swollen in the mud in front of us. "Fuck you, fuckers!" he screamed. "Burn in hell!" The cadaver jerked amid a small fountain of pebbles. "I am sorry." The soldier looked at me, composing himself. "I can't bear losing any more friends."

We got back into the car and kept driving in silence until we reached a small village that housed the battalion's command post. The house was nearly empty. With all the top officers engaged in the battle for Terny, only a British-educated Kyiv lawyer manning the radio, Radoslav, and the battalion's deputy chief of staff, Ruslan Andriyko, remained in the building.

We sat in the courtyard, listening to the radio traffic. The battalion's troops had just entered Terny from the southeast, maneuvering through the forest. Drone footage showed a dozen or so Russian troops retreating on foot to Russian positions to the north. Andriyko asked for an artillery hit on them. It seemed Carpathian Sich had achieved a major success with minimal losses. "Terny is ours," Andriyko said, beaming.

"We had waged a positional war for half a year, and if we moved then it was only with tiny steps," he added as we shared lunch. "But these days, you go out for a smoke, and two more villages have been liberated by the time you come back. Things change every second." He took me to a car parked nearby to show his recent trophies—a decked-out sniper rifle taken from the Russians, Russian medals, and combat patches. Carpathian Sich also had bulkier trophies—T-80 tanks, BMPs, and MT-LB armored vehicles.

It was frustrating to sit at the command post without being able to witness the action a few miles to our east. The updates ceased. The field radio's signal, perhaps because of Russian jamming, no longer reached all the way to Terny.

Andriyko wanted to send Maria, one of the battalion's medics, with a radio handset to the first stabilization point in a grove between us and Terny. Medics there could serve as an improvised relay station for information. We offered to take her in our armored car: it was our only way of getting closer to the battle.

Chapter 41

THE BATTLE OF TERNY

aria climbed into the front seat, put her rifle by the door, and ordered everyone to switch off location tracking services on their iPhones. Only twenty-five years old, she was slender, with an almost translucent pallor. Blond hair poked from under her helmet, and a Punisher skull patch was attached to her first-aid pouch. During the drive, she kept speaking in the choicest profanities, perhaps to conceal her stress.

As we stopped at the stabilization point—a pickup truck with three medics under a tree—we watched the Russian strikes on Terny just two miles to the east. First there was an artillery barrage, with plumes of smoke rising in the air. Then two Russian jets flew low in front of us, firing flares and lobbing missiles. Behind us, Ukrainian howitzers fired toward Russian lines, shells hissing overhead. "They have deep basements in Terny, so our guys are holding out pretty well," Maria said.

Taking advantage of a lull, we headed back. Maria was visibly more relaxed now. I asked why the call sign on her body armor read "Vozhata," Ukrainian for camp counselor. She laughed for the first time.

When the war began, she said, she had told her mother that she would go to western Ukraine to work in a camp for children who had escaped the fighting. Maria's mother was very protective. In 2015, afraid that Maria would get involved with volunteer units in Donbas, she had sent her only child to study in Poland, "so that you don't do anything stupid." Armed with a Polish university degree but eager to live in her homeland despite having a high-paying job in Cracow, Maria returned home to Kyiv in late 2020. Her mother, she reckoned, didn't need to know that she was serving as a combat medic on the most dangerous stretch of the front.

In June 2022, once Carpathian Sich was formally absorbed by the Ukrainian Army, Maria became a service member, and she finally traveled home to break the news. Aware of the likely reaction, she had brought along an IV drip and sedatives. "I had to tell Mama face-to-face," Maria recalled. "She always worries about me, and I knew what would happen. What can I say? The IV turned out to be necessary." With my own daughter just two years younger than Maria, I could relate.

✦

The strikes we had just observed were of Russian warplanes trying to hit the battalion's commander and other senior leaders as their convoy approached Terny from the west, along a muddy dam over the Zherebets.

As the convoy turned around and raced to safety, one vehicle hit a Russian land mine on the dam. The radio crackled with the dreaded number "200," the military code for fatality. "Who?" Andriyko asked. "Tur." He forced himself not to cry, but small tears appeared at the corners of his eyes. He wiped them off. "Tur?" he repeated, shaken. "This will be tough."

Tur was the call sign for forty-one-year-old Vitaliy Benchak, one of Carpathian Sich's original founders who in February had rushed with Rusyn to Kyiv from Transcarpathia to resurrect the unit. An entrepreneur, he didn't hold a formal command role. But Carpathian Sich, by now officially known as the 49th Separate Battalion of the Ukrainian Armed Forces, was not an ordinary unit. Its history as a volunteer formation meant that all its commanders were elected by soldiers, and informal authority often outweighed formal rank.

"He was one of the pillars of Carpathian Sich," Rusyn later told me. "From the very beginning, he was fighting with the boys in the trenches. He was so valuable that we had tried to pull him from the front line to diminish the danger. But that's a paradox of life. As long as he was on the front line, he was alive, but once we pulled him back, he died."

Rusyn was in no mood to talk that evening. Shortly after dusk, he brought Tur's body to the battalion command post. The bloodied stretcher was propped by the fence. I saw Rusyn helping to reload the corpse into another car that would take it all the way back home, to Transcarpathia. He paced furiously inside the garden, stopping to punch a half-broken door.

An hour later, Svat, the battalion commander, was ready to see me. Nearly fifty-nine years old, Svat was clearly in pain. He was traveling in the same vehicle as Tur. Luckily, he suffered only a mild concussion and a few scrapes. "It's a miracle I am still alive," he told me. "The explosion had propelled me into the grass. The car, it has been torn to shreds." He asked Maria for pain medication and then explained how the day's battle unfolded.

The orders to attack Terny had come shortly after midnight, and the operation plan hinged on forecasts of morning fog that would conceal the 5 a.m. approach of Ukrainian attackers from the south. But the forecasts were wrong. There was no fog, no concealment. Russian tanks had a clear line of fire, making the original plan near-suicidal.

Reshuffling the operation on the go, Svat ordered his men to loop through the forest east of Terny, between Russian lines, with the support of two trophy BMPs. The gamble worked.

"We had come through the woods and surprised the orcs," he said. "And we won the firefight. For us, this kind of full-contact battle is something new. This is a unit of volunteers, they aren't used to this kind of storm operations. For our level of training, this was unreal. But we have fulfilled the mission. I am so proud." The battalion had six wounded and one fatality, he said. Dozens of Russians had been killed.

Participants in the assault told me that the Russians had created an entrenched position on Terny's main crossroads, with two machine-gun nests that controlled the main access routes. A Ukrainian platoon leader, Lybid, managed to creep up to one of the nests, throwing hand grenades into the trench. "I don't know what they were doing in that nest, but somehow they just didn't notice us," he recalled. "And once we've hit them with grenades, chaos in their trenches erupted. They no longer had any idea about what was happening around them."

A drone flown by Carpathian Sich provided an overview of Russian movements, allowing Ukrainian soldiers to encircle the ten Russian troops who remained in the crossroads position. "We shouted at them, 'Russian Ivan, surrender, we guarantee you warm food,'" recalled Simpson, the soldier who had stopped a lost Russian BMP near Izyum. "But they refused, even though they knew they were surrounded."

With Terny gone, a much greater Russian force found itself nearly surrounded in Lyman that day. In the evening, Russian media started reporting that Russian troops had been ordered to withdraw from the city. I asked Svat, the battalion commander, if we could go there in the morning. It wasn't in his area of operations, but he didn't object. "Come here," he said, beckoning, and showed me on a large, printed map which circuitous but mine-free road could take us to Lyman at dawn.

❖

I scrolled the news before falling asleep that night. The Russian *voenkors* were in fury and despair, while Ramzan Kadyrov, the Chechen strongman, and Wagner's Prigozhin had already found a scapegoat: Colonel General Lapin, the commander of Russia's Central Military District. "What's stinging is not the fact that Lapin is inept, but that it is being covered up by the leaders of the General Staff," Kadyrov thundered on Telegram. "If it were up to me, I would have busted Lapin to private, stripped away his medals, and sent him to the front, a rifle in his hands, to wash off his shame with blood."

"Ramzan, good lad, keep up the fire," Prigozhin responded. "All these fuckwits—to the front, shoeless and with a rifle."

The cracks in the once-monolithic Russian state were now visible. The war that was meant to implement regime change in Ukraine was eroding Russia's own regime instead.

Lapin was removed days later and sent on leave. He was down, but not out.

Chapter 42

THE FALL OF LYMAN

M ist rose from the ground as we started the drive to Lyman on October 2. As the early-morning darkness dissipated, a couple of Ukrainian soldiers stepped out from behind bushes, signaling us to halt, their fingers on the triggers. "Journalists?" one of them breathed out with relief after seeing our ID cards.

"Yes," I replied, fearing that they would turn us around. The soldiers lowered their barrels. They weren't there to obstruct the press. "Careful," the trooper warned me, "there may still be some Russians on the roadsides out here. We haven't fully cleared the area yet."

A quarter hour later, we entered a birch and pine forest west of Lyman, driving along a winding road. We hadn't encountered any other cars that morning. The first that we saw had been sprayed by gunfire and shrapnel; a Russian convoy had been ambushed just hours earlier.

We stopped our car, switching off the engine. There was an eerie silence, not even the chirping of birds or the rustling of mice. The Russian cadavers that I had seen up until this point had been bloated, so disfigured by decomposition that they almost didn't seem human. But the men sprawled on the asphalt ahead of us seemed alive, as if taking a quiet nap. Two soldiers had gripped each other in a final embrace in the morning cold. One was lying on his back, his arms on his chest, a strange serenity in his features.

The other trooper was missing a hand. Severed by shrapnel, a clump of flesh containing four of the five fingers was propped up on the asphalt, right next to a primed antitank mine. A wedding ring was still on one of the fingers. The Russian soldiers had traveled in several civilian vans and cars, likely a rearguard unit. Or maybe some unlucky troops who hadn't received the withdrawal orders in time.

BEING IN A COUNTRY AT WAR, ONE IS RARELY DISTRESSED BY THE CASUAL-ties of the invading army. Many Ukrainians, including people who wouldn't even watch action movies before the war, found solace in viewing hours of drone footage of Russian soldiers getting killed and maimed. But in the forest outside Lyman, these freshly dead Russian men, with their civilian backpacks containing their meager possessions, with their sleeping bags and pouches of fever and pain medication, were no longer anonymous and generic invaders. I looked at their faces and felt anger. What had they died for? Putin's megalomania? The wounded pride of old men whose empire collapsed in 1991, just as they were supposed to inherit it? The Russian idea, whatever that may be? The wife of the owner of the severed hand was probably desperately calling and texting her husband, praying and praying that one tick on his WhatsApp or Telegram messenger would turn into two.

WE GINGERLY CHECKED THE WAY AHEAD FOR LAND MINES AND GOT BACK into our Land Cruiser. The rest of the way to Lyman was uneventful. Civilians were already out and about, on bicycles and on foot. One of the grocery stores was open, and a small market operated in the middle of the road. There were no troops to be seen, Russian or Ukrainian. "Russia, forward," proclaimed the leftover graffiti on walls. "The Russians are coming." I was surprised to see other graffiti cursing Putin's spokesman, Dmitry Peskov, presumed by Russian nationalists to be a relative moderate, as a "Ukrainian fascist."

The locals were disoriented and didn't seem to know who was in charge. In fact, several assumed that we—with our mud-spattered armored car, helmets, and body armor, with radios and patches proclaiming our blood types—were the new authority. "We still can't figure out who is what," a young man named Dmytro Hontar told me on Lyman's main square, where a small crowd had gathered by a two-story building that had served as the warehouse for Russian humanitarian aid distribution, across from the city hall. "Are those soldiers down the street Russian or Ukrainian?" he asked me. "Ukrainian, I hope," I replied. Running into living Russian troops wouldn't be optimal.

Emboldened, one man pried open the door of the warehouse, then another. The crowd surged in. The sacks of flour inscribed with the word "Russia" were the first to go, precariously attached to bicycles, then the large plastic bottles of oil, bags of sugar, boxes of bread. "People are just looting everything," Dmytro said, shaking his head in disgust. A few minutes later, he, too, joined the frenzy.

"We had no aid from anyone here. We were just eating whatever reserves we had stockpiled before the war," Tamara Kozachenko explained as she dragged out two bags of flour. "The Russians, we didn't even see how they vanished. Is it final now?" she asked, the fear of a Russian return—and retribution for looting—flashing in her eyes.

A quarter hour later, all the food was gone. The latecomers had to make do with rolls of Russian toilet paper. Then came the turn of whatever useful furniture remained inside, of door handles and light bulbs. This was the kind of looting I had seen in Iraq in 2003.

I crossed the street and wandered into the city hall. Its facade was still plastered with billboards for the referendum on joining Russia, carried out in Lyman barely a week earlier. "Russia, Donbas, Forever," they promised. Notices informed residents on how to register their property under Russian law, listed job vacancies in other parts of the Donetsk "people's republic," and urged parents to sign up for gift packages marking the new academic year in Russian-run schools.

Turning the corner into Lyman's main street, I saw a couple of Ukrainian soldiers, members of the 25th Air Assault Brigade. The rest of their team was boarding a pickup truck. They were just starting to clear Lyman's central areas. I asked to tag along. Giddy with victory, the soldiers gave a thumbs-up. The ambushed Russian column we had just seen at the entrance to Lyman was their overnight work, they told me with pride.

There was another firefight in Lyman early that morning. "Then the bastards just evaporated," said Serhiy, the team leader. We followed the pickup down several blocks, to a local hospital compound. Several decomposing bodies were stacked in one of the storage buildings outdoors, but the stench was too overpowering to investigate further. No living Russians were to be seen.

As we moved away from the smell, the soldiers asked me about Hutch, whose military build left no doubts about his former profession. As it turned out, most members of that team had just trained in England. One of them pulled out a Union Jack from his pocket and insisted on taking a group photo. Another tore off a handful of patches from his uniform and gave them to us as presents. "MILF Hunters," one read, with a woman's silhouette. Another was more subtle: "Lyman forestry management."

We kept going, stopping by a large mansion with solar panels on the roof. Its gate was marked with the letter "Z," the symbol of Russian troops. The Ukrainians started off by spraying over it with white paint and writing down their own marker, "ZSU"—the acronym for Armed Forces of Ukraine.

"Tripwire!" one of the men shouted, noticing an explosive device the Russians had left at the gate. As some soldiers disabled it, others jumped over the wall and into the compound. We followed suit.

The mansion's inhabitants had left in haste. The soldiers climbed through a second-story window and started passing down their finds. There were boxes of Russian medication and canned meat that, Serhiy decided on the spot, would be distributed to local civilians. To general laughter, one of the troopers threw out of the window another trophy—a large transparent dildo. "Are they bringing these to their wives?" a soldier asked, puzzled. "Nah, they must be having fun with it themselves," another trooper quipped.

Next came a large cloth sack that, I initially assumed, was full of potatoes. It contained hand grenades, and was followed by a box of fuzes. "No better lend-lease than Russian lend-lease." Serhiy smiled, ordering his men to put the weapons into the pickup. "It's great that we get help from the Russians."

We followed his men back to the main square, where they searched the city hall once again, hauling out Russian flags and referendum materials to fuel a small bonfire outdoors. By then, other Ukrainian units had appeared in town, as well as a handful of Ukrainian police officers.

"How long are you here for?" one of the local men asked a police officer.

"Forever," he replied.

BEFORE LEAVING, I WANTED TO SEE THE ROAD EAST FROM LYMAN, THE ONLY one that Russian troops could have used to flee the city overnight. Did the bulk of them manage to withdraw, or were many of them killed on their way out?

Manu was nervous about venturing that far. We set out to drive slowly. There was nobody else on that road, always a bad omen. Just a few hundred yards east of Lyman, we came upon a smoldering Russian armored vehicle, then another. Beyond them there was a small minivan, its doors twisted by an explosion but still bearing the Russian "Z" mark. We almost drove past it as we saw a man in black crawling out from under the van, waving a bloodied hand at us. I noticed that he was missing a foot. Just a bloody stump poked out from the end of his Adidas tracksuit trousers. There was also a hand grenade lying on the asphalt, within easy reach of him. "Should we stop and help?" Manu asked. "We're not stopping here, reverse, reverse!" I yelled. Hutch threw the gear into reverse and screeched back.

"He's probably going to die," Manu reckoned. Manu and I had just taken a hostile-environment course supervised by Stevo in a retreat outside London, where we had refreshed our skills in stopping catastrophic bleeding and administering first aid. Another key lesson drilled into us during that course, however, was to offer help only if it was sufficiently safe to do so. We had no idea what had happened to the Russian troops in the two recently hit armored vehicles. They could still be hiding in the tall grass on the sides of the road. Was the man in the tracksuit trousers one of these Russian survivors? Or a Lyman civilian who stepped on a land mine as he tried to loot these vehicles?

"We're going to get him help," I replied.

I had seen a Ukrainian military pickup truck parked under a tree just before the exit from Lyman. Indeed, as we returned to that area, two soldiers were still there, one of them surveilling the road with binoculars.

"There's a guy without a foot out there, bleeding out," I told them. "He needs to be taken to medics."

"A civilian or an orc?" one of the soldiers asked.

"I don't know." I spread my arms.

"Okay, we will follow you."

We led the troops back to the destroyed minivan. "He's probably bled to death by now," Hutch said on the way. But the man was still there, slowly crawling in the middle of the road and leaving a small trail of blood behind himself. It looked like a zombie movie. The explosion must have cauterized his stump, stopping most of the blood loss.

The soldiers jumped out and tore a piece of tarpaulin from the minivan. "Do you have a cigarette?" was the man's first desire. The soldiers gave him one. As he lit up, he explained that he was a civilian, originally from Belarus. Maybe it was true, maybe not; one of the soldiers shook his head as he put on surgical gloves and examined the wound. Months later, looking at his photo taken by Manu, I realized that the man was wearing two watches on his right wrist, the mark of a looter. "Okay, buddy, now try to roll onto the tarp," the soldier said, picking up and pocketing the hand grenade that remained on the asphalt. Moaning, the man turned around and the soldiers hoisted him into the back of their pickup truck. "You'll be fine, we're taking you to the hospital now," the soldier said to calm him down.

We followed the troops back to the exit from the city and decided to wait until a Ukrainian military convoy traveled on that road. But an hour later, the road remained deserted. We turned around and headed back to the Carpathian Sich's command post. Andriyko was there, but the other commanders had gone to Terny to fortify the village against a possible Russian counterattack.

❖

Dozens of soldiers and officers of Carpathian Sich had set up a new base that morning in the abandoned main school of Terny, near the village's onion-domed church. As several commanders were wrapping up their meeting, Svat, the battalion chief, received an important phone call. Giving him some privacy, the other officers began to walk out of the building. Most remaining troops were in the basement at the time, while about a dozen others were scattered throughout the school.

Nobody heard any warning sounds before the school imploded in a deafening, blinding fireball.

"The moment I stepped out, there was just dust and dust from everywhere," recalled Brytanets, a former Ukrainian worker at Rolls-Royce in the UK who commanded a company mostly made up of English-speaking recruits. "It was a feeling that there was suddenly a vacuum and everything got sucked inside."

He and others ran inside to look for Svat. The battalion commander had sustained his second concussion in twenty-four hours, but otherwise avoided serious injury. "We saw that the school is almost flattened," Brytanets recalled. "The explosive wave had gone inside and almost no shrapnel flew out. Otherwise, none of us would be alive now."

The Russians likely had dropped a potent thermobaric bomb on the school, the kind of weapon that creates a vacuum and sucks in all available oxygen. The light-blue inner walls of the school's gymnasium, with the remains of a basketball hoop and a mural of athletes, now stood at the edge of a smoldering crater. Soldiers who had sheltered in the basement survived. But troopers elsewhere in the building had little chance.

Zhenya, a slim combat medic who was on duty that afternoon, ran to the site, helping to dig out survivors. Rainy conditions meant that the rescuers had to work with their hands. An MT-LB tracked armored vehicle that Carpathian Sich tried to send to Terny, hoping to use it to pull the ruins aside, got stuck in the mud on the way. Russian shelling made the route too dangerous for pickup trucks.

Zhenya was small enough to fit between concrete panels as she tried to get to some of the men, pinned down by the wreckage. "The walls were cracking, the ceiling was crumbling, as I kept squeezing inside," she recalled. "I could because I was small, and maybe also because I was nuts." Two men were pulled out alive. One, with a smashed hip, survived. Another died shortly thereafter, one of the battalion's seven fatalities in Terny that day.

⬦⬥⬦

On October 5, we ran into Maria as we passed by Carpathian Sich's rear base. The medic no longer cursed, speaking softly between fits of coughing. "How's the camp counseling going?" I joked. She had caught a cold, she said. Almost automatically, she reached out to fix the strap of the tourniquet that was attached to my body armor.

Other soldiers at the base had just returned from Terny. I saw one of the men, his hands red with blood, taking two assault rifles out of the car by their barrels. Three Russian soldiers had strayed into Terny hours earlier, likely stragglers from the Lyman retreat who sought a way to rejoin Russian lines. They had come within a hundred yards of the bombed-out school and, after being spotted, tried to escape. In a two-hour firefight, the Russians managed to kill one soldier of a Territorial Defense unit that had just been sent to reinforce Terny and to injure another. One of the Russians was killed quickly, and two others ended up in the basement of one of the abandoned homes, the Ukrainian soldier told me.

I noticed his accent and an unusual patch on his uniform—the word "Ukraine" in Cyrillic atop the Arabic of the Muslim profession of faith. The call sign on his body armor read "Ermak."

Where are you from? I asked him. He was originally from Tunisia but had been living in Ukraine for years and fought in a Carpathian Sich company made up of Ukrainians rather than foreigners.

"So what happened to the two Russians in the basement?"

"They didn't want to surrender, and so they shot themselves, with these guns," he said, pointing to the two propped-up Kalashnikovs. Ermak showed me a blood-soaked Russian passport he said he had found on one of the men. Georgiy Sokolov, from the Magadan region on Russia's Pacific coast, died in a Ukrainian basement nearly 4,000 miles from his home. He was thirty-three.

PART 10

RESILIENCE

CHAPTER 43

"HAPPY BIRTHDAY, MR. PRESIDENT"

On the morning of October 8, Ukrainians woke up to spectacular news. Putin's pet project, the bridge from the Russian mainland to Crimea that he had personally unveiled in 2018, was on fire, the result of a daring Ukrainian attack. One side of the highway had collapsed into the sea. Several fuel cisterns smoldered on the buckled rail line. The explosions had occurred only a few hours after Putin finished celebrating his seventieth birthday.

The twelve-mile-long Kerch Bridge was meant to be the symbol of Russia's newfound greatness, and of its success in annexing the peninsula in 2014. An entire romcom about its construction, *The Crimean Bridge: Made with Love!*, had been filmed, its script written by Margarita Simonyan, the chief of the Russia Today TV network and one of the Kremlin's main propagandists. The movie, one of the most expensive ever made in Russia, never recouped its costs.

Beyond political symbolism, the Kerch Bridge served as a crucial lifeline to the tens of thousands of Russian troops in southern Ukraine, particularly in Kherson. On that front, Ukraine in previous days had achieved fresh successes, breaking through Russian defenses in the northern part of the region and advancing about a dozen miles closer to Kherson city.

Ukrainians had long fantasized about a strike on the Kerch Bridge, loathing the structure as a monument to their national shame. Just outside the Kyiv municipality building on Khreshchatyk Avenue, a billboard showed the bridge, with its curved span, exploding in two separate fireballs. Within minutes of hearing the news, a line of Kyivites appeared in front of the billboard to take celebratory photos for their Instagram feeds. The attack took place on the part of the bridge that was wholly within internationally recognized Ukrainian territory. Even though it was carried out at just after 6 a.m., the predawn hour when traffic was lightest, it still killed civilians—five by Moscow's count.

Ukrainian officials, while stopping just short of taking official responsibility, couldn't contain their glee. Oleksiy Danilov, the national security adviser, posted on Twitter a video of the burning bridge, next to footage of Marilyn Monroe singing "Happy Birthday, Mr. President." The Ukrainian mail service announced that it would issue a new postage stamp to commemorate the event, following a stamp of the sinking of the cruiser *Moskva*, which had become a collector's item.

In Moscow, Putin was silent as Russian social media erupted with rage and calls for revenge. The only announcement that day was the appointment of General Sergei Surovikin as the first overall leader of Russian forces in Ukraine since the invasion began. Russia finally had unity of command— and, in the bald, broad-shouldered general, a recognizable face of its war. A hard-liner among hard-liners, Surovikin was the only Russian commander whose men killed pro-democracy protesters during the failed putsch by Soviet military and intelligence chiefs against President Mikhail Gorbachev in August 1991. Once a badge of shame, it was now a distinction.

Russian soldiers in Ukraine "are in secure hands," Ramzan Kadyrov exulted once Surovikin's appointment was announced. Yevgeny Prigozhin recalled that in August 1991, he was on the side of the pro-democracy crowds. "We were in the thrall of a profound delusion at the time . . . We executed an order from the US and destroyed the greatest empire of modern time to the benefit of a gang of greedy, treacherous beasts," Prigozhin wrote on October 8. "Surovikin is an officer who, after receiving an order, didn't think twice and jumped into a tank, rushing to save his country . . . Surovikin is the most skilled commander in the Russian Army."

I went out for dinner that night in Podil with Stevo and a couple of our Ukrainian friends—a Kherson-born photographer, Anastasia Vlasova, and her boyfriend, who had begun sniper school. Everyone was in a giddy mood, drinking cocktails to celebrate Russia's humiliation in Crimea. Bathed in lights, Kyiv was bustling with life. It had been months since the last Russian missile targeted the Ukrainian capital.

⊰⊱⊱

Putin remained out of sight until the evening of the following day, October 9. Then Russian state TV showed a short clip of his meeting with the head of the country's Investigations Committee. "There is no doubt that this is a terrorist attack aiming to destroy critically important civilian infrastructure of the Russian Federation," Putin said about the Kerch Bridge explosion. "And the authors and executors are Ukrainian special services."

I had just left Kyiv on the morning of October 10, when Stevo went for a run through Shevchenko Park in the heart of the city. Favored by kissing couples, crusty chess players, and parents with boisterous children alike, the leafy park is fringed by the red-painted main building of Kyiv University on one side, and by a street containing some of Kyiv's most important art museums on the other. A statue of Taras Shevchenko, the national poet, stands in the middle. It had been shielded by sandbags and plywood since the beginning of the war, a precaution that now seemed obsolete.

Half an hour later, in the middle of the morning rush hour, a Russian cruise missile slammed into an intersection on the northwestern corner of Shevchenko Park, sending debris and shrapnel into cars, passersby, and neighboring buildings. Six people were killed on the spot, lying in pools of blood around car wrecks and a fuming crater in the middle of the asphalt. Many more were injured. That day, other Russian missiles struck around Kyiv and other cities across the country.

For the first time, Moscow also unleashed a swarm of Iranian-made Shahed suicide drones on the capital. One aimed at a power station in central Kyiv, hitting the recently built steel-and-glass Samsung skyscraper. Hearing the lawnmower-like whine of drones overhead, police officers and soldiers jumped out of their cars, raising their Kalashnikov rifles to spray the sky with lead. Some of the drones that were hit above the city lost control and veered off course, but still inflicted damage as they smashed into buildings.

It was the worst Russian attack on central Kyiv since the war's start. A total of eighty-four missiles and twenty-four drones, by Zelensky's count, had targeted primarily Ukraine's energy infrastructure, aiming to replicate on a national scale the blackout that Russia had caused in Kharkiv and Dnipro in September. It was a partial success. Several cities, including Kyiv, were without electricity or water for the night. For the first time in living memory, only the headlights of cars illuminated the city's streets. As services were slowly restored, electric utilities warned that they would have to ration consumption in the weeks ahead.

But the mood among Ukrainian officials was more of relief than fear. "It's all they can do? Makes me laugh," the interior minister's adviser, Anton Gerashchenko, texted me that afternoon. Ukraine had just inflicted the most humiliating blow to Russia, and the Russian response had caused only a mild and temporary disruption.

Putin addressed his nation the evening of October 10. "The Kyiv regime has put itself on the same level with international terrorist formations, the most odious groups. Leaving such crimes without a reply is no longer possible," he said, adding that he had ordered a strike on "energy, military command, and communications" targets in Ukraine. This was the first time the Kremlin acknowledged that it was in fact waging a war on Ukraine's civilian electrical network. Russian media celebrated Surovikin as "General Armageddon," with hosts of TV shows anticipating how Ukraine would be pushed into a preindustrial age, freezing without electricity and heating in the winter months ahead.

Zelensky recorded a video that night from Shevchenko Park, as workers behind him removed the wreckage and filled in the crater left by the Russian missile. The St. Sophia Cathedral, just 700 meters away, had been built long before Moscow existed, he noted. "They say they want to push Ukraine back into the eighteenth century, but they have regressed much further back, turning into savages by their own will," he said. "It's impossible to make Ukraine afraid, they can only make it more united." Zelensky was speaking that night with President Biden and a slew of other world leaders, asking them to rush more sophisticated air defenses to Ukraine. That day, Ukraine had failed to intercept nearly half of the Russian missiles.

The Russians fired yet another barrage of missiles and drones the following morning, aiming to finish off the parts of Ukraine's electrical grid that they had missed in the initial salvo. There would be more and more such barrages in the following weeks. The Russian strategy was to deprive Ukrainians of the will to fight by rendering their cities uninhabitable. More than two-thirds of Ukrainians live in cities, usually in apartment blocks, where everything from heating to water and sewage to elevators depends on centralized power supplies.

"The absence of electricity means the absence of water, the absence of refrigerators, the absence of sewage, and a week into a blackout the city of Kyiv will be swimming in shit, with the clear danger of pandemics," Russian lawmaker and retired general Andrey Gurulyov gloated on one of the most-watched shows on state TV. "The strikes are extremely effective."

"Why do we need residential buildings in Kyiv to be without power and water?" another panelist asked. "Aren't we fighting against the military, not against the civilians?"

"Because how would they live? We forecast an outflow of refugees to the western border," Gurulyov replied.

"About the civilians, we are not gloating, we are compassionate, we love everyone, but we have been pushed to do this, we have no choice, they want to exterminate us and we must react," the show's host, Olga Skabeeva, concluded with a grin.

Ukrainian repair teams worked around the clock after each wave of strikes, and the apocalyptic scenario forecast by Gurulyov never materialized. But rolling blackouts became a feature of Ukraine's everyday life that fall. People woke up to wash, cook, and charge their devices in the middle of the night, during the few hours when their apartments had electricity. Generators appeared on sidewalks to power restaurants and shops. Special blackout menus offered meals that could be put together without electricity.

CHAPTER 44

"THE MOST DIFFICULT DECISIONS"

S tanding in front of a screen showing the world's most famous landmarks, Kirill Stremousov, the deputy head of the Russian administration of Kherson, recited a poem on October 17. The entire universe, he predicted, would soon be conquered by Moscow. "I see Prague and Warsaw, Budapest and Bucharest. All of this is Russian state," he crooned in a video that quickly went viral. "From the pagodas of Sri Lanka, to Korea, and to China, my beloved homeland lies wherever my tank goes." While Stremousov was a jesterlike figure, he channeled Russia's new brazen, thuggish imperialism. These ambitions, however, were ludicrously out of sync with Russia's abilities.

Surovikin made his first public appearance the following day. Downcast and unsmiling, "General Armageddon" issued a shockingly sober assessment after months of triumphalist propaganda. The situation on the front, he said at a small press conference with Russian media, was difficult. Kherson faced a particular risk after Ukrainian Himars attacks rendered the Antonovsky Bridge and the dam over the Kakhovka hydropower station impassable.

"Further plans regarding the city of Kherson will depend on the unfolding military and tactical situation. It is already very complicated today," Surovikin explained in slow, deliberate sentences. "In any case, we will be guided by the need to maximally preserve the lives of civilians and of our service members. This is our priority. We will act in a conscious, timely manner, without excluding the most difficult decisions."

That phrase—"the most difficult decisions"—spread like wildfire as soon as the video of Surovikin's remarks was released. To some, it was a clear indication that Russia, faced with the risk of having tens of thousands of troops stranded in Kherson, had decided to vacate the city and the surrounding foothold on the right bank of the Dnipro. The more nationalist Russian commentators heard a threat to use tactical nuclear weapons.

Hours later, the Russian-appointed administration of Kherson urged all civilians living on the right bank of the Dnipro to relocate to Russia, where they were promised free housing and jobs. Russian troops started removing the contents of Kherson's museums and archives, and even exhumed the coffin of the city's founder, Count Potemkin.

⊲⊳⊳

Throughout October, the Himars unit under Valentyn Koval's command continued its strikes on Kherson. Though the precious Himars machines were supposed to operate in the rear, sometimes the need to hit faraway Russian command centers and ammunition depots required them to conduct missions much closer to the front line. On one such mission in late October, two Himars trucks, with Koval in the lead vehicle, crept to within about a mile of Russian troops ensconced in a strip of forest north of Kherson. It was dark. The headlights were switched off as the lead Himars driver navigated with night-vision goggles.

Once in position, the two trucks delivered a salvo of twelve missiles soaring into the sky with a blinding, deafening swoosh. The Russians realized that Himars were in range. "The entire forest strip just lit up with fire in our direction. They shot at us with everything they had," Koval recalled. Making a quick exit, the two trucks escaped undamaged into the night.

On one of the next missions, Koval's Himars team blocked off traffic as it prepared to fire from a road north of Kherson. The other vehicles stalled on the road were packed with soldiers going to and returning from the front line. Many were damaged by shrapnel and covered with dirt and debris, their windows cracked. As Koval walked to one of these cars, asking troopers not to film the Himars operations on their phones, an infantryman leaned out the window. Deaths among his comrades had become much less frequent since the Himars began operating, he said.

"We worship you guys. Just keep on working."

Koval looked at his own clean, fresh uniform and at the sweat-soaked, tattered fatigues worn by the infantryman. He was taken aback. "If you weren't in the trench over there, we wouldn't be able to drive so freely around here," he replied.

❖

I had been introduced to Koval by Amed Khan, an American philanthropist whom I first met in Kyiv in August 2021, when he had worked with Zelensky's administration to evacuate Afghans in mortal danger from the Taliban. An amiable fifty-year-old who once served in the Clinton administration, Amed remained in close touch with his new Ukrainian friends. Once the invasion began, he spent most of his time in Ukraine, helping wherever he could. He had sent some five hundred pickup trucks to the Ukrainian Army, including four to Koval's Himars unit, and had purchased a mobile CT scanner for the Mykolaiv military hospital. Realizing that Koval's team hadn't been outfitted with proper warm clothes, Amed also bought the men winter gear.

In the first week of November, Koval took a quick trip to his home village. He took Amed along. The Himars team leader had been asked to speak at the school from which he had graduated not so long before. To Koval's shock, the teachers, the students, and scores of villagers who had gathered around all knelt as he arrived, a sign of respect for warriors in Ukraine. "Me? A hero? Are you kidding?" The young officer blushed. "Please stand up, stand up!"

The next day, as Koval's grandmother was making a hearty lunch for Amed, the lieutenant pulled out the yearbook of his military academy. "This one is dead. This one is dead. This one is wounded. This one was in the ICU." He went on one by one, with a slight frown. "Oh, this guy was the best student, he got the gold medal. All the girls used to love him . . . He was killed during the first days of the war."

❖❖❖

On November 9, Russian defense minister Sergei Shoigu, surrounded by other top commanders, sat in the middle of a long wooden table at his headquarters in Moscow. Facing them, Surovikin stood by a podium, a Russian flag and a large map of the "special military operation" behind him.

The general started off with good news, talking about how the mobilization of 300,000 reservists had stabilized the front line, stopping Ukrainian offensive attempts in Donbas and achieving successes on the outskirts of Bakhmut. Then he mentioned the bitter truth. Because of constant Ukrainian Himars strikes on crossings over the Dnipro River, the city of Kherson could no longer be adequately supplied. Ukraine, he warned, might be planning to blow up the Kakhovka Dam, flooding the low-lying areas in the Dnipro estuary and causing "full isolation" of Russian troops on the right bank of the river, including in Kherson city. Under these circumstances, Surovikin added in his choreographed remarks broadcast on Russian TV, the preferred course of action would be to organize a defense on the left bank of the Dnipro, evacuating the city of Kherson.

"I understand it is a very difficult decision, but we will preserve what is most important—the lives of our service members and the overall combat capacity of our grouping of troops. Keeping it on the right bank, in a limited area, is futile," Surovikin said. Pointing to Donbas on the map, he added, these troops "could be freed up to be used for active operations, also of offensive nature, in other directions."

"I agree," Shoigu replied. "Begin the retreat."

"The maneuver will be executed in the nearest term," Surovikin snapped back.

THE SAME DAY, STREMOUSOV, THE RUSSIAN-APPOINTED DEPUTY GOVERNOR of Kherson, was speeding in an armored vehicle on the left bank of the Dnipro. Posting optimistic assurances up until the final days that Kherson would never be surrendered, he was one of the last senior collaborators to leave.

Stremousov's car crashed and flipped on the road, according to an official announcement. The man who embodied to many Russia's brief, chaotic rule in Kherson quickly died of his injuries, at the age of forty-five. Footage that surfaced later showed bullet impacts on the vehicle, and speculation was rife that Russia's own security services had assassinated the talkative Stremousov because his services were no longer required. Officially, there was mourning. Putin that night published a decree that awarded Stremousov posthumously with Russia's Order of Courage. Russian Orthodox priests declared him a saint and made icons with his likeness to bless the troops. Occupation authorities announced that they would name a street after him in Kherson and build a statue to him in the city.

But the following day, on November 10, the remainder of the Russian military was busy abandoning Kherson. Unlike the rout in Kharkiv and northern Donetsk, this was a prepared and well-organized retreat. This time around, the Russians didn't leave behind hundreds of brand-new tanks, howitzers, and BMPs. The Russian troops even had time to blow up Kherson's electrical installations, and to remove the remaining monuments to Russian generals in the city. One of the final acts of theft was the stealing of a raccoon, a llama, and a wolf from the Kherson Zoo. The animals were sent to Crimea, ostensibly to protect them from torture by Nazi Ukrainians. The Kherson raccoon, which bitterly resisted removal and bit a Russian man's hand, predictably became a meme on both sides of the border.

The last of the Russian troops on the right bank of the Dnipro walked across the river on pontoons under the Antonovsky Bridge in the dawn hours of November 11. Then the bridge was blown up, one of the spans closest to Kherson falling into the water. For nearly 200 miles, from the Black Sea estuary to the outskirts of Zaporizhzhia, the broad, fast river, with its sealike Kakhovka Reservoir, became the boundary between government-controlled Ukraine and Russian-occupied lands. Both sides knew that crossing it for an offensive would be a complex endeavor, likely to result in immense casualties with no guarantee of success.

CHECKING THE ROADS FOR MINEFIELDS AND BOOBY TRAPS, THE FIRST RE-connaissance units of the Ukrainian military gingerly approached Kherson in the following hours. Instead of the enemy, they had to deal with crowds of celebrating locals who mobbed the advancing soldiers to take selfies and to smother them with hugs. In one of the villages on the way to Kherson, the forward unit, ready for battle, was startled to find a young woman in the middle of the road, a violin in her hands. Without speaking, she started to play Ukraine's national anthem, a melody banned for the past eight months. "Ukraine is not dead yet," it began.

By the time Ukrainian soldiers reached Kherson's main square, the site of courageous protests in March, local civilians had already raised the blue-and-yellow flag. The colors proliferated quickly. It turned out that many people in Kherson had kept Ukrainian flags at home during Russian rule.

The celebrating crowds picked up a young female Ukrainian soldier and started carrying her on their shoulders, as if at a rock concert, chanting "ZSU"—the acronym for the Ukrainian Armed Forces. Later in the day, several dozen young women, waving blue-and-yellow banners and some wearing the traditional Ukrainian flower wreaths on their heads, chanted "Thank you, thank you" at the troops. They started dancing, with small children joining an improvised street party. One of the women waved a homemade poster proclaiming, "Putin has a small dick."

At night, despite the blackout, the party went on around a bonfire, as more and more Ukrainian songs blared into the night. Stenciled images of General Zaluzhny appeared on walls in the city center and by the Antonovsky Bridge as troops began to tear down billboards proclaiming, "Kherson is a Russian city" and "Russia is here forever!"

Oksana Kocherenko, an assistant in a grocery store, hadn't seen her son, a Ukrainian soldier, since the war's outbreak. All these months, he was on the other side of the front line, in Mykolaiv. He managed to stop by for a few minutes, a quick reunion. "After that, I was crying and crying," she recalled. "So happy." Anastasia Vlasova, my photographer friend originally from Kherson, hadn't seen her mother since the invasion and worried about what might happen as the city changed hands. There was no phone service in Kherson just yet, but Vlasova's mother asked a female soldier, who had access to Starlink, to send her daughter in Kyiv a joint selfie—proof that she was alive, well, and happy. The soldier had a flower stuck under her body armor.

Confronted by footage of joy in a city that had supposedly voted over-whelmingly to become part of Russia just over a month earlier, Russian TV propagandists claimed that it had all been staged by professional actors and outsiders. But the scope of Russian humiliation was impossible to hide. Despite Putin's nuclear threats, despite the mobilization and the change in military command, the capital of what the Russian constitution had declared to be one of the country's unalienable regions had been handed over to the enemy.

"Surrendering Kherson is the biggest geopolitical defeat of Russia since the breakup of the USSR," lamented Sergei Markov, Putin's former adviser who had predicted at the beginning of the year that the Ukrainian Army would quickly switch sides and join the Russian "liberators." Anna Dolgareva, the favorite poet of the Russian far right, described the abandonment of Kherson as "the worst betrayal of the war."

Wagner's Prigozhin declined to join this chorus. Surovikin, he wrote, knew that withdrawal was necessary when he accepted command in Ukraine, and was "a man" for having assumed the required responsibility.

CHAPTER 45

KHERSON, FREE BUT EMPTY

Zelensky arrived in Kherson on November 14 for yet another victory speech, addressing the troops on the city's main square. The Kremlin's spokesman, Dmitry Peskov, protested that the Ukrainian president had illegally entered the territory of the Russian Federation. It was the best Moscow could do.

The Russians had left behind a web of minefields and booby traps. The local police headquarters in Kherson had to be blown up because Ukrainian explosive ordnance teams determined that it couldn't be safely demined. Many roads were blocked off.

On the day of Zelensky's visit to Kherson, Valentyn Koval and his Himars unit commander drove into the town of Snihurivka, which had just been vacated by the Russians. Their Nissan Navara pickup truck, one of a batch brought by Amed Khan, the American philanthropist, was laden with drones and other equipment. The vehicle hit an antipersonnel mine, a light pop that damaged the wheel but caused no injuries. As Koval jumped out to pick up a spare tire, he heard another pop. His commander had stepped out of the car and triggered another mine. His foot had been blown off. He was bleeding out and they had no tourniquets.

After trying to stabilize the wound with a cut-off seat belt, the young lieutenant raced through the minefield and then along railroad tracks to seek assistance. He braved the mines to return, and helped evacuate the officer to a hospital. The commander survived.

THE PACE OF UKRAINIAN RECONSTRUCTION EFFORTS WAS STUNNING. IN just five days since liberation, Ukrainian Railways rebuilt the damaged line to Kherson, with the first passenger train arriving in the city on November 19. Phone service, including data, was back. Road repair crews cleared up the highway to Mykolaiv, creating a temporary bypass as they repaired bridges that had been blown up by retreating Russian troops.

When I came to Kherson on December 3, I was surprised by the contents of Silpo, a large supermarket on the city's main square. Under the occupation, Silpo had been rebranded and managed by the Russians, its shelves stocked with expensive produce trucked from Crimea. Manager Tetyana Prylutska told me that the original staff worked day and night as soon as the Russians departed, clearing out the shelves and donating all the Russian- and Belarusian-made products to a food bank. Ukrainian and European food was trucked in to replace it, along with generators to keep the lights on.

"I had spent the months of occupation sitting at home, just waiting for our boys to come back," Prylutska said. "Everybody is happy that we have returned, with Ukrainian food and Ukrainian prices."

Despite the occasional bangs of artillery outside, the reborn Silpo was indistinguishable from any large European supermarket. There were fresh strawberries, pineapples, avocados, and persimmons, smoked fish and meat, and a variety of dairy and cheeses. "Oh, look, fresh yeast, I haven't seen it in nine months," exclaimed one of the shoppers, Alyona Kotalo. The cashiers once again accepted Apple Pay.

⊲⊳

The war wasn't over for Kherson.

The river had become the front line, with Russian positions hidden in the bushes across the water. Once easily crossed in a few minutes, the Dnipro now was an impenetrable obstacle. On the day we came to Kherson, rumors swirled about an agreement between the two sides that would allow civilians to traverse the river on small boats to reunite with their families. Many people in Kherson had their summer homes on the left bank of the Dnipro and were now stuck on the wrong side.

The agreement, if it existed, was never implemented. A small crowd that gathered behind the river port terminal waited in vain. Maria, a cake-shop employee before the war, told me her husband had crossed to the left bank in early November because his father, who lived in a village just south of Kherson, was on his deathbed. By the time the man died, on November 11, there was no longer any way for her husband to return. Maria was stuck in Kherson with a teenage son, hoping to rejoin her husband somehow. They owned a house in the village. The trip to the village used to take just twenty minutes. "We don't want to go to the Russian world, we just want to go to our home, where there is at least a way to get heating," she told me. "What can we do here, sit in our apartment where all the walls are now covered with mildew because there is no power and no heat, and where we get shelled all the time?" Realizing that the boats would not come, Maria said she would try another route—overland to Poland, by plane to Russia via Turkey, and then into the occupied part of Kherson via Crimea. A journey that used to take twenty minutes was now several days long.

Once prime real estate, the riverside parts of Kherson were now the city's most dangerous because they faced Russian guns. Not far from the river port, we saw smoke in the sky and found a fire truck extinguishing the consequences of an artillery strike. A shell had hit a small building in the courtyard of several apartment blocks, blowing out windows. The Russians were determined to take their revenge by destroying the city they couldn't have. Kherson now faced the same grim daily toll that Kharkiv and Mykolaiv used to endure before the Russians were pushed outside artillery range.

"Every time our troops manage to hit the Russians, they respond with chaotic fire, shooting at random at residential areas, just like this one," one of the firefighters told me.

Around the corner, another house had miraculously survived two Russian strikes, each of which landed just to the side, shearing off outer walls. Viktoria Ivanova, a sixty-five-year-old pediatrician and amateur pianist, said she had been saved by a piano that her father had purchased. During the night, at the time of the Russian attack, she was sleeping next to it. The instrument was crushed, but it protected her when the ceiling caved in. I saw Ivanova and her adult son searching through the rubble to pick up family mementos. They were now living in a friend's apartment. "This is all we have left." Ivanova sighed as she pointed to her ruined home. Despite the risks, she had decided to stay in Kherson: "This is my hometown."

Many others in Kherson weren't as fearless. At the train station, I watched as family after family arrived, with their bundles of possessions, for the daily evacuation train to Kyiv. Ambulances kept bringing the old and the infirm who couldn't walk on their own. They were laid out in the departure hall, wrapped in shiny space blankets. "I will buy Putin's corpse" was daubed on the side of one of the ambulances.

Yanina Deychenko told me at the train station that she was thrilled when the city was liberated. But since then, one Russian shell had wrecked her house, while another had severed her neighbor's legs. Eight months pregnant, Deychenko pointed to her belly. "Delivering a baby in these conditions? No way." She shook her head. "We've held out long enough, but now the jokes are over."

Kherson was finally free, but it was quickly emptying.

❖

On the way out, we stopped by Buzki Park, the site of the heroic but futile attempt at resistance on the first day of Russian occupation in Kherson. There was a small, improvised memorial there: a Ukrainian flag, flowers, and a cross with the words "March 1, 2022. Kherson's Territorial Defense fighters reached the sky." Otherwise, the park looked unremarkable, save for the trees damaged by Russian machine guns. As military positions go, it was hopeless.

In Mykolaiv farther north, people started adjusting to the idea that they were no longer in a frontline city. A slew of new restaurants and coffee shops opened. Briefly, clean water appeared in taps, replacing the brackish liquid from the Southern Buh estuary to which the city's residents had grown accustomed. The water-filtering station near Kherson, disabled during the

Russian occupation and repaired after that city's liberation, didn't last long. Within days, it was destroyed by a Russian missile strike. Moscow wanted Ukrainians to remain in misery.

As we sat in a Mykolaiv restaurant in early December, the familiar sequence of a Russian missile and drone barrage began. Mid-meal, warning apps on everyone's phones started ringing with air-raid alerts. Telegram channels lit up with notices of missiles heading toward Ukrainian cities, with estimated impact times. The waitress asked us to settle the bill before the lights went out. Everyone rushed to charge their phones while they still could. I went to the bathroom before the water supply would be cut off. Half an hour later, the restaurant's chandelier flickered and died. The Wi-Fi disappeared, and data services on our mobile phones vanished another hour later.

The heaviest Russian missile barrage, on November 23, had caused such power imbalances in Ukraine's national grid that it forced the shutdown of all three nuclear power plants under Kyiv's control, an unprecedented event. It had taken three days to power them up again, using one of the hydropower stations to restart the grid. The resulting blackout was the longest and most widespread in the country's modern history. Trying to prevent a repeat, Ukrainian energy system operators now disconnected the power lines to consumers preventively, as soon as massive missile barrages began.

Even though Moscow's stockpile of cruise missiles was dwindling, Russia kept lobbing them at Ukrainian cities, hoping for a strategic breakthrough. Sergei Markov, the former Putin adviser, predicted in late November that Kyiv would be soon on its knees. "Logistics will be disrupted, conditions will become maximally unfavorable, which will cause a new exodus of citizens. Ukrainian cities will turn into an environment in which there are no chances for survival. It's the lack of communications, infrastructure, heating, electricity, and food," he gloated in an interview with a Moscow newspaper.

"The Ukrainian Army and the Ukrainian state will not survive this winter," echoed Vladimir Bobkov, the deputy speaker of the Russian-picked parliament of Crimea.

But the Russians, once again, underestimated Ukrainian resilience. There was no exodus. Gritting their teeth, Ukrainians procured a staggering number of generators in the weeks after the strikes on the energy infrastructure began—a total capacity of one gigawatt, or the equivalent of an entire nuclear reactor. New government-operated "Resilience Centers" with electricity, heating, Wi-Fi, and free food popped up in city squares across Ukraine.

The Ukrainians also found surprising ways to strike back. On December 5, long-range Ukrainian drones targeted two bases from which Russian strategic bombers launched cruise missiles, in the cities of Engels and Ryazan. This attack, and a repeat run three weeks later, destroyed several Russian aircraft and killed air force personnel. The Russians were shocked. Engels is the home of the Russian bombers equipped to carry nuclear weapons, part of Moscow's strategic nuclear triad. It is farther away from Ukraine than is Moscow. The fact that Ukraine had the capacity to strike so far reshuffled Russian calculations. A large part of the bomber fleet based in Engels had to be withdrawn beyond the Urals.

When we returned to Kyiv in mid-December, the city was making its best effort to carry on as usual. The Opera Theater still had its daily performances. The Pinchuk Art Centre put up a new contemporary art exhibition. The Zhovten cinema restarted its evening screenings. When power was cut off, moviegoers sat in their winter overcoats, waiting for staff to start up the generator for the rest of the film.

The only strategic consequence of the Russian missile campaign was to persuade Western governments to consider providing Ukraine with sophisticated air-defense systems, which up until then had been deemed too expensive and complicated. Year after year, Ukraine had been asking for Patriot missiles to replace its aging—and dwindling—Soviet-vintage S-300 air-defense batteries. The scenes of misery and blackouts in freezing Ukrainian cities, and the fear of yet another massive exodus of Ukrainian refugees, proved a convincing argument. In December, after two months of Russian strikes on Ukrainian infrastructure, the Biden administration and its allies finally took Ukrainian pleas seriously.

PART 11

UNBREAKABLE

CHAPTER 46

THE BAKHMUT MEATGRINDER

By mid-December, the focus of the war swung back to the eastern Donetsk region, with the city of Bakhmut becoming the main battlefield. Ukrainian brigades freed up by the takeover of Kherson redeployed to the Bakhmut front line, taking with them artillery pieces, tanks, and infantry fighting vehicles. Russia, too, moved many of its units to Donetsk. Hostilities in the Kherson region from now on were limited to artillery exchanges and an occasional raid by Ukrainian special forces, who used speedboats to briefly cross the Dnipro.

Bakhmut was Wagner's area of operations, and Yevgeny Prigozhin's private army had been fighting to capture the small city since the summer. "Our aim is not Bakhmut itself, but the destruction of the Ukrainian Army and lowering its combat potential," Prigozhin explained in late November, dubbing it "Operation Bakhmut Meatgrinder."

Thanks to its prison recruitment drive, Wagner had plenty of cannon fodder to expend. Prigozhin's private army now numbered some 50,000 troops, according to Western intelligence estimates. Faced with execution in case of desertion or unauthorized retreat, Wagner's men kept slowly but surely advancing in the Bakhmut area, creeping a mile or two every week while sustaining tremendous casualties. Hardly anyone mourned these rapists, murderers, and robbers inside Russia. In fact, some of their hometowns even refused to bury them. As far as many Russians were concerned, Prigozhin was killing two birds with one stone: destroying the Ukrainian enemy and purifying Russia of its criminal underclass.

A gruesome video released on Wagner-affiliated social media channels in November left no doubt about the fate that awaited traitors within its ranks. Yevgeny Nuzhin, an inmate recruited by Wagner and then taken prisoner by Ukrainian forces, had been traded back to Russia for a Ukrainian POW. While in Ukrainian detention, Nuzhin had made the fatal mistake of speaking ill of Wagner. The Wagner video showed Nuzhin's head tied with plastic shrink-wrap to a surface, and then bashed in with a sledgehammer as he spoke.

The execution, of course, was a crime under Russian law. But nobody was going to go after Prigozhin, who seemed untouchable because of his direct connection to Putin. He taunted his critics by demanding an investigation. "I'd call this movie 'Dog's death to a dog,'" Prigozhin said with a chuckle when asked about Nuzhin's death. "Excellent director's work, you can watch it all in one breath. I hope no animals were harmed during the filming."

Soon, Wagner started giving its trademark sledgehammers, decorated with a carving of a mountain of skulls, as gifts to Russian politicians. Parliament member Sergey Mironov, the head of the Just Russia party, posted a photo of himself grinning as he held one specimen. "It's a useful instrument," he wrote.

UNLIKE WAGNER, THE REGULAR RUSSIAN MILITARY HAD LITTLE TO SHOW for its efforts, even as it also sustained astounding losses. Several attempts to attack the strategic town of Vuhledar southwest of Bakhmut ended in spectacular failure as Ukrainian forces used precision artillery and remotely laid mines to destroy advancing columns of Russian tanks and BMPs.

Marines of the 155th Brigade of the Russian Pacific Fleet, a unit that had lost much of its strength in Moshchun near Kyiv in March, sparked an outcry in November. In a letter to the governor of their home region in Vladivostok, they complained of inept leadership and suicidal missions after the first attempt at a Russian Vuhledar offensive collapsed. In just four days, the letter read, the Marines lost 300 men either killed, wounded, or missing, and half of their vehicles. The Marines' wrath was focused on two natives of the North Caucasus republic of Dagestan bordering Chechnya: the new commander of the Russian Eastern Military District, Lieutenant General Rustam Muradov, and their direct commander, Colonel Suhrab Akhmedov. The two officers had sent the Pacific Marines to slaughter, hiding true casualty statistics, to get promotions and awards from Valeriy Gerasimov, the chief of the Russian General Staff, the letter accused: "They couldn't care less about anyone as long as they can showcase themselves. They refer to our people as meat."

Earlier in the war, such a letter would have been suppressed. The governor in Vladivostok tried to do just that, quickly dismissing the complaint as inaccurate and exaggerated, and posting a video with other Marines of the 155th Brigade claiming successes in Vuhledar. But it was too late. A slew of *voenkors* and bloggers now on Prigozhin's payroll quickly fanned outrage across Russia.

The political goal of Wagner's owner was to contrast his own achievements, no matter how costly and small, with the ineptitude of Russia's regular military. Soon, Prigozhin started releasing videos of Wagner's men insulting Gerasimov and complaining about the lack of support from the ministry of defense. Initially, he issued coy no-comment statements when asked if he shared their feelings. It wouldn't be long before Prigozhin himself started shouting profanities aimed at Shoigu and Gerasimov. Such open fractures at the core of the Russian state were unprecedented under Putin's twenty-three-year rule—a warning of more trouble ahead.

⋄⋄⋄

One of the units that Ukraine redeployed to Bakhmut from the Kherson front was Terra, the drone reconnaissance team made up of onetime Flemish knight reenactors. Mykola Volokhov, the commander, was away on a trip to Kyiv as we headed east: the unit was being merged into the newly formed 3rd Storm Brigade, which absorbed many veterans of Azov.

A keen student of military history, Volokhov was worried that Russia was forcing Ukraine to fight in Bakhmut on its own terms. Throughout the

war, Ukraine had managed to outsmart the Russians by avoiding the kind
of set-piece battles where Moscow could leverage its advantage in firepower
and men. But now, tens of thousands of Ukrainian troops, brigades that had
little experience working together, were being sucked into Prigozhin's meatgrinder. Running a centralized campaign in a contained area was one thing
that the Russians were good at. Ukraine, Volokhov worried, wasn't ready.

"Some of the things that make us strong, such as independence, initiative, the ability to act even without clear orders, can also become our weak-
nesses when many units are in the same place, and each has its own view,"
he told me. "The outcome in Bakhmut will depend on the ability of our
forces to achieve coordination."

On that score, the record was not encouraging. Wagner had just made
a breakthrough southwest of Bakhmut, seizing the high-ground village of
Kurdyumivka. It happened because a battalion of unprepared Territorial
Defense recruits holding that stretch of the front simply walked away in
early December, without warning Ukrainian units to their flanks. "We just
saw them leave in the morning, with their backpacks, on drone footage, and
when we called to ask what was happening, they told us: nothing," reminisced a company commander on one of the flanks. "The Russians were
there an hour later."

Volokhov offered to set me up with his friends in another infantry unit
operating south of Bakhmut, not far from Kurdyumivka. When I texted
these soldiers, they were reluctant, saying that the situation in the area had
become too dangerous. By the time we arrived in Bakhmut on December 12,
Volokhov told me that his friends' positions had been overrun in yet another Wagner breakthrough. The men we were supposed to see had gone
missing, either imprisoned or dead.

Advancing to the north and the south of the city, Wagner was inching
closer and closer to the two main roads linking Bakhmut with the rest of
Ukrainian-controlled territory. The main highway was no longer safe, so we
had to use a secondary route through the village of Khromove. The city was
filled with troops. Tanks roared through the main thoroughfare, and teams
of soldiers were digging trenches in the central square, in the once-quiet
park across from Bakhmut's city hall. "Make it pretty, you're in the army
now," a sergeant shouted at one of his men shoveling the cold ground.

From the square, the front line was only a few hundred yards away. At what used to be Bakhmut's market, closer to the Wagner lines, I ran into anti-Kadyrov Chechen fighters. They had already spray-painted graffiti in Chechen all over the neighborhood. "It's like Mariupol all over again. The Russians are wiping this city from the face of the earth," said one of these men, whose call sign was Bess.

Standing by two American-made MRAPs around the corner, soldiers from a different unit were catching their breath after a firefight, shouting at me to stay behind a pockmarked building because a Russian line of fire had opened beyond its edge. The enemy was making progress, Yuri, the commander, told me as he lit up a cigarette. "Nobody cares about their lives. We shoot them, and they keep coming back, like cockroaches. The fields all around us stink because of their corpses, but there is still one wave coming after another."

The central third of Bakhmut, with the main square and the market, is bounded on the east by the shallow Bakhmutka River, and on the west by a railway line and berm, beyond which lies a fortresslike neighborhood of high-rises. The Russians were already in many parts of the eastern third, across the river. With all the bridges blown out, the Ukrainians used a pontoon crossing to get to the other side, but it had just been damaged.

We raced and plunged into a trench right by the disabled pontoon; Ukrainian soldiers at the position paid little attention to newcomers. A pickup truck came to the pontoon from the other side, its driver not realizing that it was no longer possible to cross. Then a handful of soldiers on foot ferried across a plastic bag with the body of one of their comrades. We had seen a pile of such bags at a newly set up field hospital on the western entrance to the city. The main hospital where we stayed in August was too close to the front line and had been abandoned.

Minutes after the body was carried across, Russian shells—likely mortars—started landing in front of us, with a flash followed by plumes of smoke. The strikes missed the crossing, but they were close. Too close.

We jumped out of the trench and ran back to our armored car, which had been shielded behind a wall. There was no longer any phone signal in central Bakhmut, so we headed back to the western part of the city, behind the railway line, where our phones came back alive.

Vsevolod Kozhemiako, the commander of Khartiya in Kharkiv, had connected me with one of his friends, tennis player Sergiy Stakhovsky, who now fought in Bakhmut with a unit of Ukrainian special forces. "Come," Stakhovsky texted me, sending me the location on the southern edge of the city.

The unit to which he was attached operated a 120mm mortar that they carried in their pickup truck, shifting from one position to another every day. The targets were fielded by a drone reconnaissance unit elsewhere, now standard practice for Ukrainian troops.

The compound where we met was an abandoned corporate office, with a burned bulldozer in the courtyard and occasional craters from Russian shells nearby. Stakhovsky took me upstairs, to a window from which we could see Russian positions. A prewar map of Bakhmut on the wall, still with its Soviet name of Artemivsk, was filled with ads for local businesses that no longer existed, and probably would never exist again. Computer repair. Construction materials. Cosmetics and massage.

Stakhovsky, who had formally retired from professional tennis the previous month, lived in Hungary with his Russian wife, and focused before the war on his winemaking business in Transcarpathia. As the father of multiple children, he was exempted from mobilization. He happened to be in Dubai when the war broke out. Without much reflection, he rushed to return to defend Ukraine, running into Kozhemiako at the border crossing with Poland.

The situation in Bakhmut made him gloomy. "The Russians are emptying their prisons and sending their worst to die here, while we are losing some of our best," he said. "It's not at all a fair trade."

In the westernmost third of Bakhmut, there was still some semblance of life. Two elderly women, dressed in ancient fur coats, sat on a bench outside their high-rise despite heavy shelling. There was a Ukrainian military position in a nearby basement, but the troops, wary of artillery fire, remained underground. "We're so used to it, we no longer pay much attention," one of the women, seventy-six-year-old Ludmyla Bondarenko, said, pointing to a crater left by a Russian round that had hit the courtyard in the morning. "It's been going on for months. When is it going to end?" she asked me.

"It's probably never going to end," replied the other woman, seventy-five-year-old Zoya Shilkova.

A few blocks away, a "Resilience Center" created by volunteers in an abandoned store had put up a Christmas tree. A few dozen civilians, some bandaged, lounged inside charging up their phones, browsing the internet on Starlink Wi-Fi, and drinking tea. A TV on the wall broadcast Ukrainian news. One of the volunteers had a box with some of the most widely used medications in front of him, to disburse to anyone who needed them.

The woman who ran the center, Tetyana Shcherbak, was on the verge of tears as we spoke. A native of the city, she refused to contemplate the idea of leaving. "Of course, Bakhmut will hold out. We believe in our soldiers, in our eagles, in our falcons. We're Ukrainian," she said. "Our enemies will vanish."

"Like the dew at sunrise," I replied without thinking, mouthing the Ukrainian national anthem's next line. She started crying and hugged me.

The "Resilience Center" lasted another two months. In April, the neighborhood was obliterated as Wagner troops conquered its scorched ruins.

ON THE WAY BACK TO KYIV, WE STOPPED IN TERNY, OUR FIRST VISIT TO THE village for which Carpathian Sich's soldiers had shed so much blood. The battalion was engaged in grinding forest warfare with Russian troops entrenched a few miles to the east. Two trophy Russian T-80 tanks were in its possession. The first of the tanks had an unexpected engine problem and wouldn't move when we were offered a ride to positions. "A tank is like a woman. It doesn't always get turned on," quipped Vasylyna, the battalion's press officer. The second one worked, racing through chilly mud.

A rock band was visiting the village that afternoon for an improvised concert to cheer up the troops. There were no civilians in Terny. One of the band's numbers was the battle song of Ukrainian nationalists, first performed in 1932. In the ruins of a bombed-out village home, the lyrics seemed particularly poignant:

> No one has gained their liberty by weeping,
> But those who fight, they gain the world.

❖

To the Ukrainian generals, Bakhmut was of secondary importance. The town of Chasiv Yar just to the west sat on higher ground, and could be used to set up the next, easier line of defense, preventing a Russian breakthrough to the rest of the Ukrainian-controlled Donetsk region. "From the military standpoint, Bakhmut doesn't have strategic significance," Oleksandr Syrsky, the commander of Ground Forces, told Ukrainian TV in December. "But at the same time, it has psychological significance." In private, General Zaluzhny was also wary of committing so many resources to the city and falling into Prigozhin's "meatgrinder" trap.

But unlike in the early days, the war was being run at the weekly meetings of the Stavka, with Zelensky making the strategic decisions. He wasn't about to give up. A fall of Bakhmut would mark the first Ukrainian retreat since July, reversing the narrative of Ukrainian victories—and potentially endangering the crucial Western support for Kyiv. He decided to turn the city into a symbol of Ukrainian toughness. Cabinet ministers started wearing sweatshirts proclaiming "Fortress Bakhmut" and a pop song with the same name became a mainstay of TV and radio programming.

Zaluzhny, the chief commander of Ukrainian forces, alarmed Ukrainians that week in a rare interview with *The Economist*. The Russians, he said, were preparing resources and men for a major new offensive, which he expected sometime between January and March. "The Russian mobilization has worked," Zaluzhny warned. "I have no doubt that they will have another go at Kyiv."

Ukraine's need to prepare for that Russian push—and to plan its own offensives to retake occupied land—meant that men, equipment, and ammunition had to be withheld from places like Bakhmut. "Our troops are all tied up in battles now, they are bleeding . . . May the soldiers in the trenches forgive me," he told the magazine. "It's more important to focus on the accumulation of resources right now for the more protracted and heavier battles that may begin next year."

To beat the enemy, Zaluzhny said, he needed more resources from the West: 300 tanks, 600–700 infantry fighting vehicles, and 500 artillery pieces. At the time, Biden, Scholz, and other Western leaders kept saying that Ukraine wouldn't be getting any Western-made tanks and IFVs. Only a fraction of the requested artillery was on the way.

Foreign Minister Kuleba complained to me that Western decision-making on weapons supplies was based on a perverse logic: no help forthcoming when Ukraine had momentum, but a move to step in when the situation became critical and the Ukrainian military faced collapse. "This is how it worked in the beginning of the war with 155mm artillery, this is how it worked with Himars," he said. "We need to completely change the optics. Instead of waiting for a crisis in order for them to make a decision, they need to make decisions now in order to avoid a crisis."

❖

A few days after we left Bakhmut, Zelensky arrived in the city to meet Ukrainian troops. He handed out medals and honored the fallen with a moment of silence. He joked that he couldn't promise uninterrupted electricity to their families, one of the men's top concerns. "It's a complicated situation. Sometimes there is light, and sometimes there isn't," he said. "What's important is to have a light inside."

The soldiers gave Zelensky a big Ukrainian flag inscribed with their names and asked him to take it to the US Congress. Another officer handed him one of his medals. Zelensky's convoy raced west after the meeting, making a 920-mile-long overnight journey by train and car across Ukraine to the Polish airport of Rzeszów. The following day, the Ukrainian president disembarked in Washington, DC—his first trip abroad since the war began.

CHAPTER 47

LEOPARDS FREED

The meeting in the Oval Office, by a burning fireplace in the afternoon of December 21, was full of symbolism. Zelensky wore combat boots and an olive-drab sweatshirt emblazoned with the Ukrainian *tryzub*. President Biden put on a striped tie in blue and yellow Ukrainian colors. Zelensky repeatedly thanked the American president for the weapons deliveries and then passed along a medal that he had brought from Bakhmut.

The military cross had been earned by a captain named Pavlo, the commander of a Himars missile battery.

"He said that so many of his brothers were saved by this system," Zelensky told Biden as he handed over the medal.

"It's an honor," the US president replied.

Earlier that morning, while Zelensky was still flying across the Atlantic on a US Air Force C-40, a military version of the Boeing 737-700, the White House released long-awaited news. Ukraine would finally receive a battery of Patriots, a powerful defense against Russian cruise-missile barrages.

Zelensky's message in Washington was simple: the tide of war had turned again, with Russia regaining the initiative. Ukraine needed Western weapons, fast. Not just Patriots, but tanks, infantry fighting vehicles, artillery, aircraft, and all the other things that the West until now had denied because it needlessly feared provoking Russia.

Zelensky arrived in Washington at a delicate political moment. The previous month, Biden's Democratic Party had lost control of the House of Representatives. A small but vocal part of the Republican Party now in charge of the federal government's purse strings was bitterly opposed to American military aid to Ukraine. Some lawmakers, such as Marjorie Taylor Greene of Georgia, kept repeating almost verbatim Putin's talking points about alleged Ukrainian Nazis. The incoming Republican Speaker, Kevin McCarthy, was more supportive of Ukraine but insisted that Kyiv would no longer be getting a "blank check."

There were still a few more days to go before the new Congress was seated, and the White House tried hard to make sure that Biden's $1.7 trillion appropriations bill was passed before Christmas by the lame-duck session. Among other things, this legislation funded military help for Ukraine at least through the summer of 2023. Zelensky's visit focused their minds.

At 7:38 p.m. on December 21, members of the US Congress gathered in a joint session gave a standing ovation as the Ukrainian president came up to the podium. He smiled as thunderous applause went on, and on, and on. "I think it's too much." Zelensky turned to Vice President Kamala Harris and Speaker Nancy Pelosi, who presided over the event.

The American military support, while indispensable, was insufficient, he said bluntly.

"Next year will be a turning point, when Ukrainian courage and American resolve must guarantee the future of our common freedom, the freedom of people who stand for their values," he explained, in heavily accented but fluent English. "You can speed up our victory. I know it . . . So much in the world depends on you. Decisions can save millions of people. Let these decisions be taken."

Then Zelensky spoke about Bakhmut, comparing the Ukrainian effort there to the Battle of Saratoga, the pivot in America's own War of Independence against the British. At the end of the speech, Zelensky handed the large Ukrainian flag signed by Bakhmut's defenders to Pelosi, who immediately raised it above the podium. "Outstanding," Vice President Harris leaned in to whisper.

Zelensky departed for Kyiv, with stopovers for more meetings in London,

Paris, and Brussels. American lawmakers pushed through the appropriations bill before Congress recessed. Ukraine was guaranteed another $44.9 billion in American assistance, enough to fund its planned offensive.

Zelensky's visit to Washington and European capitals underscored that, after nearly a hundred billion dollars spent, the conflict had become the West's own war. True, no Western soldiers were fighting and dying in Ukraine, except for volunteers in units like the International Legion and Carpathian Sich. But a Russian success after such a commitment to Ukraine would have devastating consequences for the West's own credibility and deterrent capacity around the world.

"Beijing is watching closely to see the price Russia pays, or the reward it receives, for its aggression. What is happening in Europe today can happen in Asia tomorrow," NATO secretary-general Jens Stoltenberg warned. "If Putin wins in Ukraine, the message to him and other authoritarian leaders will be that they can use force to get what they want. This will make the world more dangerous and us more vulnerable."

⦁⦁⦁

Modern tanks and infantry fighting vehicles, indispensable for any offensive, were among Ukraine's top requests. Just a few months earlier, Germany was refusing flat-out to supply its modern Marder IFVs to Ukraine, devising instead a complicated scheme under which the Marders would be shipped to Greece and the Greeks would send to Ukraine outdated Soviet-designed BMP-1s instead. Berlin had also warned other European nations, such as Poland and Spain, which considered sending German-made Leopard tanks to Ukraine, that it wouldn't permit such a move.

The big breakthrough came on January 5. German chancellor Scholz and President Biden announced that Berlin would ship a fleet of Marders to Ukraine while the United States started supplying its own Bradley IFVs. A decision on tanks took three more weeks, with Britain and France breaking the taboo by announcing that they would deliver fourteen Challenger 2 tanks and fourteen AMX-10 armored fighting vehicles. Despite growing public pressure to supply Leopards, including a "Free the leopards" meme campaign involving celebrities wearing leopard-patterned clothes, Scholz refused to budge until, once again, Washington took the lead. On January 25, Biden announced that the United States would be sending thirty-one Abrams tanks to Ukraine. The same day, Scholz declared that Germany and its European allies would be providing Ukraine with dozens of Leopards.

All in all, the United States and NATO allies started training and equipping nine brand-new Ukrainian brigades. With more than 200 tanks, nearly 900 fighting vehicles, and 150 artillery pieces, these brigades would be the core force of the planned offensive. In Kyiv, satisfaction with this breakthrough was tinged with sadness. These numbers weren't too far from what the Ukrainians had asked for in May, a request rejected at the time as unrealistic. If these weapons had been supplied in August, when Russia's military was stretched thin, they could have ensured a strategic Ukrainian victory and possibly ended the war. But Russia had since mobilized hundreds of thousands of soldiers and erected a system of fortifications and minefields all along the front line. The cost of any Ukrainian advance would now be exponentially higher—in equipment, and in lives lost. Because of Western prevarication, a strategic opportunity had slipped away.

⚬⚬⚬

On the ground in Bakhmut, Ukrainian commanders weren't thrilled with Zelensky's branding of the city as a Ukrainian Saratoga. To many of them, continuing to cling to the city, despite mounting losses, distracted Ukraine from the bigger prize—preparations for a campaign to retake the coastlines of the Black and Azov seas, strategic terrain with much more importance for the state's viability than the blighted post-industrial cities of Donbas.

Wagner's successes in entering the urban tissue of Bakhmut, where Russian troops engaged in street-to-street fighting, meant that the ratio of casualties was no longer disproportionately skewed in Ukraine's favor. In early January, Wagner broke through Ukrainian lines north of Bakhmut, to the salt-mining town of Soledar, a move that threatened the remaining supply routes to the city. The Ukrainian retreat from Soledar was disorganized and Prigozhin delighted in showing footage of rigid, frozen cadavers of Ukrainian soldiers. With his characteristic panache, he recorded a video in Soledar's giant salt mine, holding a packet of the town's main product.

The loss of Soledar meant that Ukrainian troops in Bakhmut increasingly faced the risk of being cut off, as Wagner's men kept inching closer to the one remaining safe route into the city. When I spoke to Volokhov that week, he—like many other Ukrainian officers and soldiers on the Bakhmut front—was perplexed by Zelensky's decision to keep battling for the city.

"It's not me, it's King Leonidas who has figured out that you should fight the enemy on the terrain that is advantageous to you," Volokhov told me, a reference to the Battle of Thermopylae, a narrow pass between the mountains and the sea where the Greeks tried to stop the massed armies of the Persian Empire in 480 BC. Russia's bigger size meant that even with lopsided casualties, Moscow was still winning the attrition war over the long run. "The exchange rate of trading our lives favors the Russians," he said. "If this goes on like this, we could run out."

WAGNER, HOWEVER, WAS ALSO RUNNING OUT OF MEN. EVEN THE POPULA-tion of Russian prison camps was not endless. After initially refusing to re-cruit prisoners with HIV and hepatitis C, Prigozhin allowed them to replenish the dwindling ranks in late December. One of these recruits, forty-eight-year-old Yevgeny, had been convicted for murder, robbery, and drug offenses. Rejected in October, he was told to pack up on New Year's Eve, then fly to Rostov and transfer to a training camp called Druzhba. All seventy of the recruits in the camp had HIV or hepatitis, or both; they wore color-coded wristbands to identify their infections.

Yevgeny's three-week training was focused on one disposable mission: how to storm a Ukrainian position in the forest using small-group tactics. His group of twelve men was ordered to crawl toward a Ukrainian outpost north of Bakhmut, which immediately opened up with machine-gun and mortar fire. "This was dumb. People were blown into pieces in front of my eyes," Yevgeny, who was captured by Ukrainian forces months later, told me. Of his group's members, most were killed that day. Yevgeny was injured in his arm. Only four men were unhurt. But the next wave of Wagner attackers quickly replaced the casualties, continuing to inch ahead. Retreat was not an option. "If you don't push forward and do what you're told, you simply get nullified," Yevgeny said, using Wagner's term for on-the-spot executions.

Some Ukrainian soldiers started experiencing signs of psychological distress after machine-gunning dozens of Wagner's convict-recruits every day. But overall, the tactic worked. "It's a zombie war," explained Senior Lieutenant Petro Horbatenko, an Azov veteran who had fought in Moshchun and now commanded a 3rd Storm Brigade battalion on the Bakhmut front. "They are throwing cannon fodder at us, aiming to cause maximum damage. We obviously cannot respond the same way because we don't have as much personnel—and we are sensitive to losses."

⟡

On January 7, Valentyn Koval and two men in the Himars battery traveled back to Snihurivka. On the way, the lieutenant sent a video to Amed Khan, the American philanthropist. Sappers had demined the area. "It will be a pity if one of us loses a leg there," Koval joked. "We have this dark humor. But how can we do it otherwise?"

Hours later, his left leg was blown off just below the knee. His right leg was peppered with shrapnel, bones broken, the foot hanging just by the flesh. "Just tear it off," Koval yelled at a fellow soldier evacuating him. The trooper tried to pull, but failed. Tourniquets on his thighs, Koval was brought to a hospital in Mykolaiv, then Odesa. His mother came to the city from Poland, his girlfriend from his village. Koval had told his father to remain in Poland. "If you come back here, they'll draft you in no time and will send you to die in Bakhmut," he urged.

One of the first things the injured soldiers did was to check whether their genitals were intact. Everyone was fine on that score in Koval's hospital ward, an unlikely coincidence. Those who had lost their reproductive ability, a nurse explained to him later, had been segregated in a separate ward.

Several surgeries in Odesa saved Koval's right leg. Pulling all possible strings, Khan arranged with Zaluzhny to allow the lieutenant to be transferred for more surgeries and rehabilitation in Switzerland. The American philanthropist and his friends picked up the tab. The private plane that took Koval to Geneva stopped for refueling at the same German airfield where he had trained to operate the Himars.

❖

Apart from Wagner's advances on the Bakhmut front, Russia had no successes of note that winter. Before midnight on December 31, as hundreds of mobilized soldiers were ordered to watch Putin's New Year's Eve address in a former vocational school in the city of Makiivka, a particularly well-timed Ukrainian Himars strike hit the building. The Russians had kept their ammunition and fuel in the same compound, something that only inexperienced commanders would permit. Secondary explosions engulfed the building in a ball of fire, causing the single largest recorded loss of life for the Russian military since the war began. The Russian ministry of defense acknowledged 89 fatalities in Makiivka, including the regiment's deputy commander. Russian media reported 140 soldiers were killed, while Ukraine estimated the total fatalities at some 400 men. Trying to quell public outrage, the Russian ministry of defense promised an investigation, which was then promptly forgotten.

With no battlefield victories, Surovikin also had little to show for his campaign against Ukrainian infrastructure. By January, as Moscow started to run low on cruise missiles, the frequency and intensity of these barrages had to be reduced. Ukraine's electrical system, meanwhile, hadn't been destroyed and blackouts had become more and more infrequent. The only lasting consequence of "General Armageddon's" war on Ukrainian power stations, it turned out, was Biden's decision to start supplying Kyiv with Patriot air defenses.

The public support so generously offered to Surovikin by Prigozhin and Kadyrov, meanwhile, had turned into a kiss of death as Wagner's owner engaged in increasingly public conflict with the ministry of defense, accusing it of deliberately withholding ammunition to sabotage his men.

On January 11, Russian defense minister Shoigu had had enough. He appointed Valeriy Gerasimov, the chief of Russia's General Staff, to take direct command of Moscow's "special military operation." Surovikin was demoted, no longer the public face of the war, to become one of Gerasimov's three deputies. A day earlier, Shoigu also tapped Colonel General Aleksandr Lapin—whom Kadyrov and Prigozhin had wanted to see busted to private and sent to the trenches—to become chief of staff of Russia's Ground Forces.

Weeks later, Lapin resumed command on the Luhansk front. The generals in Moscow weren't going to surrender authority to Putin's former cook and to a former Chechen jihadi so easily. Another decision they made was to bar Wagner from recruiting prisoners, depriving Prigozhin of his main source of manpower. The ministry of defense established its own prisoner units, called Shtorm-Z. Without Wagner's experience, command structure, or cohesion, these prisoner forces proved nowhere near as efficient.

SHOIGU AND GERASIMOV WANTED A VICTORY, SOMETHING THAT WOULD end Prigozhin's boasts about how only Wagner had the capacity to advance. They chose as the main target the town of Vuhledar, where the ill-fated 155th Marine Brigade had been decimated in November. With its labyrinth of high-rises that effectively turned the town into a fortress, Vuhledar protected the Ukrainian-held part of the Donetsk region from the south. It also sat uncomfortably close to the only railway line linking Russia with Crimea that also avoids the Kerch Bridge—so close that the line couldn't be used.

On February 2, Lieutenant General Muradov, the commander of Russia's Eastern District, issued orders for tank and BMP columns to attack Vuhledar, moving in open terrain. Ukrainian defenders watched the attack using a swarm of commercial drones. They also had a new weapon in their arsenal—the US-supplied RAAMS, anti-armor mines that can be laid remotely and use 155mm artillery shells.

As the Russian column began to advance, the front vehicle was hit. Panicked, other tanks and BMPs started turning around, running into minefields, and blowing up. Some drove over infantry soldiers, smashing them into the mud with their treads. Ukrainian artillery started to shell the now stalled column. Drones hovering above it all filmed scenes of carnage, including a sequence in which a Russian tank driver, his uniform on fire, runs away from a tank just seconds before it blows up, killing the rest of the crew. Other Ukrainian drones, armed with bomblets, finished off the survivors.

But the Russians didn't relent, and kept launching wave after wave of similarly suicidal assaults in the following days. By February 8, an entire brigade's worth of tanks, BMPs, and other armored vehicles lay smoldering in the fields outside Vuhledar, as did dozens, if not hundreds, of bodies. It was probably Russia's single biggest loss of equipment since the failed river crossing in Bilohorivka in May.

Wagner-affiliated media didn't bother disguising their gloating. "Muradov is a cowardly bitch, sitting behind in the command center and sending column after column to Vuhledar," the Grey Zone Telegram channel affiliated with Wagner wrote on February 10. "This cowardly bitch is lucky that he isn't in the vicinity of fighters who would frag him, as they already fragged similarly smartass commanders locally." Russian casualties in these failed attacks included Colonel Sergey Polyakov, commander of the 14th Special Purpose Brigade, an elite special forces unit of the GRU military intelligence.

"The Ukrainians shot up the attackers like in a shooting gallery, and our fighters weren't able to cause them casualties in return," summed up Igor Girkin, the former defense minister of the Donetsk "people's republic."

The extent of the disaster in Vuhledar, however, seemed to go unnoticed in the Kremlin. On February 17, Putin signed a decree promoting Muradov in rank, to colonel general.

Things didn't get much better for the Russian Army at other points on the front line. A push to take the city of Adviivka caused huge losses to Russian infantry, with only minor gains. Piecemeal attempts at an offensive in Zaporizhzhia proved futile. The much-feared incursion from Belarus into Kyiv also didn't occur. By mid-February, it became clear that Russia had wasted its window of opportunity, at a time when it had finally enjoyed numerical superiority in troops while Ukraine still awaited the training of new brigades and the delivery of Western-made tanks, fighting vehicles, and artillery.

Sergei Markov, the former Putin adviser who had predicted a Ukrainian collapse, noted the disappointing reality. "The absence of a big offensive by the Russian Army, which was expected by everyone," he wrote, "has become the most important event of the winter."

CHAPTER 48

"NOBODY LOVES LOSERS"

When Manu, Stevo, and I returned to Kyiv in late February 2023, ahead of the one-year anniversary of the war, the mood in the Ukrainian capital was of quiet triumph and grief.

Ukrainians had survived the winter. The St. Sophia Cathedral outside the Intercontinental Hotel was illuminated at night, just like during peacetime. President Biden had just deposited flowers on the square outside at a monument to Ukraine's defenders, a few steps away from the display of destroyed Russian tanks, howitzers, and troop carriers.

A year earlier, the hotel was empty and the American embassy abandoned because of the looming Russian threat. Even as the war continued to rage, Biden had endured an overnight train journey to come and show solidarity with Ukrainians. "Ukraine will never be a victory for Russia," he pledged in Warsaw the following day. "Appetites of the autocrat cannot be appeased. They must be opposed."

In the days before February 24, 2023, the Intercontinental turned into the heart of global diplomacy. As I checked in, the Italian prime minister, Giorgia Meloni, swept through the lobby with her retinue of advisers, security men, and camera crews. The Spanish prime minister came the next day. The following day, as I walked out of my room, I bumped into the Polish ambassador; his prime minister was staying down the corridor. Pretty much every foreign correspondent I knew was in the breakfast restaurant in the mornings, sipping cappuccinos with fixers and interpreters.

The hotel's basement was packed with international celebrities, in Kyiv for a high-profile conference. In the evenings, lawmakers from Britain, France, and other nations congregated at the packed hotel bar, which served Negronis and whiskey sours well past the 11 p.m. curfew hour.

As I sat down with Stevo and Manu for a drink on the evening of February 23, I watched the French philosopher Bernard-Henri Lévy, with his unruly hair, gesticulating with animation across the hall. A bunch of International Legion fighters made friends with VIPs at the nearby table. Vsevolod Kozhemiako stopped by. Khartiya, the unit he had founded, was in the process of being transformed into a full-fledged brigade of the National Guard, part of the new grouping being prepared for the offensive. Serhiy Zhadan, the Kharkiv novelist who also led a rock band, had already written a catchy battle song for Khartiya. "The truth of the Ukrainian East is with us," it went. Zhadan and his band were holding a concert in Kyiv a few days later, a packed event where they were fundraising for drones. "Do you want to see Moscow burn?" the promotional leaflets asked.

Kozhemiako was worried about the tightening noose in Bakhmut, showing me how far Wagner's men had advanced in their quest to surround the city. Some of his soldiers were there that night. It seemed evident that, sooner or later, Bakhmut would fall.

But a year into the full-fledged invasion, it was also clear that Ukraine had won the war for its independence. It wasn't certain in what borders the country would remain, with or without Bakhmut or the Azov Sea coastline. Bloody battles lay ahead. But Ukraine wasn't going to disappear from the map once again. It wasn't going to be swallowed and digested by Russia. This, by itself, was worth celebrating.

⋘⋙

Many Kyivites left the city for a few days around the war's first anniversary, fearing that Putin would unleash deadly barrages to vent his rage. But the night was quiet, and in the morning, Zelensky, Zaluzhny, and much of the Ukrainian leadership stood ramrod-straight on St. Sophia

Square, facing troops who had assembled for a televised commemoration. None of these men felt the need to be hiding in bunkers anymore. The fear was gone.

Zelensky found the precise words to express Ukrainians' feelings that day. "We didn't get scared, we didn't break, we didn't surrender," he said. "Ukraine has surprised the world . . . This was a year of fortitude, a year of endurance, a year of unity, a year of being unbreakable, a cruel year. Its main conclusion is that we have held out and haven't suffered defeat. Now we will do everything so that, this year, we achieve a victory."

The phones of every Ukrainian now contained at least one contact who would never reply to calls or messages again, Zelensky noted. "We will not erase their names from our phones, or from our memory," he pledged. "We will never forgive or forget."

I drove around the city at lunchtime. There was traffic, and shops and restaurants were busy, with their lights on. As happened almost every day, a funeral for a fallen soldier was taking place in St. Volodymyr's Cathedral, a ceremony attended by several hundred people. "The Muscovite is not a brother to us," the priest, Father Bohdan, told mourners as he recited the prayer. "It is Cain who has gone after Abel."

A couple of blocks away from Khreshchatyk, a museum had mounted an exhibition of posters with quotes from former Israeli prime minister Golda Meir, who was born just around the corner in 1898. "To be or not to be is not a question of compromise," said one, with a painting of Meir in a Ukrainian dress. "Either you be or you don't be."

Down in Podil, I stumbled upon a newly opened bookstore and coffee shop. The staff were busy putting on temporary tattoos to mark the day. One of the co-owners, Ivana Lishnevets, had chosen the image of a Molotov cocktail. Creating another Ukrainian-language bookstore was by itself an act of resistance against Russia, she said. "The main feeling we have today is a huge sense of gratitude to everyone who has gifted us this year of life," she said. "Those defending our land, and those who have already fallen."

Down the street from the bookstore, I started speaking with Anastasia Lisnychenko, a young mother pushing her daughter in a stroller. On the scale of the horrors inflicted by Russia, she was lucky. True, she and her child had had to flee Kyiv to the countryside in central Ukraine a year earlier, while her husband stayed behind to defend the city. But now they were all reunited, back in their home, in good health.

I asked Lisnychenko how she felt. "The fury, it hasn't gone away," she said. "I hate the Russians with all my heart and I wish them all the worst things in the world because of what they have done to us," she went on, her eyes welling up. "I didn't use to feel that way about them," she added, trying to wipe away tears that were now out of control. I also felt tears in my eyes, and so we just looked at each other, surprised by the intensity of our emotions in what seemed to be such a simple conversation.

✧

Zelensky's anniversary press conference took place downstairs in the Intercontinental's basement hall. Foreign dignitaries packed the front rows. The stage was inscribed with the motto "The Year of Resilience" and *Liuty*—a Ukrainian word that means both February and ferocious. Tired but enjoying the moment, Zelensky held court for nearly three hours. He indulged an Azerbaijani reporter who had promised his son he would take a selfie with the president. He listened politely as a Dutch journalist offered him a painting, though security stepped in to prevent the thick frame from reaching the stage. He teased a Chinese correspondent: How come Beijing was not siding with Kyiv if it stood for respect of sovereignty and territorial integrity?

The only moment Zelensky lost his cool was when a correspondent for the Channel 5 TV network owned by Petro Poroshenko was called on for a question. It was a moment when it became evident that Ukraine's bitter domestic politics, suspended for the past year, had reawakened after a long slumber. Standing up, the correspondent asked Zelensky whether he had any regrets about lulling Ukrainians into complacency about the looming invasion a year earlier, and what punishment awaited his "childhood friend" Ivan Bakanov, the dismissed head of the SBU intelligence service.

Ignoring the question about Bakanov, Zelensky stiffened, speaking with cold fury. "It seems to me that I was here on February 24. I didn't run away anywhere. I believe it is important that we didn't lose the state . . . I am not a hero, but maybe I did something right if we are here now," he replied. Then came the parting shot: "We shall win with the president that we happen to have. With the one that we used to have, we didn't."

The main thrust of Zelensky's remarks, however, focused on something else. Ukraine, seen as a hapless victim a year earlier, was now a force to be reckoned with. The courage of its people and their successes on the battle-field had transformed minds around the world. A year into Europe's blood-iest war in living memory, Zelensky—like many Ukrainians—was a man shorn of illusions. "Nobody loves losers," he said. "As horrible as it sounds, this is the truth. Everybody wants to be with the winning side."

EPILOGUE

The war continued to ravage Ukraine through 2023, killing its best, destroying its cities, and turning swaths of once-prospering countryside to waste. Though more military aid poured in from the US and NATO allies, Russia's mobilization and new defensive fortifications made any Ukrainian attempts to regain lost land much costlier than the successful counteroffensives of 2022. Still, as one self-imposed taboo after another disappeared, Kyiv gained approval to get American-made F-16 jets and received cruise missiles from Britain and France, as well as previously denied American ATACMS missiles, that extended its reach to all the occupied parts of the country. More Russian command centers and weapons depots came under fire, and more Russian generals and senior officers died.

Prigozhin's Wagner finally managed to capture the ruins of Bakhmut in late May 2023, at the cost of what he acknowledged were 10,000 dead prisoner recruits and 10,000 dead volunteer mercenaries. The real toll was likely higher. No longer allowed to tap the Russian prison system, Wagner pulled out of Bakhmut that month, leaving the regular Russian military in charge. Ukraine, which also lost thousands of troops in the battle for the city, began counterattacks in the area, slowly retaking lost ground. The city's civilian population had declined to zero, with hardly any building left standing. There was no Bakhmut anymore.

As the Russian ministry of defense tried to take away Wagner's autonomy,

Prigozhin launched a mutiny, creating the most serious political crisis in the twenty-three years of Putin's rule. In a rambling video on June 23, 2023, he questioned the foundational myths of Putin's war, saying that the Ukrainians hadn't shelled civilians in the Russian-occupied parts of Donbas, and hadn't planned to attack these areas prior to February 2022. Zelensky, he added, would have accepted a deal with Putin, averting the war, if "someone had climbed down from the Olympus" to negotiate. The only reason for the invasion, Prigozhin added, was a desire to sate the egos of generals and to line the pockets of oligarchs. This was a remarkable thing to say for the man responsible for some of the worst atrocities of the war.

After seizing the southern city of Rostov on June 24, Prigozhin sent his columns toward Moscow, advancing hundreds of miles with little resistance, before aborting the rebellion and agreeing to relocate to Belarus. Putin had unleashed the war with the goal of regime change in Ukraine, but now it was his own regime that, for one day, tottered on the brink of collapse. Purges after the putsch drew in some of Russia's leading generals, further corroding morale. Surovikin, the onetime "General Armageddon," was suspected of abetting the Wagner uprising, and disappeared immediately after the putsch. Less than a month later, Igor Girkin, the former defense minister of the Donetsk "people's republic," was thrown behind bars after condemning Putin for being too soft on the mutineers. From his cell in Moscow's Lefortovo Prison, he announced plans to challenge Putin in the 2024 presidential election. The fragility of the Russian system was there for everyone to see.

Prigozhin himself proved to be tragically naive in trusting Putin's guarantees of security. On August 23, exactly two months after the mutiny began and on the same day when Surovikin was officially dismissed as commander of Russia's air force, Prigozhin landed in Moscow after surveying his African operations. Hours later, an Embraer business jet took him, Wagner's military commander Dmitry Utkin, and other leaders of the group to Saint Petersburg. The jet fell out of the sky over the Tver region northwest of Moscow that afternoon, disintegrating midair and killing all ten people aboard. The debris was consistent with an air-defense missile strike or a bomb planted on board. Wagner supporters immediately accused Putin and the ministry of defense of assassinating Prigozhin. The Russian president, after maintaining silence for twenty-four hours, offered terse condolences—but didn't miss a chance to note that Prigozhin "was a man of complicated life who had committed grave mistakes." Defying wartime prohibitions, some people in Kyiv celebrated that night by launching fireworks.

Violence spilled into Russia in other ways, too. In May, Ukrainian-backed Russian insurgents seized and briefly captured border towns in Russia's Belgorod region. Ukrainian drone attacks on targets in Russia became commonplace, including a symbolic strike that inflicted minor damage to the Kremlin on May 3, and that was followed by several more serious attacks on the Russian capital. The war had come to Russia. Moscow responded by intensifying missile hits on Kyiv, which was now protected by Patriot batteries that deflected most of these barrages. Still, Moscow managed to strike, once again, the GUR military-intelligence headquarters compound. Russian officials insisted for weeks that they had killed Kyrylo Budanov—who later emerged very much alive.

On June 6, just as Ukrainian forces began the big counteroffensive in the south, backed by Leopard tanks and Bradley fighting vehicles, the Kakhovka Dam burst, flooding vast areas downstream and emptying the wide Kakhovka reservoir. Tens of thousands of people were displaced and southern Ukraine faced an ecological disaster. Kyiv and Moscow accused each other of destroying the dam. Independent experts, however, concluded that it could only have been blown up from within, likely with explosives placed in a passageway under the structure. That passageway was under firm Russian control.

In the Black Sea, Ukraine used naval drones in July to strike and disable once again the just-repaired Kerch Bridge to Crimea. Russia responded by bombing Ukrainian ports and pulling out of the grain deal. Showing its reach, Kyiv then attacked Russia's biggest port, Novorossiysk, putting a major warship out of action, and then struck a Russian oil tanker and the headquarters of the Russian Black Sea Fleet in Sevastopol. No longer able to approach the Ukrainian shores, Russia's Navy watched from afar as Ukraine unilaterally reopened the ports of Odesa to international commerce.

As expected, the Ukrainian offensive that aimed to retake occupied parts of Zaporizhzhia and Kherson was bloody and difficult. Prigozhin's "Bakhmut Meatgrinder" had had its effect, and the Ukrainian military faced a severe shortage of experienced troops. The Russians had used the time to learn and prepare, and managed to inflict significant casualties with minefields, drones, and aircraft. Ukraine, with no modern aircraft of its own because of delays in providing F-16s, had difficulty protecting its skies. Destroyed Ukrainian Leopard tanks and Bradley fighting vehicles littered the emerald-green fields of Zaporizhzhia. The death toll mounted on both sides, and the Ukrainian counteroffensive had made only minor gains by November. Russia, meanwhile, had gathered forces for offensives of its own in Donbas.

Though no longer in the headlines as the world focused on the fresh horrors in Israel and Gaza, the war in Ukraine wasn't anywhere near over. A long, grueling fight lay ahead.

ACKNOWLEDGMENTS

A book like this is an acknowledgment by itself. To everyone who spoke to me, who let me into their lives, who allowed me to watch them fight, grieve, and celebrate in a Ukraine battling for survival, thank you. This book wouldn't have been possible without your help.

My editor at Penguin, Will Heyward, was enthusiastic about this project since we first talked in the middle of the Ukrainian counteroffensive in Kharkiv, and masterfully steered the manuscript, with invaluable help by Natalie Coleman.

My agent, Elias Altman, provided brilliant advice throughout the process. Thank you.

The book's cover art is the work of Rufina Bazlova, one of many Belarusians who support the Ukrainian cause and the artist who designed a *vyshyvanka* embroidered shirt worn by Zelensky. For your and our freedom!

The Wall Street Journal, one of the world's greatest news organizations, was fully committed to the story of Ukraine, making it possible for me to report far and wide—and to come back in one piece. My thanks go to my direct editors, Gordon Fairclough and Deborah Ball, who worked with dedication and grace around the clock as the story unfolded, and to everyone else in the newspaper's management. My comrades under fire in Ukraine—Paul Hutchinson (aka "Hutch"), Ben Cunningham, Serhiy Khomyshynets—stay safe. My wartime colleagues Alan Cullison, Brett Forrest, Ian Lovett,

Isabel Coles, James Marson, Marcus Walker, Matthew Luxmoore, Vivian Salama—it has been an honor. Evan Gershkovich—I hope to see you free and home by the time this book is published.

No words can describe the debt I owe to Manu Brabo and Stevo Stephen. I have tried in this book. Manu's heartrending photographs, which he has graciously allowed to be reproduced in this book, are a testament to his courage and talent.

Last but not least, my resilient partner, Agata, has had to put up with my doing two wars back-to-back, and was always full of sage advice, on this book's contents and the cover design. Thank you.

NOTE TO READERS

Journalism, as *Washington Post* publisher Philip L. Graham noted in the 1960s, is the first rough draft of history. This book is the second draft of the history of the full-out Russian war against Ukraine, spanning the first decisive year of the conflict. I had the opportunity to revisit events that I had witnessed, talking to participants weeks and months later, at a time when they could tell me some of the things that had been secret before. But as I finished writing this book, the war in Ukraine continued. By necessity, many other details remain hidden, perhaps for decades to come. This book tells the story of Ukraine's fight for independence based on what can be known at present. A final account of this war will have to be written once archives open up in the future.

Whenever possible, I used full names as provided to me. For most soldiers, only the first name or a call sign were available. In line with military rules, the soldiers were not allowed to disclose their full details as long as they remained in active service, so that the Russians wouldn't be able to target or blackmail their families. When civilians are identified only by their first name, that's because they had declined to provide their full identity—usually because of fear of reprisals.

Most of the narrative in this book is based on eyewitness observations and hundreds of interviews I conducted all over Ukraine in 2022 and early 2023. This includes conversations with President Zelensky, National

Security Adviser Danilov, Foreign Minister Kuleba, GUR military intelligence chief Budanov, and countless other military officers and civilians, as well as interviews with senior officials in Washington, Paris, and London. I used direct quotes when reporting what people said in their social media posts, in videos posted by the government or the military, or during televised events. The references at the end of the book are limited to remarks cited from other news sources.

The vast majority of conversations in this book were conducted in Ukrainian or Russian, and appear in my translation. The translations of other remarks and statements in either language, and of literary works cited in the book, are also mine. The spelling of place names in Ukraine generally follows Ukrainian transliteration rules, and the same is done with personal names. I used Russian transliterations for Ukrainians who joined the Russian administration and adopted Russian citizenship.

NOTES

CHAPTER 3: THE LAST DAYS OF PEACE

30 **"I was afraid that"**: Simon Shuster and Vera Bergengruen, "Inside the Ukrainian Counter-strike That Turned the Tide of the War," *Time*, September 26, 2022, www.time.com/6216213/ukraine-military-valeriy-zaluzhny.

31 **"Most of the Ukrainian Army"**: "Политолог заявил о готовности украинских солдат перейти на сторону России," *Lenta*, February 22, 2022, www.lenta.ru/news/2022/02/22/osvobozhdenie.

CHAPTER 4: "WE WILL FIGHT. WE WILL NOT SURRENDER."

38 **"Some of the defense intelligence people"**: "In Full: Exclusive Interview with Boris Johnson," Sky News, November 2, 2022, news.sky.com/video/in-full-exclusive-interview-with-boris-johnson-12736232.

38 **"For God's sake"**: *Putin vs. the West*, Series 1:3, "A Dangerous Path," BBC, www.bbc.co.uk, January 30, 2023, www.bbc.co.uk/iplayer/episode/p0dlzdwr/putin-vs-the-west-series-1-3-a-dangerous-path.

CHAPTER 5: UKRAINE BARES ITS TEETH

42 **"For eight years"**: "Year. Off-screen. General. Special project of Dmytro Komarov. Part three [ENG + RU SUBTITLES]," YouTube video, 51:20, www.youtube.com/watch?v=TadXxP_26V8.

43 **"He doesn't need to understand"**: Simon Shuster and Vera Bergengruen, "Inside the Ukrainian Counterstrike That Turned the Tide of the War," *Time*, September 26, 2022, www.time.com/6216213/ukraine-military-valeriy-zaluzhny.

CHAPTER 6: "RUSSIAN WARSHIP, GO FUCK YOURSELF"

48 **Before dawn, the brigade's:** "Гостомель. Перший бій українських строковиків з російськими десантниками | 'Таємниці війни,'" YouTube video, 18:06, www.youtube.com /watch?v=ebcXLxfq_o0.a.

48–49 **"You can hit them!":** "Вони горять!—кричали захисники аеропорту Гостомеля, збиваючи російські 'Алігатори,'" Ukrinform, May 12, 2022, www.ukrinform.ua/amp/rubric-ato /3481713-voni-gorat-kricali-zahisniki-aeroportu-gostomela-zbivauci-rosijski-aligatori .html.

51 **"It is clear":** Roman Romanyuk, "Битва за Зміїний. Героїчна історія: як Україна втратила і повернула надважливий острів. Реконструкція," pravda.com.ua, November 7, 2022, www.pravda.com.ua/articles/2022/11/7/7375232/index.amp.

CHAPTER 7: "WE ARE ALL HERE"

57 **"I don't understand you":** Simon Shuster and Vera Bergengruen, "Inside the Ukrainian Counterstrike That Turned the Tide of the War," *Time*, September 26, 2022, www.time.com /6216213/ukraine-military-valeriy-zaluzhny.

57 **The Ukrainian state had only:** Livia Gerster, "Sie wollen seine Worte nicht hören," *Frankfurter Allgemeine*, March 18, 2022, m.faz.net/aktuell/politik/ausland/ukrainischer-botschafter-andrij -melnyk-verhasst-bei-politikern-17909743.amp.html.

CHAPTER 10: SOUTHERN BETRAYAL

78 **"For the Russians":** ОЛЕКСІЙ БРАТУЩАК and КОСТЯНТИН РЄУЦЬКИЙ, "Подвиг у Бузковому парку. Невідома історія окупації Херсона," pravda.com.ua, November 8, 2022, www.pravda.com.ua/articles/2022/11/8/7375378/index.amp.

CHAPTER 14: RUSSIAN TANKS CATCH FIRE REALLY WELL

108 **"They are cowards":** Юлія Ткач, "Генерал Марченко розповів, як вдалося захистити Миколаїв: 'Мені 8 разів давали команду підірвати Варварівський міст,'" *Никвести*, May 23, 2022, www.nikvesti.com/news/public/248649.

CHAPTER 17: RUSSIA'S ROUT IN VOZNESENSK

132 **"The enemy ended up":** "Ігор Скибюк, командир 80-ї окремої десантно-штурмової бригади," Ukrinform, July 22, 2022, www.ukrinform.ua/amp/rubric-ato/3534491-igor-skibuk -komandir-80i-okremoi-desantnosturmovoi-brigadi.html.

134 **Ukraine lost forty-three:** "'Битва за Вознесенськ': вийшов документальний фільм про те, як українське місто успішно відбило наступ росіян (Відео)," texty.org.ua, April 15, 2022, www.texty.org.ua/fragments/106382/bytva-za-voznesensk-vyjshov-dokumentalnyj-film-pro -te-yak-ukrayinske-misto-uspishno-vidbylo-nastup-rosiyan-video.

CHAPTER 18: "THE CITY IS BEING LEVELED"

139 **"We thought, this is it":** Дмитро Джулай, "Мощун—тут Україна розбила еліту армії РФ та зупинила наступ на Київ (розслідування)," radiosvoboda.org, March 12, 2023, www

.radiosvoboda.org/amp/moshchun-tut-ukrayina-rozbyla-elitu-armiyi-rf-ta-zupynyla-nastup
-na-kyyiv-rozsliduvannya/32305176.html.

CHAPTER 20: THE ISTANBUL SURPRISE

150 **"The situation was close to critical"**: Власта Лазур, "Денис Кірєєв—співробітник ГУР, якого
вбили в автівці СБУ, а тіло викинули на вулицю». Інтерв'ю з Кирилом Будановим," Radio Liberty, January 22, 2023, www.radiosvoboda.org/amp/вбивство-кірєєва/32233661
.html.

CHAPTER 22: HOWITZER TIME

163 **"Cruiser *Moskva* was like"**: "Year. Off-screen. General. Special project of Dmytro Komarov.
Part three [ENG + RU SUBTITLES]," YouTube video, 51:20, www.youtube.com/watch?v
=TadXxP_26V8.
164 **"Denazification will inevitably be"**: Тимофей Сергейцев, "Что Россия должна сделать с
Украиной," ria.ru, April 5, 2022, www.ria.ru/amp/20220403/ukraina-1781469605.html.

CHAPTER 23: AZOVSTAL

167 **"Rockets were flying like sparrows"**: "ЕКСКЛЮЗИВ. Виліт на бойовому МІ-24 в
Маріуполь—пілот армійської авіації | Воїн—це я," YouTube video, 15:06, www.youtube
.com/watch?v=qxYn202PyYg.

CHAPTER 26: THE BILOHORIVKA CROSSING

191 **"I have to admit"**: "Це була суцільна стіна вогню: командир ЗСУ про важкі бої за
Білогорівку," fakty.com.ua, July 13, 2022, www.fakty.com.ua/ua/ukraine/20220713-cze
-bula-suczilna-stina-vognyu-komandyr-zsu-pro-vazhki-boyi-za-bilogorivku/amp.

CHAPTER 30: KYIV LIVES

218 **"an element of surprise"**: "Ми їх дотисли і змусили покинути ці території," Буданов |
СПЕЦОПЕРАЦІЯ "ЗМІЙНИЙ." @Raminaeshakzai, YouTube video, 1:22:13, www.youtube
.com/watch?v=2U7QtZ4YHAY.

CHAPTER 36: INTO THE STEPPES OF KHERSON

265 **"When they started"**: Matthew Luxmoore, "Ukrainian Soldiers Say They Are Advancing
in the South, but at a Cost," *Wall Street Journal*, August 31, 2022, www.wsj.com/articles
/ukrainian-soldiers-say-they-are-advancing-in-the-south-but-at-a-cost-11661983338.

CHAPTER 45: KHERSON, FREE BUT EMPTY

331 **"Logistics will be disrupted"**: Рафаэль Залян, "'Нет шансов выжить': почему Украина
замерзнет этой зимой," Вечерняя Москва, November 29, 2022, www.vm.ru/news/1014844
-net-shansov-vyzhit-pochemu-ukraina-zamerznet-etoj-zimoj/amp.

CHAPTER 46: THE BAKHMUT MEATGRINDER

342 **Zaluzhny, the chief commander:** "An Interview with General Valery Zaluzhny, Head of Ukraine's Armed Forces," *Economist*, December 15, 2022, www.economist.com/zaluzhny -transcript.

LIST OF MAPS

INDEX